Intercollegiate athletics is in crisis. Drug abuse, illegal recruiting, poor academic standards for athletes, racism, sex discrimination, and the growing power of agents and the media have made many question the value and integrity of what was founded as an amateur game. *THE RULES OF THE GAME: Ethics in College Sport* looks closely at the issues and offers sound, workable solutions for putting college sport in its proper place in American higher education.

The perspective comes from the frontline. The principals contributing to this impressive volume include: former athletes and their agents, coaches, college presidents, athletic directors, journalists, and administrators. These experts consider their situation vis-à-vis the current crisis as it is received in America's living rooms. Highlights include:

• Charles Farrell, **Washington Post**, characterizes the history of college sport as being steeped in controversy, from its inception in the 19th century leading up to today's drug, recruiting, and eligibility problems.

• Bob Woolf, preeminent sports attorney, views the evolution of the role of agents and the effects their power and proliferation have had on intercollegiate sport.

• Donna Lopiano, Director, *Intercollegiate Athletics for Women at the University of Texas*, writing on women's athletic programs, presents arguments that are ethically on target and practically useful in the face of financial adjustments and discriminatory hiring practices.

• Sandy Padwe, Senior Editor, **Sports Illustrated**, reveals the underlying dilemma of sports journalists, who are at once promoting sport and acting as its social conscience.

• Jack Bicknell, football coach, *Boston College*, offers advice on how to establish and uphold integrity within the coaching ranks, emphasizing the roles of president and athletic director in maintaining university standards, and the coach as educator.

of awards and honors in education, scientific research and public service during his distinguished career. Among his many achievements was a Presidential appointment to the National Science Foundation, where he later served as Director. He was Chancellor of the University of Maryland at College Park, and six years later, became the eleventh president of Occidental College, where he continues to serve today. Dr. Slaughter has chaired the President's Commission of the NCAA.

THE
RULES
OF THE
GAME

ETHICS IN
COLLEGE SPORT

THE RULES OF THE GAME

ETHICS IN COLLEGE SPORT

Richard E. Lapchick

John Brooks Slaughter

AMERICAN COUNCIL ON EDUCATION

MACMILLAN PUBLISHING COMPANY

New York

Collier Macmillan Publishers

London

Macmillan Publishing Company
866 Third Avenue, New York, N.Y. 10022

Collier Macmillan Canada, Inc.

Library of Congress Catalog Card Number: 89-6743

Printed in the United States of America

1 2 3 4 5 6 7 8 9 10

Library of Congress Cataloging in Publication Data

The Rules of the game : ethics in college sport / [edited by] Richard
   E. Lapchick, John Brooks Slaughter.
      p. cm. — (American Council on Education/Macmillan series in
   higher education)
   Bibliography: p.
   Includes index.
   ISBN 0-02-897401-8
   1. College sports—United States. 2. College sports—Moral and
ethical aspects. I. Lapchick, Richard Edward. II. Slaughter, John
Brooks, 1934- . III. Series.
GV351.R85 1989
796'.071'173—dc20   89-6743
                                                          CIP

*For future student-athletes in the
hope that our institutions of higher
education will help them to reach their
full human potential—academically as
well as athletically.*

CONTENTS

FOREWORD

ERNEST L. BOYER

American universities are confronting, in a climate of crisis, the moral dilemmas inspired by college sport. Some observers of big-time athletics believe such dilemmas are no more serious than was the case in earlier years. They point out that in 1905 President Theodore Roosevelt called university representatives to the White House and cautioned that unless they took action to reduce injuries to players in intercollegiate football games, he would do so by executive decree. Observers note, too, that in 1929, the Carnegie Foundation examined the problem of college sport in a comprehensive published report called *American College Athletics*. In that hard-hitting critique of abuse on athletes, the Foundation reached the following conclusion:

> More than any other force, [athletics has] tended to distort the values of college life and to increase its emphasis upon the material and the monetary. Indeed, at no point in the educational process has commercialism of college athletics wrought more mischief than in its effect upon the American undergraduate. And the distressing fact is that the college, the Fostering Mother, has permitted and even encouraged it to do these things in the name of education.

It is true, of course, that ethical issues in sport predate our own time. But it is also true that violations are more

serious than before. Changes in degree have become changes
in kind. Now, sport programs involve staggering amounts
of money, television contracts, and mass audiences. Now,
there are agents to guide athletes—not through their academic
programs but through their years of eligibility and into the
ranks of the professionals. Now, in addition to the so-called
recreational drugs, there are performance-enhancing drugs.
Now, the ethical problems of big-time sport have reached
into the community colleges, the high schools, and even the
junior highs or middle schools. Now, the professionalization
of coaching has led to tighter and tighter specialization with
the result of more and more coaches for each team. Now,
racial, gender, and legal issues are as conspicuous as they are
complex. Now, the definition of unsportsmanlike conduct
seems to have been radically constricted.

Certainly not everything has turned negative. Players once
denied the right to participate because of race or social class
are conspicuously among the best players. Women, too, are
involved in many more sports, and with the belated opportunities to compete they have become much better players.
Many more concerned officials are aware of the commercialization of sports and want to keep the cherished notion
of the "student-athlete" alive. Not all has gone wrong. Not
all is lost. Nevertheless, there is a strong undertow of fatigue
and even fatalism among many of our most honorable and
sophisticated observers. It is as though the ethical problems
in college sports are endemic—a condition with which we
must come to terms after the way we come to terms with
human nature. Evil, some would argue, is built in. But here
is the question: because ethical issues have plagued college
athletics for a long time, and may be more widespread and
deeper than before, should we despair of ever making the
situation better?

In other important areas of modern life, in religion and
politics and business, the persistence of an ethical problem
is not sufficient reason to give up. Of course the solutions
we find are almost always provisional. Still, we keep at the
job. That is where we are, I believe, with regard to big-time
college sport. The magnitude of the problem and its persistence are no justification for surrender. This is no time

for flippant wisdom such as "We have met the enemy, and it is us." The challenge now is to redouble our efforts to protect the integrity of the institution as well as the rights of students.

But how, more specifically, do we go about strengthening ethics in college sports? In the essays to follow, there is broad consensus that publicly legislated morality will not solve the problem. The preference among our authors is for our responses to remain within the institutions, led by colleges and universities themselves. Of course, we need vigorous leadership from within. However, we need not regard the situation as either-or. As educated persons we do not feel that way about, say, civil rights; there, we want action on all levels, from individual to judicial. Indeed, in recent decades, we have relied heavily on Congress and the courts to enforce individual and institutional compliance to civil rights in the achievement of human justice. Can we not agree that, similarly, all available resources should be brought to bear to help us in the struggle for ethical behavior in another dimension of college life?

Big-time sport, collegiate and professional, is becoming the new civil authority in our culture. It draws the pride and unifies the community in the same way great cathedrals did in earlier times. Today, successful coaches have an importance that would rival that of priests and bishops of the church. And they are accorded salaries, promotional contracts, and visibility that few educators or politicians can match.

Athletics, university administrators say, is the "window through which the people see the university." They believe that sport is the best way to catch the attention of prospective students, the media, and wealthy donors. The old call to arms, attributed to several college presidents—"Let us build a university of which the football team will be proud"—has now been verified too often in practice to be dismissed by laughter. The ethical and moral questions introduced by big-time athletics are too important to be ignored.

But, again, what can be done? Among the forces available for the work of reform are the National Collegiate Athletic Association (NCAA) and National Association of Intercollegiate Athletics (NAIA), including the NCAA Presidents Commission. That commission, to which John Slaughter makes reference in his essay, involves forty-four presidents/chancellors who are committed to increasing the academic performance of prospective athletes, to instituting the so-called "death penalty" for institutions found to be in repeated violation of NCAA rules (a penalty that has already been applied to Southern Methodist University), and to conducting national forums for the discussion of athletic reforms.

The media are part of the solution, too. Remember that it was *Sports Illustrated* and certain newspapers that exposed excesses back in 1980 when five major schools in the Pacific Ten Conference were declared ineligible for league championships and bowl games because of rules violations. And we should not ignore state legislatures. In Texas, the "No-pass, no-play" high school legislation is gaining increasing approval. The work of the Arkansas Business Council, giving impetus to athletic reforms in that state, shows that business leaders will participate, will in fact take the lead.

I also am convinced that the health professions have an important role to play. As John Hoberman points out in his contribution to this volume, the availability of performance-enhancing drugs at a time of emphasis on high-performance sport raises a tide of ethical issues. How shall we respond when athletes with the complicity of coaches and researchers decide that they are no longer content to achieve the best results available within accepted physiological limits, but instead they commit every resource, including genetically engineered substances, to refine—if not actually alter—human physical growth patterns? We need health professionals to help us define, sort, and meet these challenges.

The resources of institutional accreditation are available as well. In *College,* I challenged the accrediting bodies to stand up for reform in athletics:

> When serious athletic violations are discovered, the accreditation status of the institution should be revoked—along with the eligibility status for the National Collegiate Athletic Association. It is ironic that one hears that a university has lost its athletic eligibility but never hears that a college has been on accreditation probation or suspended because of unethical

behavior in athletic procedures or its abuse of students.
(pp. 184–85)

Faculty are especially crucial to the cause of ethics in
athletics. The faculty athletic committees on our campuses
are charged with policy formation and program supervision.
Their records, generally, are embarrassingly weak. They have
been manipulated by athletic directors, coaches, and other
sport advocates. They should be more responsible and provide active leadership. If faculty will not defend the academic
calendar, if they allow basketball teams to travel during big
portions of term time, what hope is there of restoring the
concept of the student athlete and removing the charge that
universities exploit team members?

Directors of athletics and team coaches must know and
accept the terms under which an honorable athletic program
can proceed, and then they must function accordingly. In
the essay provided by Jack Bicknell, football coach at Boston
College, and in the one prepared by Douglas Single, new
director of athletics at Southern Methodist, we have good
examples of clarity in understanding and full commitment
to ethical behavior.

Still other valuable resources in our push for progress are
brought by women. They are increasingly active as team
members, as coaches, and as leaders in the formulation of
athletics policies. To date, most of their attention has been
directed toward achieving parity in budgets and developing
competitive teams and supportive constituencies. All of this
is good. But beyond access, and beneath performance, and
indeed running throughout the entire endeavor is the basic
issue of integrity: how to deal with moral dilemmas in order
to assure ethical standards.

It is my conviction that women who are coaches and
athletes have important contributions to make. Yes, they are
competitive. Yes, they want to succeed by traditional measures of success. Yes, they demand a fair share of the action.
But they can also help us strengthen the commitment to
community and build up collaboration as a countervailing
force to rampant individualism and raw selfishness. They
care about integrity and know that their behavior should be

based not on imitation of the worst current practices but on a willingness to be courageous in the service of better practice.

Students are essential, too. I believe undergraduates have a legitimate complaint when they are held to a standard of honesty in class work and exams in the context of documented institutional dishonesty in intercollegiate athletics. Regarding such ambivalence I wrote in *College*, "Integrity cannot be divided. If high standards of conduct are expected of students, colleges must have impeccable integrity themselves. Otherwise the lessons of the 'hidden curriculum' will shape the undergraduate experience."

Students who want to graduate with a degree that is above reproach should care about whether the institution likely to confer that degree is also above reproach. Furthermore, realistically, students should care when $500,000 or $1,000,000 are diverted from the educational budget to cover deficits in the intercollegiate budget. This diversion of funds is happening, and it comes at the cost of teaching and learning. It comes as an unacceptable cost to students.

Finally, but actually of first importance, there must be firm leadership at the top from the board of trustees and the president of the college or university. Ethical direction for the coaches and athletic directors, for the faculty athletic committees, for student athletes, for the fans and especially the alumni, must come from the board and president. The buck stops there.

If all of our resources could be made to work together, I am confident we could meet the challenge of ethics in college sport. Indeed, we must, for if the institution of higher education allows unscrupulous practices and athletic scandals to undermine the integrity of the enterprise, that college or university loses its authority in society. How can its educational integrity be assured if one of its major programs is untrustworthy? It should be remembered that what is at stake is nothing less than the basic definition of the institution of higher education. What should the college do? Is there anything that it should not do? What does it in fact do, and are things being done that should not be done? We cannot answer those questions until we are clear about our underlying convictions. Only then can we hope to bring our behavior into the service of our best values.

To review, the modern college or university cannot escape ethical norms and moral dilemmas. These confront the institution in its dealings with politicians in the State House as well as with athletic boosters in the campus field house. To avoid a tragic outcome, we must renew and extend our efforts to keep intercollegiate athletics within the mission of the institution of higher education. The problems are persistent, but the complexity of an issue has never been a sufficient reason to abandon the search for an honorable solution.

In the end, there is one issue that stands above all other issues. It is the integrity of the university—integrity that cannot be conferred but must be earned. The institution of higher education must make itself worthy of trust. Students, faculty, administrators, business and political leaders, parents, media representatives, and the general citizenry must believe that the enterprise will show moral seriousness in dealing with problems about which people differ. Anything less will make a mockery of sports and bring disgrace to one of our most cherished institutions.

We have the resources to succeed. But do we have the will? To succeed, we must be truly convinced that just as the game cannot continue unless the rules are honored, so the pleasures and benefits of intercollegiate athletics cannot be realized unless the rules are ethical—and are obeyed.

ACKNOWLEDGEMENTS

We would like to thank all of the people involved in the production of this book. While it would take pages to list everyone, many need to be singled out.

First, we were the recipients of the work of the leading thinkers on ethical issues involving college sport: educators and administrators Roscoe Brown, Donna Lopiano, Dick Schultz and Doug Single (with Cynthia Patterson's assistance); scholars John Hoberman, Alan Sack and Connie Zotos; coach Jack Bicknell; former athlete David Meggyesy; sports agent Bob Woolf; and Charles Farrell and Sandy Padwe from the media.

We would also like to thank Ernest Boyer, one of our nation's leading educators, for writing the foreword for this book and Lloyd Chilton of Macmillan for approaching the Center for the Study of Sport in Society at Northeastern University with the concept of such a book.

We want to thank Ray Gillian of the Chancellor's Office at the University of Maryland for technical support and advice.

In addition, the entire staff of the Center for the Study of Sport in Society participated in this project in some fashion. In particular, we thank Jacques Eusebe for technical help and Ann Pasnak for technical assistance, advice and suggestions.

However, if we had to single out one person who contributed the most to the overall effort, it would be Joseph Panepinto, formerly of the Center. Joe helped with fine-tuning of the entire manuscript, assisted in researching the chapters on high school athletes and race, and drafted the introduction.

INTRODUCTION

RICHARD E. LAPCHICK
WITH JOSEPH PANEPINTO

There is a great deal of debate over whether college athletics has changed significantly since its first appearance. Some wonder whether college sport is at all as they like to remember it—amateur, fun, and secondary to academics. The real question is, was it ever really that way?

The question becomes especially relevant at the 100 plus colleges and universities with big-time athletic programs. In reviewing the history of sport at those schools, we would do well to be cautious in assigning sainthood to ancestors and damnation to contemporaries. Conflict and controversy have followed the development of sport in America just as surely they have followed the development of any social institution. Nostalgia often blurs our vision of the negatives and brings into greater resolution those things we miss most of all—particularly innocence, spontaneity, and a clear sense of values and worth. Today's problems in sport are not new, nor have they just recently bloomed. In unearthing the precursors to today's problems, we must be careful to realize that, in reconstructing their contexts and environments, we tend to ignore the clouds for the sunshine and the hardships for the joys.

Indeed, on many campuses around the country, where the athletic tail is purported these days to be wagging the academic dog, the truth is that it has been doing so in some respects for over a hundred years. The 1984 formation of the National Collegiate Athletic Association (NCAA) Presidents Commission in direct response to the "crisis of integrity" in college sport is a move toward remedying the perceived widespread problems of cheating and educational neglect, but the decade of the 1980s has not been the first, nor will it be the last, to witness such problems.

The 1940s and 1950s brought an incredible growth in the size of the thirty-year-old NCAA and the scope of its powers. By the 1960s the NCAA was regularly performing legislative and punitive functions. The NCAA's "Sanity Code," which eliminated athletic prowess in the giving of financial aid, was overruled in the 1960s, and in its stead grew today's highly publicized recruiting, payoff, and transcript-tampering scandals. Temple University President Peter Liacouras relayed the sentiments of a 1980s colleague regarding his problems with the athletic department when he said, "I fought the dragon, and the dragon slew me."

Today, while administrators are pushing for stricter admissions and eligibility requirements, some coaches are demanding more freedom in the administration of their programs; some players are calling for their rights to play regardless of academic inabilities; and the headlines are calling for a return to integrity. Yet they may have to look very hard to find any renewable sanity from the past. Sport in colleges had some of the same ethical problems at the formation of the first association in the 1880s as it does today. Contemporary spectators are simply deluding themselves when they wax nostalgic for a time when things were better.

Section I of this book presents historical backgrounds of the present-day problems in sport ethics. The first chapter, "An Overview," is contributed by Charles Farrell, who built his reputation as an honest and hard-hitting investigative journalist during his tenure as sport writer and editor at the *Chronicle of Higher Education*. Currently with the *Washington Post*, Farrell regularly writes about the relationship of broader social issues, such as drugs and declining values, to sport. In Farrell's opinion, money—a fairly recent but over-

whelmingly prominent player on the college sport scene—
has led to a situation wherein "the incentive to win has often
taken precedence over sportsmanlike behavior."

After listing just a few of the scandals that large amounts
of television and promotional money have wrought on college
sport, Farrell goes on to characterize the history of the NCAA
as an organization steeped in controversy. From its formation
in 1906, through the point-shaving and illegal inducement
problems of the 1930s and 1950s, to today's drug and eligibility problems, the evolution of the NCAA has been partly
in response to an evolution in institutional cheating. It seems
as though many organizational strategies designed to curb
unethical behavior have thus far been ineffectual. It remains
to be seen whether the NCAA, as the major legislating body
in college sport, can bring honesty and integrity back to the
college game. Most authors in this book believe it is up to
each institution to do so on its own.

Very often we get the impression that monetary inducements in college and professional athletics are the only source
of all of the problems in sport. It is sometimes forgotten
that all of the college and professional athletes we read about
so often in such an unflattering light are products of our
high school system. Richard Lapchick's chapter entitled "The
High School Student-Athlete" shows how the ethical poisons
produced by some university athletic departments are seeping
down to the high schools and producing cynicism and equally
appalling problems at that level. Claims that the academic
accomplishments of high school athletes match or exceed
those of nonathletes are true but misleading. There *are* academic problems, and they are centered on the highly publicized, revenue-producing sports of football and basketball.
Up to 30% of all high school seniors who play football and
basketball are reportedly functionally illiterate. The complex
problems of instituting minimum academic standards for
extracurricular activities are highlighted in the chapter through
examples from schools nationwide. One of the strongest
arguments against minimum standards is that they discriminate against minority students; and Lapchick provides the
numbers that could bear this fear out. Yet Lapchick supports
a more flexible brand of standards for their proven success
in raising high school athletes' grade point averages; a method

that works equally well with white and black students. Around the country, school districts are looking hard at the question of minimum academic standards for their athletes. Lapchick's recommendations should allay the fears of those high school administrators about to institute standards—and should encourage those who are hesitant about such action to take another look at the debate. The ethical problems of college sport, especially in regard to academic violations, will be easier to address if the academic caliber of collegiate student-athletes is raised while they are still in high school.

Section II of this book explores ethical dilemmas of the 1980s and 1990s. Among them, one of the most prevalent concerns of college athletic departments is women's sport. Women are losing ground in the coaching and administration of women's athletic programs even as they become more popular and visible in the 1980s. The 1988 NCAA Division I women's basketball final was broadcast on national television, a historic first. However, a quick look at the benches showed that the coaches for both teams were men. Men are coaching women's programs in unprecedented numbers.

In her present position at the University of Texas at Austin, Donna Lopiano acts as director of Intercollegiate Athletics for Women, and many consider her to be the unofficial spokesperson for the rights of women in intercollegiate athletics. Together with Connee Zotos, assistant professor of Kinesiology and Health Education at the same institution, Lopiano analyses matters for concern in this field. Their chapter, "Equity and Policy Problems in Intercollegiate Women's Athletics," is compelling in the way it presents both the legal obligations of universities to insure equal opportunities for women and the philosophical and ethical arguments. Title IX of the 1982 Educational Amendments Act is the most widely cited legal standard by which equality in athletic departments is judged, but in addition to this Lopiano reveals other state and federal statutes that apply not only to the administration of intercollegiate athletic programs but to the broader hiring and discrimination practices. The measurement of "equality" within programs presents the most stubborn problems in the application of such legislation.

Lopiano is direct in her explanation that the redistribution of "existing financial resources" within athletic departments could reduce opportunities for men, adjust the "standard of living" for men's programs, and force a new frugality in areas of the athletic department. However, she is unflagging in her push for a more equitable distribution of athletic department resources. Her article presents arguments that are ethically on target and practically of great use.

Another major concern of athletic departments is the racial factor on college campuses. The television screen belies the fact that in the 1980s, although the majority of players in the National Basketball Association and the National Football League (NBA and NFL), have been black, significant equality has not been achieved. The high visibility of the black athlete in America conceals the discrimination that blacks suffer in sport as in other areas of employment. The fact is, black coaches and administrators account for dismally low percentages of employees in franchises in each league. At the college level, where we would expect a greater degree of equality, the situation is even worse. In "Race on the College Campus," Richard Lapchick examines the racial hiring practices of college athletic departments in light of renewed interest in reform—and in the light of comments emanating from Al Campanis and Jimmy "the Greek" Snyder. The exposed racial nerve was again exacerbated with the debate and protest over NCAA Proposition 42.

Until recently, reform efforts have been concentrated on the professional athletic leagues, where minority hiring in nonplaying positions is dismal. The NFL has still never had a black head coach. Lapchick examines the relegation of black players to nonthinking positions on the field, the tendency of professional athletic team owners to keep marginal white players over marginal black players, and the persistence of genetic explanations for black success; all these tend to keep the number of black coaches artificially low.

However, even more scandalous are the hiring figures for colleges, where up to 54,000 head and assistant coaching positions offer far more opportunities for aspiring blacks— but less than 2% of these positions are filled by blacks. Moreover, black athletes account for less than 10% of athletic scholarships awarded each year; if we thought the percentage was higher, it may be because those scholarships are in the more widely telecast and revenue-producing sports of football and basketball. Yet the proceeds from these sports are used to support other sports from which blacks are virtually excluded. Perhaps because of this perceived hypocrisy in hiring in athletic departments, a larger percentage of blacks than whites favor monetary compensation for intercollegiate scholarship athletes.

Newspaper headlines decrying the "illegal" activities of college student-athletes most often cite violations of the NCAA amateur code. Monetary inducements in recruiting as well as compensations beyond tuition, room, board, and books are deemed "illegal." However, in a chapter contributed by Allen Sack ("Recruiting: Are Improper Benefits Really Improper?") we learn that a large number of student-athletes competing in intercollegiate athletics do not agree. Rather, they would point out that although the scholarship is a form of compensation, it does not provide compensation in the event of injury, nor money to cover normal college expenses, nor any guarantee of a truly genuine educational opportunity. In short, many athletes believe that NCAA amateur rules are not fair.

Citing the historical example of Prohibition as a non-publicly supported law that bred corruption, Sack analyzes the current state of university sport under NCAA rules. While 43% of the athletes surveyed felt that the amateurism rule was unfair, there were discrepancies among the various racial, socioeconomic, and gender groups. Eighty percent of lower-income black male athletes felt that some type of revenue-sharing policy should be instituted in college sport, while only 28% of upper-income whites agreed. Sack concludes that since the rule is anathema to the beliefs of so many—and has been such for the almost hundred-year-long history of intercollegiate sport in America—some adjustments must be made in the NCAA legislation.

Yet another major concern of college athletic departments is drug abuse, the subject of John Hoberman's chapter. The deaths of Len Bias and Don Rogers and the highly publicized legal conflicts involving hundreds of athletes with drug problems have brought us to the point at which we clearly recognize the dangers of so-called recreational drugs among athletes. Yet athletes, it could be argued, do not abuse drugs with any greater frequency than nonathletes. The 738 nationwide cocaine-related deaths in 1986 attest that fact. However, their prevalence does not diminish the need to act against these drugs in sport. In addition to recreational drugs, an area of equal concern that is virtually an exclusive one for athletes is the abuse of performance-enhancing drugs. John Hoberman, an international spokesman against such drug use, explores today's controversies over both recreational drug use and drug-testing. Drug use will almost certainly become a primary issue for colleges and universities as scientists push for higher levels of human athletic achievement through the use of performance-enhancing substances. Ben Johnson's demise in the 1988 Olympics underlines this.

The final contribution to Section I comes from Bob Woolf in a chapter entitled "Agents on Campus." The name Woolf has been associated with superstars in each of the four major sports since 1965. As the first, and still most preeminent sport attorney, Bob Woolf has seen the evolution of the role of agents and he understands their unwelcome contribution to the decline of ethics in professional and college sport today. Woolf follows his premise that "the evolution of the player agent followed the evolution of money" with a brief history of his own involvement in negotiating professional sport contracts, and a formula for addressing current issues of import.

There are, according to Woolf, 11,000 agents to negotiate 3,000 contracts. In spite of the seeming saturation of the sport representation market, Woolf suggests we will see a continued growth in numbers of agents and their effects on sport unless current problems are addressed. Based on insights afforded him by his experience, Woolf suggests a number of changes in both college and professional athletics that would limit the detrimental effects of agents.

Section III discusses the principals in the equation of reform. In this context, David Meggyesy became convinced—after a lifetime of athletic participation extending from little league through college and into the ranks of the NFL—that championing the cause of athletes' rights would be his life's work. His book Out of Their League was one of the first honest and critical books on sport written by an athlete, and he continues his work in the present chapter, "Still Out of Their League." Meggyesy has had a distinguished All-Pro career for the Saint Louis Cardinals of the NFL, and recently, he has been an instrumental player in the administration of the NFL Players' Association. Acting consistently on behalf of the rights of players, Meggyesy has a history of insightful and challenging views regarding the crises of ethics in college and professional sport.

Meggyesy opens his chapter by assuming a well-thought-out, but widely criticized, stand on the nature of the athletic scholarship as employment contract. Although some states, California in particular, have acted to categorize the athletic scholarship as a contract for employment, most people would claim that such a stand overburdens financially ailing athletic departments. Meggyesy refuses to allow the argument to come around to the point at which we are essentially blaming the victim. Athletes, as the only unrepresented members of the college sport business community, are repeatedly pressed by increasing athletic demands—to satisfy athletic department budgets—and unrelenting academic demands, in spite of diminishing study time. As solutions to these complex problems Meggyesy suggests a number of practical options that would hardly touch off a full-scale college sport revolution.

In the world of sport—a highly promoted and visible social institution—the ebbs and flows of activity are recorded with particular acuity and in exceeding detail. Sandy Padwe earlier developed a reputation as one of the most honest and critical sport editors in the United States when he guided the brilliant sport department of *Newsday*. His chapter, "The Media's Responsibility in College Sport Coverage," points up how the media can contribute to problems of ethics in college athletics. The underlying dilemma of sport journalists is that they must act—simultaneously—as social conscience for sport and as sport promoters. Padwe, now senior editor at Sports Illustrated, delves into the specific areas where sport journalism has special conflicts: covering the inadequate educational preparation of athletes, publishing and commenting on point spreads, reporting incidents involving drug and alcohol abuse by athletes, and opposing the racial stereotyping of blacks. All aspiring journalists should look hard at the issues Padwe broaches as they go beyond sport and into the realm of journalistic responsibility and commitment.

Coaches and athletic administrators deal heavily with the press, and their position as educators may easily be compromised to the end of increased monetary gains both for the athletic program and for themselves. Jack Bicknell, head football coach at Boston College, explores the scope of a major college coach's interests and concerns in a chapter entitled "The Coaching Responsibility." Bicknell is a veteran of four post-season Bowl Games, including BC's final-play Sugar Bowl victory. During the Doug Flutie era, Boston College established itself as a nationally recognized Division I football program and an excellent example of a program with integrity and concern for its players. Bicknell reveals that there are no secret formulas to establishing and maintaining integrity. The coach's responsibility begins with choosing quality people and knowing the university philosophy and expectations, and ends once his players have had meaningful college experiences and graduated. In addition to advice on dealing with the media, Bicknell offers guidelines on a number of other issues facing contemporary coaches. Throughout the chapter Bicknell emphasizes the role of the president and athletic director in dictating and enforcing university standards within the athletic department, and on the role of the coach as educator.

A related topic is examined by Doug Single of Southern Methodist University in "The Role of Directors of Athletics in Restoring Integrity to Intercollegiate Sport." When the flag went up on repeated NCAA violations at SMU resulting in the NCAA's first-ever imposed "death sentence," it seemed to the naive observer that the head was lopped off all the cheating in college sport. However, those close to college sport knew that SMU was paying for the collective sins of many programs. Ironically, SMU has now emerged with the opportunity to reassemble its athletic department with full benefit of recent debate and policy recommendations regarding ethical problems in athletics. As newly appointed athletic director, Single has assumed center stage with President Kenneth Pye in SMU's athletic reorganization. In his chapter

Single displays a knowledge of both the philosophical and the practical issues facing contemporary directors of athletics, and he makes recommendations with his gaze squarely fixed on the educational goals of the university. In Single's view, the successful management of university athletic departments requires the development of a national philosophy and model of university sport, as well as the implementation of policies based on that model. In addition, the move toward ethical regeneration requires a measure of equity and nondiscrimination within athletic departments. Single's observations support the contention advanced in the chapters by both Lopiano/ Zotos and Lapchick: the establishment of equitable and fair practices within athletic departments will reduce the ethical problems of college sport.

Media and educational exposés of the problems within college sport have often focused on the role of the NCAA. This is the subject of a chapter by Richard D. Schultz, entitled "The Role of the National Collegiate Athletic Association." In 1987, Schultz became the second executive director in the history of the NCAA. His appointment and his initial actions as executive director offer encouragement to those seeking a remedy for the problems that plague college sport. Certainly the NCAA will be the biggest single player in the future of athletics on campus. However, Schultz is quick to remind us that the NCAA is merely the representative of its individual members.

Schultz offers a sense of history and philosophy regarding the NCAA's role in reinstituting ethics in college sport. He explains the association's policies regarding drug testing, academic progress, eligibility, and institutional responsibility. Essentially agreeing with John Slaughter and Roscoe Brown, contributors of the final chapters in this book, Schultz maintains that the NCAA "cannot legislate integrity"—a statement that highlights the state of college sport today and suggests the direction we have to take in order to renew faith in the college athletic system. Schultz suggests that as each individual institution assumes responsibility for policing its athletic program, the overall problems of sport on campus will diminish.

Issues in the athletic department are no longer simply the concern of the four-year university president. The Interas-

sociational President's Committee on Athletics, chaired by
Roscoe C. Brown, was formed to examine the role of college
presidents in the administration of athletic programs. Brown's
chapter, "The Role of the Community College President,"
points up the pervasiveness of the problems in college sport
and reiterates Schultz's emphasis on the responsibility of
individual institutions to police themselves.

Brown tells us that the most straightforward and oft-
shirked responsibility of college presidents, regardless of level
of competition, is to "know what is going on." Some NCAA
rules, such as Proposition 48, have had a special impact on
community colleges. However, Brown suggests that the solutions at the two-year and four-year colleges are largely the
same: presidential awareness of and concern for integrity
issues within the athletic department, combined with academic support and counseling services for incoming student
athletes. While Brown believes that four-year institutions
should consider reinstating the freshman ineligibility rule, he
believes that a large number of the problems can be halted
at the community college level if "presidents accept responsibility for athletics and monitor athletic programs closely."

While many decry the state of college sport and focus on
how far we have strayed, Occidental College President John
Brooks Slaughter shows how little distance we have put
between ourselves and the problems that have existed
throughout the history of college sport in America. In "Where
Was the President?" he points out that power over the athletic
department was not wrested from the offices of university
presidents; rather, it simply grew up outside their windows.
Slaughter argues that the energies of American intercollegiate
sport reformers would be better spent looking at present-day
solutions to institutional management problems than looking
back for a time when things were more sane. The job of
university president has grown more complex, and the delegation of authority has increased. However, delegation without accountability is the error of former years that has led
to the present-day ethical problems in college sport.

By tracing the evolution of college sport from the late
1800s to today, Slaughter reveals that the university president
has never really been in control of athletics. The 1984 formation of the NCAA Presidents Commission, which Slaugh-

ter chaired, was a direct response to the problems of athletics in higher education. Although the results of the commission's forums, debates, and comprehensive surveys are not completely in, Slaughter reveals how the commission's own naiveté regarding the infighting in college sport administration has led to a diminution of the commission's power as well as to skepticism about its ultimate reforming effect. Slaughter advises concerned college presidents to stay involved at the national and regional level but also to focus their energies on intrainstitutional management and accountability.

The policy recommendations given in Section IV, comprising the final chapter of this book, will no doubt become the longest-lasting contribution of our writers. The credibility and stature of every one of the authors lends enormous weight to these recommendations, and the ethical problems now plaguing college sport will undoubtedly be diminished if the recommendations are adopted on a widespread basis.

Historical Background

1

Historical Overview

CHARLES FARRELL

> There are a growing number of coaches and administrators
> who look upon NCAA penalties as the price of doing
> business—if you get punished, that's unfortunate, but that's
> part of the cost of getting along.
>
> WALTER BYERS
> EXECUTIVE DIRECTOR, NCAA, 1952–87

The ancient Mayans played a crude game that combined some
of the skills of both football and basketball. The often-violent
contests frequently lasted for days, and deaths and serious
injuries were common. But to the victor went the spoils:
the winning team and its fans were permitted to chase the
losers and their fans, taking whatever clothing or jewelry
they desired. Talk about an incentive to win!

The ancient Greeks tried to make sport civilized, a test
of individual achievement and strength, glorified through
Olympic competition. The ancient Romans realized the spec-
tator potential of sport—if gladiator combat and feeding
Christians to the lions can be considered sport.

Athletics and the desire to win have been with us through
the centuries, but the *business* of sport has been honed in

the twentieth century to a fine edge through the introduction of large amounts of money to the arena. With big money involved, along with the acclaim accorded to champions, the incentive to win has often taken precedence over sportsmanlike conduct—and nowhere is this phenomenon more evident, it could be said, than in American colleges, where huge sums of money and the promise of international prestige have led many people associated with sport to adopt a win-at-all-costs attitude that has sometimes challenged the basic ethical fiber that took American higher education more than three hundred years to develop. This attitude is visible in the newspaper stories that recount underhanded maneuvers to lure top athletes to a particular university by means of money, clothes, cars—even women. While it can be said with certainty that most colleges run their programs ethically and put sport in the proper framework for an educational institution, a disturbing number continue to cheat.

Walter Byers, the highly respected, recently retired executive director of the NCAA, could not conceal his shock during an interview a few years ago, when he estimated that 30% of intercollegiate athletic programs indulge in some sort of unethical skullduggery. He laid much of the blame on the large amounts of money available to colleges through lucrative television contracts and the superdollars available in salary, bonuses, and endorsements for successful coaches. All of these, he maintained, create pressure to win and pressure to cheat. "I believe there is a growing acceptance of the belief that the conditions of intercollegiate athletics are such that you have to cut corners, you have to circumvent the rules," Byers told the Associated Press. "There are a growing number of coaches and administrators who look upon NCAA penalties as the price of doing business—if you get punished, that's unfortunate, but that's part of the cost of getting along." Yet, even though the punishments have gotten heavier over the years, reports of misdeeds, such as athletes on payrolls, continue to be well documented, as the events leading to the demise of the football program at Southern Methodist University clearly indicate.

Another misfortune that has resulted from the pursuit of conference and national championships is the lessening of academic integrity. There is now a revolving door through which many athletes enter a university illiterate, and through which, after exhausting their eligibility, they leave again, still illiterate and unable to get a decent job. Steps have been taken to address the problem, but it still represents the deepest form of exploitation. Statistics exemplify the problem—such as the disclosure a few years ago that Memphis State University had not graduated a single black basketball player for nearly a decade. Many other universities bear similar shame. The fact that an average of 20-plus universities have been recently under NCAA sanctions attests to this.

Illegal recruiting and exploitation are by no means the only serious problems. Three years ago, Tulane University was forced to abandon its basketball program in the wake of a point-shaving scandal that eventually uncovered indiscretions by the coach and led to his resignation and the suspension of the basketball program. Several criminal indictments were handed down, including one to a top basketball player who was later acquitted. Drugs, too, have caused havoc, such as the tragic death of University of Maryland basketball star Len Bias in June 1986, which has left indelible testimony about the fallibility of athletes. Unfortunately that testimony often goes ignored—the headlines continue to document the prevalence of drug use by some of the nation's top athletes.

Another question that continues to be raised concerns the precarious participation in college sport by black athletes. These athletes were once scorned by most of the big-time sport factories and now are major fixtures in their success. By reason of circumstances that lie in our history, many blacks have been unprepared to handle college academics, and some black athletes have ended up uneducated and exploited—an exploitation more cruel than that practiced on white athletes, who are more likely to have a safety net to catch them if they fail in sport. The promise of helping blacks out of the ghetto is ever more cruel when 80% of black players in football and basketball return without a degree.

More serious still is the fact that the black athlete was altogether shut out from professional sport for so long a period. Since Jackie Robinson broke the color line, blacks have found great success in the National Basketball Association, the National Football League, professional baseball, and other pro sports. But the dream of professional sport as sold to most athletes is too often a pipe dream, with opportunities limited to an amazingly few each year. Yet this dream is all that some black athletes have, and all too often that dream is unreachable.

The Origins of the NCAA

Ethical problems in college sport—the threat to academic integrity, illegal recruiting, drugs, gambling, and the exploitation of athletes, particularly black athletics—have all been of major concern lately to the NCAA, the most powerful body in college sport. While college athletics unfortunately continue to be soiled by the misdeeds of a few, such concerns are within the association's tradition: the NCAA was founded as a cure for the ills of early college athletics, in particular football. It was on November 6, 1869, that Rutgers played Princeton in what is recognized as the first college football game. The final score: Rutgers 6, Princeton 4. By 1876 the Intercollegiate Football Association had been established and the game spread quickly throughout the country. Football, even in those days, was an extremely rough sport, and the flimsy protective gear of the era did little to prevent injury. And as more and more colleges discovered the inherent value of football, more and more colleges took extraordinary measures to assure victory. One easy way to accomplish this was to enlist the help of older, stronger players to wage the weekly war. Students in name only, these players could be hired per game, and many traveled from college to college each week to sell their talent.

Money was already an influence in those early days; in 1903, for instance, Yale—a leading national power at the time—made more than $105,000 on football (Rader, 1983, p. 85). That was a huge profit when measured in the value of the dollar in 1905.

Violence already abounded as the older, stronger players overwhelmed smaller and weaker opponents; death and near-fatal injuries became common. Finally, in 1905, after the deaths of numerous college football players, the situation was deemed completely out of hand. President Theodore Roosevelt stepped in and told the colleges that they must either reform the sport or give it up. Faced with these alternatives, representatives of thirteen colleges met in New York City on December 8, 1905, to decide the future of college sport. Representatives of sixty-two institutions attended a second meeting on December 28, 1905, at which they agreed that intercollegiate competition was of benefit to them all, and they formed the Intercollegiate Athletic Association of the United States, which became the National Collegiate Athletic Association in 1910.

Created specifically to control violence in football, the association originally confined itself to standardizing the rules of various sports. But over the years, the NCAA has expanded its role much farther, to the point of dominance over most aspects of intercollegiate athletics. One aspect that the NCAA has attempted to control with mixed success is the amateur status of the athletes under its governance. That position was clearly outlined in the association's eligibility code, written in 1906, which stated that the association opposed:

> The offering of inducements to players to enter colleges or universities because of their athletic abilities and of supporting or maintaining players while students on account of their athletic abilities, either by athletic organizations, individual alumni, or otherwise, directly or indirectly.
> The singling out of prominent athletic students of preparatory schools and endeavoring to influence them to enter a particular college or university. (NCAA Proceedings, 1906)

Over the next few years, the NCAA adopted more rules regarding amateurism. However, enforcing those rules was very often unsuccessful, because college presidents and faculty were unable to control overzealous alumni and fans who were willing and content to pay for good teams. Even if presidents and faculty had been in a position to control amateurism, the increasing flow of dollars to college sport would have made them reluctant to attack such large and continuous resources of money, revenue that was of benefit to an entire university.

The Carnegie Foundation Report

It soon became evident that many schools ignored NCAA regulations in their efforts to field winning and financially successful teams. In an attempt to evaluate the situation, the NCAA called for an independent commission in 1916 to investigate college sport, an undertaking finally accepted by the Carnegie Foundation.

Over the next thirteen years, the foundation went to over a hundred colleges and reviewed all aspects of their sport programs, including recruiting, coaching, and administration. When its report was issued in 1929, the foundation documented the rampant professionalism, commercialization, and exploitation that were corrupting virtually all aspects of intercollegiate athletics. Probably the subjects most harshly dealt with by the foundation were the recruiting and subsidizing of athletes—practices so widespread, the foundation said, that they showed how blatantly NCAA rules had been ignored. The report concluded: "Apparently the ethical bearing of intercollegiate football contests and their scholastic aspects are of secondary importance to the winning of victories and financial success" (Savage, 1929, p. 298).

The Carnegie Report was, and probably remains, the most thorough look ever taken at U.S. college sport, but despite the widespread attention that was paid to the report at the time of its publication, the NCAA did little to correct the situation, other than appointing vice presidents to oversee representative districts and decide whether there were violations of the rules of amateurism. The association was admitting there was a problem, but it shied away from solutions.

The Depression Era

The depression era caused colleges to reflect increasingly on their athletics programs, from the perspectives of both economics and priority. Rising costs threatened many programs, and the drive to win and to continue monetary success became even keener. The role of athletics within a university therefore became more influential and businesslike, and digression from the rules more common. By this time, college sport had clearly etched itself into the fabric of American morale and competition, and it already reflected the ethical behavior—or lack thereof—of those involved. This process went on as critics continued to question the place of sport in institutions of higher education, while supporters did all they could to secure that place.

The 1940s: An Increasing Impact of Sport with Ensuing Problems

The end of the depression brought a renewed spirit to college sport. Radio—and later television—began to have a big impact on sports, bringing them to a wider and wider audience and introducing new sources of revenue that created additional pressure to succeed. In 1934 the NCAA was still trying to cope with widespread illegal recruiting of (and payments to) college athletes. At the association's annual convention that year, still another code of behavior was adopted to govern recruiting. However, those new rules simply became additional regulations to be circumvented, since they lacked any severe penalties for their violation and relied totally on self-discipline. Finally, in 1941, colleges realized that restraints had to be imposed to corral the out-of-control breaking of rules. A new NCAA constitution was ratified that called for the expulsion of members who refused to adhere to association policy.

In 1948, in a further attempt to curb payments to players, the association adopted a "sanity code," which permitted the awarding of scholarships to athletes when it was based on financial need. The association also established a compliance committee to enforce the code. Yet this code was a failure—because many schools simply refused to comply. The University of Virginia went so far as to reject the code openly, declaring it unenforceable. Within a year, the compliance committee had gained enough evidence to charge seven institutions—Boston College, the Citadel, the University of Maryland, the University of Virginia, Villanova University, Virginia Military Institute, and Virginia Polytechnic Institute—with offering scholarships to athletes without regard for their financial need. The committee also estimated that as many as twenty other institutions had violated the code.

A motion to suspend the seven institutions for failure to abide by the code was brought before the 1950 NCAA convention, only to fall short of the two-thirds vote needed. Two years later, the NCAA repealed the sanity code and allowed for scholarship awards based solely upon athletic prowess. The association members also gave the NCAA more power to dispense sanctions against those who violated association rules.

The 1950s: The Point-Shaving Scandal and NCAA Sanctions

The bubble burst in 1951 when the New York District Attorney discovered that more than thirty basketball players from seven colleges had engaged in point-shaving—winning or losing basketball games by less than the betting point spread. There were also revelations of illegal recruitment and payments to players. The scandal severely reduced the stature of New York collegiate basketball and dramatically underscored the potential for unethical behavior in college athletics.

At about the same time, the University of Kentucky basketball team, under the direction of the legendary Adolph Rupp, was the country's premier power, producing eight Southeastern Conference championships, one National Invitational Tournament trophy, and three NCAA titles. But that success shriveled in the wake of the conviction of three Kentucky basketball players in April 1952 for gambling and point-shaving during the 1949 season. For the first time, the NCAA put a school on probation, going the additional step of canceling Kentucky basketball for a year, a move that was estimated to cost the university as much as $150,000 in lost revenue and untold damage to the respect the university had garnered through athletics. Also placed on probation was Bradley University, which had three players involved in the scandal, as well as other violations of NCAA rules, including under-the-table payments to players.

The sanctions against Kentucky and Bradley signaled that the NCAA could indeed flex its muscles, and they established the association as the power behind college sport and the defender of ethical behavior.

The 1960s and 1970s: College Sport in Its Ascendancy

College sport soared over the next two decades, enhanced by both the exposure and money that television offered. As the revenue became higher and higher, colleges jockey for advantages by continuing to resort to illegal methods of securing players to lead them to championships. Recruiting became a highly specialized endeavor. The money spent on recruiting players was as much as—or even more than—the money spent on educating them. Alumni stayed actively involved in the search, often openly offering cash inducements.

Many colleges were just beginning to open their doors to blacks, and the benefits of having black athletes became evident quickly. But black athletes tended to be less prepared for college than their white counterparts; and, because they tended as well to be less economically self-sufficient than whites, black athletes were more susceptible to the lure of cash rewards for their athletic prowess. Unfortunately, there always seemed to be someone who was prepared to change high school transcripts in order to insure their admission to a university, and there always seemed to be someone willing to take tests and prepare term papers to keep them eligible for competition. Ironically, many of those athletes found themselves out on the streets, uneducated and unprepared for life, as soon as their athletic eligibility ended.

The NCAA continued to develop more and more rules regarding the recruitment and subsidization of college athletes, ultimately churning out some forty-five hundred pages of restrictions that were complicated, confusing, and difficult to enforce. The result, of course, was that cheating continued. From 1952 to 1985, the NCAA put more than 150 schools on probation for illegal recruiting, payments to athletes, or illegal benefits to them.

But one of the difficulties was that while the NCAA could impose sanctions on a maverick university or could discipline players who were illegally recruited or who accepted payment for their athletic skills, coaches at those institutions were free simply to move on to other colleges and thus to avoid sanctions. The NCAA needed to take a bold step toward signaling coaches that they too could be held accountable for misdeeds. In 1975, the NCAA charged Jerry Tarkanian for infractions at California State University at Long Beach, where he had been basketball coach from 1968 to 1973, and for additional infractions at the University of Nevada at Las Vegas, where he became coach after leaving Long Beach. Both institutions were placed on probation, and the NCAA ordered the University of Nevada to suspend Tarkanian. However, Tarkanian appealed and won, claiming that the NCAA was practicing selective enforcement. He received an injunction. However, in late 1988 the U.S. Supreme Court decided that the NCAA acted within its powers as a private organization. This case was considered by many to greatly expand the powers of the NCAA. It is interesting to consider that college sport, which should be so uncomplicated in its scope, now required the highest court in America to be ultimate referee.

The 1980s: Unbridled Growth with TV Money

College sport continued to grow in the 1980s. So have the problems as the desire for the wealth and prestige accompanying sports continued to grow. In 1988 football teams going to postseason could expect a minimum of about $500,000 for a game, and multimillion-dollar payments were the norm. Rose Bowl participants each received more than six million. Basketball teams in the NCAA Division I men's tournament got close to $250,000 just for making the sixty-four-team tourney, while those who made it to the Final Four, the premier college championship, earned over $1 million.

Television and newspapers routinely reported on the riches of college sport, and they also turned their attention more and more to the ills that plagued college athletics. In 1980, for example, there was a rash of reports from several universities of altered transcripts, as well as credits recorded for classes never attended or extension courses never taken.

NCAA Tightens the Reins

In an effort to solve the problem, the NCAA adopted resolutions at its 1981 convention aimed at requiring athletes to make progress toward a degree and tightening other requirements for academic eligibility. Yet there was little to ensure that athletes were prepared for the rigors of college academics. After numerous stories about the academic failings of athletes and the revolving door that awaited many athletes at college, the NCAA adopted in 1983 what is commonly called Proposition 48, which required that high school students who wanted to play intercollegiate sports as freshmen meet minimum academic standards in high school. While Proposition 48 has been hailed by many as insurance against academic failure, many criticize the measure as discriminatory against blacks, who have had particular difficulty meeting the academic standards of the standardized tests. And without the incentive of competition, many of those athletes would not attend college, the critics say. The academic standards went into effect only in 1986, so the jury is still out on the effectiveness of the measure. However, early results were promising—79% of Proposition 48 students in 1986–87 and 1987–88 were in good standing in 1988–89. That put them on a par with other student-athletes.

As the NCAA continued to be faced with mavericks who broke recruiting and subsidization rules, harsher sanctions were proposed and adopted, including what has been dubbed the "death penalty," which called for the suspension of an athletics program for repeat rules violators. The revelation that Southern Methodist University continued to pay athletes even after the adoption of sanctions led to the imposition of the penalty, resulting in a ban on football at SMU in 1987 and a restriction on the 1988 season, which SMU eventually canceled.

The NCAA, which is comprised of 804 member institutions, has forced its institutions and their presidents and chancellors to be more accountable for their sport programs, a measure that many think has been needed for years and that will hopefully lead to the prevention of future problems. At the forefront of that effort is the NCAA Presidents Commission, a forty-four-member body created in 1984 to ensure presidential involvement and responsibility. Another positive move toward the elimination of problems was the total removal last year of alumni from the recruiting process.

Yet problems continue. More than twenty NCAA institutions were on in January 1989. They were primarily charged with recruiting violations and with giving extra benefits to athletes. Numerous other violations are under investigation by the NCAA's competent but small enforcement division.

Twenty institutions on probation for rules violations may not seem like many when it is considered that there are more than eight hundred NCAA institutions. However, the perception of the public is that ethical behavior is generally lacking in intercollegiate athletics. Enforcement is difficult because there are so many institutions, and, in the long run, enforcement will not be the cure for what ails college sport. Richard Schultz, the current NCAA executive director, made clear when he took office last year that it was up to individual institutions to police themselves and to weed out those who would willingly break rules in pursuit of the pot of gold at the end of the sport rainbow. Schultz maintains—and his contribution to this volume bears out his claim—that college sport will get clean and stay clean only if *all* institutions adhere to the rules.

Some of the problems troubling collegiate sport are, of course, due to the tremendous pressure to win. Drugs are an example, both the so-called recreational drugs and the performance enhancers such as steroids. A vigilant NCAA and individual institutions have taken measures to check for drug use, but the tragedy of Len Bias and scattered reports of continued drug use by athletes suggest that vigilance must be improved. Other problems may be attributed to greed. Gambling scandals arise every few years. Agents on campus are another current problem; the unscrupulous ones lure athletes to sign contracts before their athletic eligibility expires, in violation of NCAA amateurism rules. There is no easy solution to that problem, but it must be addressed as long as the association embraces strict amateurism.

It has been more than eighty years since the institution now known as the NCAA was created in order to solve the problems that accompanied college sport. Those problems have multiplied as college sports themselves have multiplied, and with them money and prestige. The money is not going to disappear, nor should it. Much of the money available from football and basketball, the top revenue-producing sports, goes to support other athletic programs and, in some cases, other university programs. Indeed, without the support of basketball and football, many institutions would be hard pressed to offer women's sports, which have expanded and gained acceptance in their rightful place alongside men's.

The pure competition and excitement generated by intercollegiate sport are desirable aspects, and they have defined standards of excellence. The Georgetowns, Penn States, and Notre Dames have shown that success and ethical behavior can survive hand in hand.

College sport has continually gone through periods of reevaluation, and there have been improvements. Where there is evidence of unethical behavior, it continues to be investigated and documented. There are no sure cures, no magic potions to eliminate that behavior; presumably there will always be some who cheat. But it is a worthy goal to strive for a time when ethics in college sport will not be questioned. Is such a goal achievable? Only time will tell.

2

The High School Student-Athlete

ROOT OF THE ETHICAL ISSUES IN COLLEGE SPORT

RICHARD E. LAPCHICK

Millions of America's youth surrender their opportunity for a meaningful education because they have bought the dream that they will beat the 10,000-to-1 odds of becoming a pro. Too many waste their shot at an education by pursuing eligibility and not educational skills.

The "dumb jock" is alive but not well. Many are alive on the playing field but dying slow deaths in the streets. The more than 250 athletes who have got into trouble with the law between 1987 and 1989 attest to this growing nightmare. Since all these athletes are products of our educational system, educators are increasingly asking, "What are we doing wrong?"

Have we created the image of the dumb jock? Do we expect less of athletes than of other students? Why do we express surprise when an athlete sounds intelligent? Educators are speculating that we perhaps create our own self-fulfilling prophecies when we do not expect intelligence in our athletes.

Ethical issues in college sport all have their roots at the high school level. Yet the academic problems of high school athletes are virtually ignored. With all our attention on problems of pro athletes in trouble with the law or the problems of colleges and universities in trouble with the NCAA, we forget that both the pros and the collegiate athletes were produced by our high school system.

Millions of America's youth surrender their opportunity for a meaningful education because they have bought the dream that they will beat the 10,000-to-1 odds of becoming a pro. Too many waste their shot at an education by pursuing eligibility and not educational skills.

College Problems in the High Schools

All the problems of college sport exist at the high school level. Notre Dame coach "Digger" Phelps could well have been talking about high school basketball when he told the *Dallas Morning News*, "We have a serious problem. We forget that national championships are moments. Education is something that lasts a lifetime. College sports are an embarrassment to all of us involved in them."

Parents redshirt promising eighth grade children in every corner of the United States. Grade transcripts are reportedly altered by high school and college officials. Agents are already courting schoolboys in hopes of future signings. The pressures will be even greater now that the National Federation of State High School Associations has signed a cable TV contract for a high school basketball and football game of the week.

No region is immune from the sport madness that has swept the nation. Twenty million children compete in youth sport programs. At the high school level, 3.3 million boys and 1.8 million girls play high school sports—953,516 boys play football and 505,130 boys play basketball. Only 17,623 play men's Division I college football and basketball, the sports most identified with the scandals. Less than 3,500 people in the entire United States earn a living playing professional sports. Approximately 150 make it into the NBA and NFL every year.

Yet contrary to the public image, the typical student-athlete performs academically as well as or better than other students at both the college and high school levels. Engagement in the "community" life at both levels through sports appears to lead to a deeper involvement in schoolwork in general. In fact, a U.S. Department of Education analysis of 30,000 high school sophomores and 28,000 seniors documented that high school athletes outperform nonathletes academically. The study found that 88% of varsity athletes had better than a 2.0 (C) grade point average (GPA), while 30% of all students had an average below C. However, the figures can be misleading. The vast majority of the educational problems of athletes exist in men's football and basketball, the revenue sports.

The illiteracy rate for high school football and basketball players is estimated to be a debilitating 25 to 30%—more than twice the national average for high school seniors! On the college level, only 27% of basketball players and 30% of football players graduate.

Black and Minority Athletes

The worst victim is the black athlete, and society's promise that sport will lift black youth from poverty to riches and fame is a cruel illusion. Yet parents, coaches, and administrators buy the media package and encourage the illusion; black athletes themselves sacrifice educational opportunities to the glittering dream of the sporting arena. The dream goes like this: even if I don't make the pros, I'll at least get a college degree!

A study of 1,359 black athletes and 4,067 white athletes by the Educational Testing Service for the NCAA showed that for freshmen entering in 1977, only 31% of blacks graduated after six years compared to 53% of whites. Again, the figures for black basketball and football players were much worse. Too many of all the blacks who graduated received their degrees in physical education, sports administration, and communications. Ironically, all the information on black opportunities in these fields that was released following the Al Campanis controversy showed that blacks, with or without degrees, *are virtually shut out of these areas.* This fact is explored elsewhere in this volume in my chapter on racism at the college level.

The Move Toward Higher Academic Standards

Higher academic standards for high school athletes have been a distant goal in most parts of the nation. As recently as 1983, fewer than 100 of the 16,000 school districts in the United States required a minimum C average for participation in extracurricular activities. However, public recognition of the problem has led to a movement for higher academic standards in colleges and, increasingly, in high schools.

College Level

It became obvious that reform was necessary as scandal after scandal unraveled at big-time sport schools. Under the leadership of the Presidents Commission, the NCAA developed rule 5.1(j)—commonly known as Proposition (or Prop) 48. Under Prop 48, an incoming college freshmen, in order to be eligible to play a sport in the freshman year at any NCAA Div I or IA program had to (1) maintain a C high school average in 11 core curriculum courses, and (2) score above a 700 on the combined verbal and math sections of the SAT or a 15 on the ACT.

The new standards referred only to the athlete's academic record in high school. The athlete could still receive a scholarship but would not be eligible to play in the freshman year. While the core curriculum and grade point standards won widespread approval, the requirement for minimum scores on standardized tests angered black educators and civil rights leaders. Many educators agree that standardized achievement tests are culturally and racially biased. Black leaders charged that Proposition 48 would limit black athletes' opportunities to obtain college athletic scholarships.

An NCAA study undertaken prior to implementation seemed to bear out that fear. The study examined the class of 1981 and showed that 6 out of 7 black male basketball players and 3 out of 4 black male football players at the nation's largest schools would have been ineligible as freshmen. At the same time, 1 out of 3 white male basketball players and 1 out of 2 white male football players would have been ineligible.

However, when implemented in the fall of 1986, Prop 48 actually sidelined far fewer athletes. Less than ten percent of football players and only 13 percent of basketball players overall had to sit the season out. While the NCAA study indicated that more than 69% of all black male athletes in the 1981 class would have been ineligible, fewer than 20% actually were in 1986–87!

The 1987–88 figures were no less dramatic. In a survey of all Division I schools (with 202 responses) only 5.9% of all enrolled freshmen were either partial qualifiers (4.5%) or non-qualifiers (1.4%). The figures were predictably higher in football (34% of all partial qualifiers) and basketball (13% were partially qualified). Of the 1,282 black football and basketball players, 199 were partial qualifiers or non-qualifiers. That represented only 15.5% of blacks in the revenue sports. While Prop 48 continued to take a disproportionately heavier toll on blacks (58 of 60 in basketball and 141 of 152 in football), the 15.5% is about one-fifth of the number predicted in the 1981 NCAA study.

The debate seemed to explode when the NCAA voted to adopt Proposition 42 at its January 1989 Convention. The new proposition, taken with the standards established in Prop 48, would mean that someone who did not qualify could not receive an athletic scholarship in the first year. Under 48, the athlete could receive the scholarship but could not play in the first year.

Considering that the overwhelming number of Prop 48 students were black, the new rule created a tremendous controversy. Temple basketball coach John Chaney called it "racist." In protest of Prop 42, John Thompson walked off the court in Georgetown's first game after the convention. His stature fired the debate and led to a decision to table Prop 42 until 1991 pending further study. Many coaches maintained that Prop 42 would deny the students the chance to get an education if they could not receive a scholarship.

They would not have the chance to prove themselves academically. Proponents said it would put increased pressure on high school players to study harder.

The facts seemed to support the opponents. The number of Prop 48 ineligible students cited above indicates that the threat of ineligibility was already effectively putting pressure on high school student-athletes, without additional pressure from Prop 42. Furthermore, of those who failed to meet the standards in 1986–87 and 1987–88, 79% were in good academic standing in 1988–89. That was on par with their fellow students who had met the Prop 48 standards. Academic advisors said that they paid more attention to the Prop 48 students because they were identified as being "at risk."

A more impressive fact emerged when that NCAA study of the 1981 class was analyzed. Of the 69% of all black male athletes who were at risk regarding Prop 48 standards, 54% graduated. This stands in dramatic contrast to the 31% of all black male athletes in that class who graduated. In other words, the black students who came in at risk graduated at a much higher rate than regular student-athletes. Many were given that extra emphasis on academics in the first year and it carried over.

The predictions of disaster for athletes who were asked to do more proved false. The players produced.

The High School Level:
Texas No-Pass, No-Play

If Proposition 48 seemed controversial on the college level, the no-pass, no-play law at the high school level hit Texas like a cyclone. House Bill 72 was passed with the strong backing of Governor Mark White and billionaire H. Ross Perot. That was only the beginning of the battle. No-pass, no-play forced anyone participating in any extracurricular activity to receive a passing grade of at least 70% in *every* class. An ineligible student would have to sit out six weeks, a large percentage of any sport season.

The move was strongly opposed by coaches and parents. The coaches formed a political action committee that eventually helped defeat Governor White in his bid for reelection.

On the national level, the National Federation of State High School Associations, a coordinating body of all the individual state associations, vigorously objected to the strenuous standards set by the Texas legislation. While the federation supported minimum standards, it objected that the requirement of a 70% average in each course and the impermissibility of failing even a single subject were too stringent. The heat was on high when the results of the first grading period were announced. Texas, where football is an exalted event, lost 19.7% of its football players for the six-week marking period. In the winter, it lost 18.97% of its basketball players. Parents of ineligible students were demanding repeal.

The parents went to court. After conflicting lower court rulings, the Texas Supreme Court determined that the act provided a strong incentive for students wishing to participate in extracurricular activities to maintain minimum levels of performance in all of their classes. Since the rule's objective was to promote improved classroom performance by students, the court found it "rationally related to the legitimate state interest in providing a quality education to Texas public school students." The decision was appealed to the United States Supreme Court but was dismissed for lack of a substantial federal question.

Parents and coaches were not convinced by the results of the legal process. Many predicted that if an athlete became ineligible to play, he would lose interest in school and possibly drop out or fail out. Some foretold lives of crime or drug use. H. Ross Perot confronted this attitude head-on at the state coaches' convention by responding: "It is like saying if a boy is not on the team, he'll be out robbing 7-Eleven stores. It's a question of priorities. We will still have athletic teams, we will still have bands, but these won't be the forces that drive education."

The forecasts of dropping out and lives of crime evaporated when the second-year results came in. Most students who were ineligible the first year were back on the gridiron or court after raising their grades. In Dallas, the rate of ineligibility for varsity football players dropped from 16% in 1985 to 7.2% in 1986. For basketball, it dropped from 17.8% in 1985 to 11.8% in 1986.

Surprisingly, public opinion began to roll in support of no-pass, no-play. A poll conducted by the Public Policy Laboratory at Texas A & M University showed that 76% of Texas residents favored the new law. Nationally, a Gallup poll indicated that 90% of adults favored requiring a passing grade for participation. A *U.S. News and World Report* survey showed that 45% of student leaders favored restricting those with less than a C average. The federation's own poll indicated that only 25% of the 7,000 high school juniors and seniors polled opposed the restrictions. In Dallas, Spruce basketball coach Val Rhodes reported a change in players' attitudes toward grades. More than half of his team began appearing in his office at 7:30 in the morning to study. Teachers knew they could contact Rhodes about potential problems and arranged conferences with parents, Rhodes, and the student. The link between academics and athletics was being reforged.

Perhaps the group that got the biggest surprise was Texas coaches. Educators said no-pass, no-play worked *because* of the academic efforts of the coaches. Goree Johnson, the Roosevelt basketball coach in Dallas, emphasized the coach's influence. He held up the start of practice until 4:00 P.M. so his players could work with teachers after school. His staff also made weekly grade checks and assigned mandatory early-morning tutoring for athletes found to be behind academically. Johnson did not lose a single player.

School administrators echoed coaches' feelings. George Reid, Dallas assistant superintendent for secondary schools, was emphatic: "No pass, no play has proven to be very effective in Texas. We have seen a definite trend toward seriousness in athletes as far as their grades are concerned. It was difficult to implement, but once we got it in place it has shown very effective results."

An analysis by Theodore L. Goudge and Byron D. Augustin in *Texas Coach*, March 1987, showed how the percentage of ineligible athletes was directly related to the size of the school: the larger the school, the higher the percentage of athletes with academic problems. The importance of the coach became the key variable, and one of the best examples of this fact comes from Dade County, Florida, where Clint

Albury took over as coach of Killian High School for the 1984 season. He discovered that his team's grade point average was 1.3. Horrified, he instituted a mandatory study hall. There was only a D average eligibility standard, but Albury brought in honor students to tutor his athletes. In specialized study hall, they taught math and English three days a week, science and history the other two. By the 1986 season, the team's GPA had been raised to 2.45. No one failed a course. At the end of the season, twenty-three players signed with colleges and universities. That was believed to be the highest number of signed players in Dade County history. Dade is football country. All were Prop 48 eligible.

Were Killian's teachers merely marking them at an easier standard? Apparently not—since all twenty-three did well enough as college freshmen to stay academically eligible. It appeared to be a testament to Albury, who has since moved into a full-time academic position at Killian so he could offer the program to all student-athletes.

But the most startling case was that of Paul Moore. He was the type of player that many would say could never be eligible under a 2.0 (C average) system. He would, according to the argument, be victimized by society's good intentions. In fact, Moore was reading on a first or second grade level in 1984. Then coach Albury got him into a program for learning-disabled students. He graduated in June 1987 with an eleventh grade reading level and a 2.3 GPA in core courses; he exceeded 700 on his SATs. He was eligible under Prop 48 at Florida State in 1987–88 but was redshirted. He was a running back for the 1989 Sugar Bowl team.

No-Pass, No-Play in Other Localities

Texas is now just one of a growing number of states where at least a C average is required. The others are California, Hawaii, Mississippi, New Mexico, and West Virginia. Innumerable local districts have acted where states have not. By 1989, the results of no-pass, no-play were evident: (1) grades will improve with increased academic standards; (2) those who participate in extracurricular activities do much better academically than those who do not; and (3) coaches will rally to assist their players academically if standards are put in place.

The Los Angeles city schools announced a blanket C average, with no Fs allowed, as early as 1982. It was called an "academic remedy for scholastically ailing students." Within a year, seven of the neighboring fifteen Orange County school districts adopted some form of C rule. Favorable results experienced in the Los Angeles and Orange county areas soon led the California State Legislature to adopt a statewide C average standard in 1987.

In Georgia, the 1987–88 school year was the fourth year wherein a C-average rule was in place under school superintendent Ronald E. Etheridge, in the Savannah–Chatham County school system. Etheridge said, "Here you earn the uniform in the classroom first and on the field second." He added:

> When these youngsters find out that we mean business, they will rise to the occasion. High expectations will bring about high achievement. For us, it was just a matter of setting a standard and sticking with it. In our public schools, having to pass a C average is now as natural as putting on your helmet before going into the game.

Maryland's Prince Georges County school board chairman, Tom Hendershot, said that the rule, after a rocky start, is now applauded. Hendershot echoed a comment that is increasingly heard: "The rule makes such good sense. Why did we have to wait so long until we asked more of our athletes? In Prince Georges County, we once again have student-athletes competing for us."

The Future

In the ideal sense, educators say there is very much to learn from sport. It teaches self-discipline; recognition of one's limits and capabilities; dealing with failure and adversity; teamwork and cooperation; also hard work, group problem-solving, competitive spirit, self-esteem, self-confidence, and pride in accomplishment. Good sport programs become an alternative for the idle time that could otherwise lead to patterns of alcohol and drug abuse.

It seems clear that the climate is strong for increased minimum academic standards. According to the National Conference of State Legislatures, 40% of states recently approved tougher graduation requirements, and 36% adopted tougher testing. Moreover, a national group of more than sixty prominent people have come together to move for the adoption of higher standards for athletes on a state and/or local level. The group includes such diverse personalities as Senator Bill Bradley, Mayor Tom Bradley of Los Angeles, NFL Player Association director Gene Upshaw, basketball coaches Dean Smith and John Thompson, football coaches Joe Paterno and Tom Osborne, civil rights leaders Ben Hooks and John Jacob, and more than forty school superintendents and college presidents.

After an internal survey was conducted to produce the most equitable standards, the group came up with a proposed combination of the eligibility elements from all the existing plans:

1. A simple C average would be required in all subjects combined.
2. A student would be allowed one F per year as long as the average remained at the C level.
3. A student would be required to take courses that are on a track for graduation and to make normal progress toward graduation.
4. There would be one probationary period. Thus, the student who dropped below a C or 2.0 average would be on probation and not ineligible—but for the first time only.
5. If the average continued below a C, that student would be removed from that activity until the grades improved to meet the minimum standard.
6. Once ineligible, athletes would receive academic help.
7. Exceptions would be made on an individualized basis for students with extenuating circumstances.
8. Administration of the rules would be left up to each principal.
9. Junior high or middle school students who fell below a C average would receive nonmandatory warnings that if

they were in high school, they would be ineligible for extracurricular activities.

If higher standards are accepted for athletes, as this national group believes they should be, then these proposed variations would help to ease the transition and provide a fair set of standards acceptable to educators, athletes, coaches, and civil rights advocates.

The academic future seems brighter for athletes. John R. Davis, former president of the NCAA, believes that increased demands on athletes' academic abilities while they are still in high school result in better preparation at the high school level: "For the first time, we're seeing a marked improvement in the types of athletes we're getting." Certainly, those college freshmen who did not surrender responsibility in high school for their actions away from the arena have dramatically multiplied their chances for success in college. When we demand more of these athletes academically, then we have helped them to keep that personal responsibility. More importantly for society as a whole, the 99% of high school players who will not play Division I college ball will have a better chance at whatever they choose to do because more will have been expected from them.

SECTION TWO

Ethical Dilemmas of the 1980s and 1990s

Equity Issues and Policy Problems in Women's Intercollegiate Athletics

DONNA A. LOPIANO, Ph.D.
CONNEE ZOTOS, Ph.D.

Rather than presenting a burden to institutions of higher education, Title IX and the demand to provide equal opportunities for female student-athletes may very well prove to be the salvation of intercollegiate athletics.

Institutions of higher education are obligated by federal law and basic doctrines of fairness to provide equal educational opportunity for both men and women. Meeting these legal and philosophical obligations in the area of intercollegiate athletics requires a redistribution of existing limited financial resources and the identification of new revenue sources in order to develop existing women's sport programs and to expand the number of athletics opportunities for female student-athletes.

Program expansion and improvements in the quality of opportunities afforded female student-athletes may require (1) a reduction in numbers of opportunities for male athletes, (2) an adjustment in the traditional "standard of living" of men's athletics programs, and/or (3) cost-cutting measures in both men's and women's athletics in order to maximize sport participation opportunities for both sexes. Chief executive officers and athletics administrators will be challenged to develop institutional policies and national sport governance association regulations that will contribute to the elimination of sex discrimination in sport and reductions in the cost of intercollegiate athletics.

The accomplishment of sex equity goals and objectives is complicated by a resistant and progressively more male-dominated athletics establishment—an establishment that has historically opposed the provision of equal opportunity for women due to fears that cutbacks in revenue-producing men's sport will undermine the financial stability of intercollegiate athletics. There is also an underlying belief among male athletics administrators that women's sports, like men's minor sports, do not deserve the financial support of major revenue-producing men's sports such as football and basketball.

Legal Obligations of Colleges and Universities

Recommended Policy: No university policy or procedure shall be in conflict with applicable federal or state statutes prohibiting sex discrimination.

TITLE IX OF THE 1972 EDUCATION AMENDMENTS ACT

Over the past sixteen years, the legal obligation of higher education institutions to provide equal athletic opportunities for women has been subject to dispute, misunderstanding, and change. Equal athletic opportunities for women are mandated by the passage of Title IX of the Education Amendments of 1972 which provides: "No person in the United States shall, on the basis of sex, be excluded from participation in, be denied the benefits of, or be subjected to discrimination under any education program or activity receiving federal financial assistance" (Education Amendments, 1972).

It took three years for the Department of Health, Education, and Welfare (HEW) to issue the regulations designed to implement Title IX (Oglesby, 1978). During that time, distortions and misrepresentations of the law were plentiful among the athletic community. The most damaging misconceptions were, and still are, that separate athletic programs would have to be merged and equal dollars would have to be allotted to both programs (Parkhouse & Lapin, 1980).

In the name of financial savings, most of the collegiate men's and women's athletics programs in the country were merged under single administrative structures with the director of the men's program taking the top administrative position. Women administrators feared loss of decision-making power and control of the development of women's programs. Martin Gerry, Director of HEW's Office of Civil Rights (OCR), issued a memorandum (Gerry, 1976) specifically addressing the permissibility of separate athletics departments and expressing concern that department mergers might violate the Title IX statute:

> OCR is concerned that department mergers may result in placement of the administrators of former men's departments in positions of more stature or pay than those to which administrators of former women's departments are assigned, although no demonstrated difference in qualifications may exist. This concern stems from current information we have received, which indicates that in merging previously separate men's and women's physical education departments, the resulting unitary departments are administered by men in a disproportionately high number of instances. . . . Title IX places on recipient institutions the responsibility to assure that the process of selecting those placed in positions of administrative responsibility does not discriminate on the basis of sex. Further, if past discriminatory practices of an institution have placed members of one sex at a disadvantage in terms of acquiring the necessary experience and/or education to make them eligible for selection or assignment to an administrative position, it is the respon-

sibility of the institution to provide promptly the training and opportunity for experience necessary to qualify these employees for such positions. (P. 1).

Both the regulations and the courts have interpreted the Title IX statute as *not* requiring equal per capita expenditures of dollars on male and female athletes. "Athletic expenditures need not be equal but the pattern of expenditures must not result in a disparate effect on opportunity" (Aiken v. Lievallen, 1979). Yudof, Kirp, van Geel, and Levin (1982) note ten factors that are considered relevant in determining the existence of equal opportunity under the Title IX regulations:

(i)   Whether the selection of sports and levels of competition effectively accommodate the interests and abilities of members of both sexes;

(ii)   The provision of equipment and supplies;

(iii)   Scheduling of games and practice time;

(iv)   Travel and per diem allowance;

(v)   Opportunity to receive coaching and academic tutoring;

(vi)   Assignment and compensation of coaches and tutors;

(vii)   Provision of locker rooms, practice and competitive facilities

(viii) Provision of medical and training facilities;

(ix)   Provision of housing and dining facilities and services;

(x)   Publicity. (P. 755)

Other important factors outlined in the regulations target availability of funds for scholarships and recruiting practices. Equal numbers of scholarships or equal dollar values of scholarships are not required for men and women. However, the regulations do stipulate that "the total amount of scholarship aid made available to men and women must be substantially proportionate to their participation rates" (*Federal Register*, 1979, p. 71415). In addition, examination of recruiting practices will take place when equal athletic opportunities are not present for male and female students (*Federal Register*, 1979).

Many disputes revolved around inclusion of intercollegiate athletics under the regulations of Title IX. In 1976, the NCAA posed the first legal challenge by filing suit against HEW (Wong & Ensor, 1986). The NCAA maintained that athletic programs with revenue-producing sports did not receive direct federal funding and should be exempt from Title IX compliance. In 1978, the district court dismissed the case on the basis that the NCAA was not an educational institution and did not have the standing to pursue the suit. The appeals court overturned the ruling and "held that while the NCAA does not have standing to sue in its own right, it does have standing to sue on behalf of its members" (Wong & Ensor, 1985–86, p. 367). The NCAA withdrew from litigation despite the appeals court ruling.

The issues raised in the NCAA lawsuit set the tone for Title IX litigation that followed. The major dispute revolved around the concept of direct versus indirect federal funding. In question was whether "Title IX applied only to the specific departments receiving direct funding (commonly referred to as the 'programmatic approach') or extended to any department within an institution that benefited from federal assistance (commonly referred to as the 'institutional approach')" (Wong & Ensor, 1986).

By 1979, HEW had accumulated a backlog of 842 complaints of sex-discrimination (Gelb & Palley, 1982). The Women's Equity Action League (WEAL) and other feminist groups took legal action against HEW for a lack of enforcement of Title IX. Despite a promise by HEW to meet specific timetables to rectify the situation, the first case involving an intercollegiate athletic program was not settled until April of 1981, almost nine years after Congress adopted equal educational opportunity legislation. The Department of Education's Office of Civil Rights (OCR), which is responsible for monitoring compliance of Title IX, found inequities between men's and women's athletics at the University of Akron. However, the University was in the process of implementing a plan to rectify the inequities and was exonerated from noncompliance. The University of Akron case was a precedent-setting decision used to settle many other complaints by allowing institutions sixty days to arrive at an acceptable solution despite the fact that they were given three years to come into compliance with the law during the 1975–78 period (Title IX: More than education, 1981).

In 1984, "Title IX was dealt a severe blow in the Supreme Court Grove City v. Bell decision" (More than education,

1987, p. 6). The court ruled that Title IX applied to specific programs receiving direct federal aid in contrast to all programs housed in institutions receiving federal assistance. Twenty-three cases pending litigation initiated by the Department of Education against athletic programs at institutions of higher education were dropped because it could not be established that the athletic departments directly received federal funds (Berry & Wong, 1986). However, a strategy immediately employed by the OCR was to pursue enforcement on student financial aid programs for nonequitable distribution of athletic scholarships. "Approximately one dollar in five of financial aid based on athletic ability is awarded to a women," despite the fact that women comprise almost 31% of the participants in collegiate athletics (Uhlir, 1987, p. 28).

Civil rights activists noted that the narrow interpretation of the Grove City ruling could be applied to many nondiscrimination statutes and began soliciting support for new legislation to counteract the potential effects of this decision. Senators Kennedy of Massachusetts and Weicker of Connecticut introduced a bill in 1984 to restore the broader interpretation of Title IX and three other civil rights statutes that prohibited discrimination in federally assisted programs (More than education, 1987). The bill was introduced in the 98th, 99th, and 100th Congress but failed to gain approval.

In 1988, the Civil Rights Restoration Act was again introduced and overwhelmingly passed by both the Senate and the House by more than a two-thirds majority vote (Lawmaker's predict, 1988). President Reagan vetoed the bill despite requests by many Republicans for approval. Congress then overwhelmingly voted to override the president's veto, a move that put Title IX back into full force and effect.

The effects of the Civil Rights Restoration Act on enforcement of Title IX in intercollegiate athletics is yet to be seen. However, since enforcement of the regulations under the Reagan administration was spotty at best and much backsliding occurred following the Grove City v. Bell decision, administrators should expect an increase in Title IX complaints and investigations. Higher education institutions are required to establish a grievance procedure for the resolution of complaints by students and employees (Oglesby, 1978).

However, there is no requirement that complaints be initially heard by the grievance committee. Title IX complaints may be filed directly with the OCR. According to Oglesby (1978):

> Complaints of discrimination can be filed by or on behalf of an individual or a group of individuals. Complaints must be filed within 180 days of the date of discrimination. The Office of Civil Rights may also initiate investigations on its own. Once a complaint has been filed, and the complaint is determined to be valid, the institution is notified that a complaint has been made and which part of Title IX applies to it. The Department of Health, Education and Welfare [now the Department of Education] will then attempt to gain voluntary compliance by the institution. If this fails, administrative hearings may begin that can lead to the termination of Federal financial assistance. (P. 214)

EQUAL PAY ACT OF 1963

The Equal Pay Act of 1963 prohibits any discrimination in salaries and fringe benefits on the basis of sex in all educational institutions. The Equal Pay Act stipulates that persons in jobs that require equal skill, effort, and responsibility under similar working conditions be given the same pay. In its simplest terms, a woman coach whose team has an equal number of contests and equal number and length of practices, who supervises an equal number of students in her charge and has equal recruiting responsibilities, equal budgets to administer, and so forth, cannot be paid less than her male counterpart (Parkhouse & Lapin, 1980):

> Although 95 percent of the complaints are resolved through voluntary compliance, the Secretary of Labor has the right to file a suit against any agency that does not comply. Individuals may also do so, should the Department of Labor decline. The employee may be awarded salary raises, back pay and interest. No institution can harass or discriminate against an employee who has filed a complaint, assisted with an investigation, or instituted proceedings. Unless the issue comes to court, the name of the complainant may not be revealed to the institution without the person's consent. (P. 38)

TITLE VII OF THE CIVIL RIGHTS ACT OF 1964

Title VII of the Civil Rights Act of 1964 applies to institutions with fifteen or more employees. Employees are protected from any type of employment discrimination such as hiring, upgrading salaries, fringe benefits, training, and other conditions of employment that are based on race, color, religion, national origin, or sex (Parkhouse & Lapin, 1980):

> Under this statute, individuals and organizations may make the complaint on behalf of themselves or a class, citing a pattern as well as individual case. . . . Individuals may also take legal action. The court may order the institution to stop its unlawful practices, initiate or step up its affirmative action program, reinstate the employees, and award back pay for up to the two years prior to the filing of charges. As in the Equal Pay Act, the institution is prohibited from harassing the participant in these matters. (P. 41)

EXECUTIVE ORDER 11246

Executive Order 11246 is a government regulation applicable to all institutions that have government contracts of over $10,000. The regulation prohibits the institution from discriminating against any employee or job applicant based on race, color, religion, sex or national origin. In addition, institutions with contracts in excess of $50,000 and more than fifty employees must file written affirmative action plans that include numerical goals and timetables for recruiting, hiring, training, and upgrading women and minorities (Parkhouse & Lapin, 1980):

> Should the institution fail to comply, OFCCP or OCR has the power to suspend or terminate federal contracts, prevent future awards, or refer the issue to the Department of Justice, whereupon it may end up in court. The school may be ordered to raise salaries, provide back pay for up to two years for a nonwillful violation and three for a willful violation, or take other remedial action. (P. 43)

TITLE VII (SECTION 799A) AND TITLE VIII (SECTION 845) OF THE PUBLIC HEALTH SERVICE ACT

Title VII (Section 799A) and Title VIII (Section 845) of the Public Health Service Act prevents discrimination in admissions, internships, and employment at schools that receive a grant, loan guarantee, or interest subsidy to health personnel training programs or that are receiving a contract under Title VII or VIII. This law is applicable to athletic programs in the areas of sports medicine or athletic training programs (Parkhouse & Lapin, 1980).

STATE EQUAL RIGHTS AMENDMENTS

While there has been no federal enactment of an equal rights amendment, some individual states (for example, Pennsylvania and Washington) have adopted equal rights amendments to their state constitutions, and several sex discrimination in athletics cases have been decided in the complainant's favor on the basis of a state ERA (Wong & Ensor, 1985–86). Other states have enacted equal rights amendments that have not yet been used to litigate athletics cases.

Ethical and Philosophical Arguments Supporting Equal Opportunity for Women in Collegiate Sport

Recommended Policy: No University policy or procedure shall limit access to or equitable participation of qualified individuals from any group of society (e.g., women, ethnic or racial minorities, or the economically disadvantaged) in any higher education program or activity.

Higher education's larger responsibility is to lead society by espousing higher-order values central to the maintenance of ethical behavior and by creating a society within the university that is, by its example, a measure of human integrity. Limiting qualified individuals' access to or equitable participation in any higher education program is anathema (Lopiano, 1988, p. 3). Women students have historically been denied equal opportunity in collegiate athletics.

Overt or covert discrimination against females within the institution of sport has serious implications and consequences for the individual as well as for women in other institutional settings, most notably in education and occupational attainment (Demo, 1985, p. 38). Such discrimination also prevents women from receiving important benefits:

First, participation in athletics may teach interpersonal skills that are readily transferable and marketable outside of athletics. Second, athletics may serve an allocation foundation by raising the visibility of participants and providing them with an early success definition or label. Third, athletics may introduce participants to interpersonal networks, contacts, and information channels that are beneficial in establishing careers. (Otto & Alwin, 1977, P. 112)

Athletics teaches participants to develop physical strength, mastery of their environment, and the will to improve themselves. The level of self-confidence produced by physical achievement is obvious to all observers. Team play in sport teaches children about group dynamics, devising strategy, and medication, while traditional girls' games of dolls, dress-up, and cheerleading encourage passive, dependent, domestic, and decorative behavior (Pogrebin, 1980, p. 347).

"Athletic competition, as a powerful social institution, is as old as civilization. In addition, athletics often mirror as well as generate the social stereotypes that dictate society's values and roles for men and women" (Like she owns the earth, 1985, p. 1). Sport has traditionally been an area wherein the stereotype of men as participant and women as cheerleaders or observers has been reinforced (Mushier, 1978). It is the responsibility of higher education to espouse a strong position on the value of intercollegiate athletic participation for men and women and to insure that the female athlete does not occupy an inferior position vis-à-vis the male athlete. Gelb and Palley (1982, p. 95) confirm this principle: "To change the society in which one lives it is first necessary to modify the belief system of the people living in that society. One institution for transforming belief systems is the school. Thus, to alter beliefs regarding equal opportunities for women, one available route is education."

Determination of Equity: The Most Problematic Issues

Recommended Policy: Equal athletic participation opportunities shall be afforded male and female student-athletes. Institutional policies and procedures shall not discriminate on the basis of sex as they relate to the nature and extent of the sports programs offered, provision of athletic equipment and supplies, practice and competition schedules, provision of travel and per diem allowances, opportunity to receive coaching and academic tutoring, the assignment and compensation of coaches and tutors, provision of locker rooms and practice and competitive facilities, provision of medical and training services, housing and dining facilities and services, publicity services and scholarships. Athletic program expenditures need not be equal, but the pattern of expenditures must not result in a disparate effect on opportunity.

Title IX's "laundry list" of areas (see recommended policy above), which will be looked at by OCR in judging whether equal opportunity is being afforded female student-athletes, is fairly extensive. Institutions of higher education should conduct a self-evaluation of compliance by using the latest regulations interpreting the statute (see *Federal Register*, Vol. 44, No. 239, December 11, 1979). Lopiano (1976) suggests a model for conducting a Title IX self-evaluation. Administrators should also be aware of the most problematic issues that will be encountered in the process of evaluating and developing equal opportunity athletics programs.

NATURE AND EXTENT OF SPORT PROGRAMS OFFERED

Equal Numbers of Sports or Equal Participation Opportunities? Title IX requires equal participation opportunities as opposed to equal numbers of sport programs for male and female athletes. Thus, the fact that the average number of sports offered for women has grown to 7.31 per school (whereas ten years ago it was 5.61 sports) is deceiving (Acosta & Carpenter, 1988). When women's sports are added to college athletics programs, they are often low-participation sports like cross-country, golf, and tennis, which require minimal funding. Even if the number of sports for men and women are equal, team rosters of 50 to 100 male athletes in the sport of football often skew participation ratios. Thus, it is very important to look at comparative individual athlete participation slots as opposed to number of sports offered.

Despite the fact that college enrollments are 52% female, only 31% of all athletes enrolled in NCAA member institutions in 1985–86 were female (Uhlir, 1987). In addition, only 30% of the athletes participating at National Junior College Athletic Association institutions were women (Uhlir, 1987). "Fewer national championships in fewer sports and in fewer divisions are available to women than were available in 1981–1982" (Uhlir, 1987, p. 28). Thus, there is little question that colleges and universities will be asked to increase athletic participation opportunities for female students.

As the economic crunch facing athletics over the past several years was confronted, it was not atypical for women's programs to share equally in budget cutbacks despite the disproportional impact of such action. "Since women's athletics programs never achieved anything close to parity (participation is less than a 1:2 ratio), participation would still be less than equitable even if all participation cutbacks came from men's athletics" (Uhlir, 1987, p. 25). College administrators should be wary of budget reduction proposals that purportedly treat men's and women's athletics equally.

The "Interest" Loophole.   Whether the selection of sports and levels of competition effectively accommodate the interests and activities of members of both sexes is a factor used to determine whether equal participation opportunities are being offered. Women's programs have not been expanded and many women's teams have been dropped or continued with minimal participants under the guise of "insufficient interest." Upon closer examination, many women's sport programs suffer from lack of institutional commitment to developing such programs. If, in the name of gradual development, a part-time, underpaid, and unqualified coach is assigned to a new or existing women's sport program, the interest of prospective athletes may be deterred. Compared to the better-paid or more competent coach of the men's team, efforts to recruit participants or time spent with student-athletes may be minimal. Often, a men's team has a recruiting budget while the women's team in that same sport has none and is dependent upon the interest of currently enrolled students. The fact of the matter is that in most Division I and a majority of Division II programs, sport program participation is not dependent on the interest of the student body. Rather, it is dependent on the coach's recruiting efforts. Salary, recruiting budgets, released time for coaching, and numbers of assistant coaches may all relate to the number of participants in a particular sport program. Thus, eliminating women's sports due to "lack of interest" should be looked upon with suspicion.

Revenue-Producing Sport Exemption Proposals.   Soon after Title IX of the 1972 Education Amendments was adopted, efforts were made to remove revenue-producing sports from the calculation of equal opportunity in athletics (for example, the Tower Amendment). These unsuccessful efforts were provoked by a fear that the growth and development of women's athletics would drain the financial resources and success from revenue-producing men's football and basketball programs. Chief executive officers of colleges and universities will continue to hear many athletics administrators lament over the need to protect "the goose that laid the golden egg." Athletics administrators may also suggest that revenue-producing sports not be included in any comparison of athletics opportunities for male and female student-athletes. OCR has clearly interpreted Title IX as having no revenue-producing sport exemption.

Orleans (1982) has suggested that the entire notion of continuing efforts to exempt revenue-producing sports might not be in the best interests of higher education:

> A revenue-producing sport exemption may not now be in the best interests of colleges that seek it. First, administrative and judicial developments suggest that a solution is possible without new legislation. Second, state equal educational opportunity laws will continue to embrace all sports as matters of state policy, particularly at public institutions, regardless of any restriction in the scope of Title IX. Third, a special exemption for revenue-producing sports may strengthen arguments for treating them as commercial rather than nonprofit activities. Finally, any attempt to insulate "expensive" men's sports from comparison with women's program would give women coaches strong incentive to initiate equal pay litigation before any Title IX change could be accomplished. (P. 41).

Administrators should have a sound philosophy on the on the proper place of revenue-producing sports within the higher education setting. There is nothing wrong with the commercialization of sport or academia as long as exploitation or protection of the means of revenue production does not come at the expense of higher education's larger responsibility, which is to guarantee access to and equitable participation in higher education programs of qualified individuals. Justification of sex discrimination in the name of maintenance of a more efficient commercial exploitation of the sport entertainment product is unacceptable.

When the educational institution produces excellence, there is a public demand to consume that educational product—

be it athletics contests, superconducting materials, or government contracts for the intellectual expertise of our faculty. However, the public cannot be allowed to dictate or limit the university's search for truth or its commitment to higher-order values. Presidents and academic deans walk the same tightrope with major donors and contractors in the arts and sciences, and they struggle with federal intervention as athletics directors and coaches walk with those alumni interested in athletics. Chief executive officers must insure that the tail does not wag the dog. Commitment to higher-order value obligations must come before commercial exploitation of the sport entertainment product (Lopiano, 1988).

OPPORTUNITY TO RECEIVE COACHING AND THE ASSIGNMENT AND COMPENSATION OF COACHES

One of the most difficult equity issues in the provision of equal opportunity women's athletics programs involves the provision of quality coaches who are compensated in the same manner as their counterparts coaching men's sports. "The top-salaried college women's basketball coach in 1986–87 earns thirty-nine cents on the dollar of the top-salaried men's basketball coach. Median salaries of directors of athletics (1986–87) are $10,783 more for men than for women" (Uhlir, 1987, p. 28).

An examination of the salaries of male and female coaches in collegiate athletics reveals that generally, male and female coaches of women's teams are paid less than coaches of men's teams (who are predominantly male), and female coaches are paid less than male coaches who are coaching the same sport. Mottinger and Gench, in a 1984 comparative study of the salaries of coaches of men's and women's basketball teams, concluded:

> The differences in salary between the male and female basketball coaches in Division I colleges and universities appear to be attributable to sex-based factors. Furthermore, the male coaches are subject to higher salaries than the female coaches without any reasonable basis for that distinction, except possibly for years of experience and number of auxiliary personnel supervised. Even though an institution may claim that it can justify its pay scales for coaches, it may not be in compliance

with federal laws requiring equal employment opportunity. Congress and the executive branch of the federal government have addressed sex discrimination in employment. Through their decisions the courts have established precedents which have held that jobs which are substantially equal in skill, effort, and responsibility should be equally compensated. [P. 26]

There are two different pools of coaching candidates in the marketplace: an all-male coaches' pool for revenue-producing men's sports and a mixed pool of men and women for men's non-revenue-producing and women's sports. The marketplace value of coaches in the former pool is two to five times higher than the marketplace value of coaches in the latter pool. However, the existence of this sex-segregated marketplace cannot be used to justify salary discrimination for women coaches. In fact, with the recent development of women's basketball as a significant revenue-producing sport, it will be difficult to justify not hiring coaches of women's teams from the revenue-producing sport pool or paying female coaches of women's teams salaries equal to those of coaches in that pool.

Equally distressing as the current salary gap between coaches of men's and women's teams is the steady diminution in the number of women coaching men's and women's sports and the number of women in professional leadership positions:

- Only 43.3% of the coaches of women's teams are female. In 1972 more than 90% of women's teams were coached by females. A sample of what has happened in the top six participation sports for women at the college level follows:

Sport	1978	1988
Basketball	79.4%	58.5%
Cross-country	35.2%	19.5%
Softball	83.5%	67.2%
Tennis	72.9%	52.2%
Track	52.%	21.6%
Volleyball	86.6%	71.0%

- Fewer than 1% of the coaches of men's teams are female.
- About 5757 jobs exist in 1988 for head coaches of women's teams. This is an increase of 52 jobs since last year, but

women did not share in any of the increase and actually hold seven fewer jobs than in 1987.

- Only 16% of women's programs are headed by a female administrator. In 1972, more than 90% were headed by a female.
- Women hold 29% of all administrative jobs in women's programs.
- No females at all are involved in the administration of 32% of women's programs. (Acosta and Carpenter, 1988)

When financial resources started flowing to women's programs in the mid- to late-1970s as a result of Title IX, men's athletics department sought to control those new resources through mergers with women's athletics departments. Up until the early 1970s over 90% of all women's athletics programs were headed by women under separately administered (independent from men's athletics) departments, and most women's athletics teams were coached by women who performed these duties gratis or for minimal stipends. Under the guise of cost savings through prevention of duplication of effort, mergers of men's and women's athletics programs were accomplished with the director of the men's program assuming the helm of the combined unit and taking control of the hiring process. Soon thereafter, women coaches were displaced by male coaches attracted by the more lucrative salaries Title IX provided coaches of women's teams.

Acosta and Carpenter (1988) offer several reasons for the declining proportion of female coaches: "the continuing influence of the 'old boys' network for male coaches; the inability of a comparable 'old girls' network to get off the ground; unconscious discrimination in the selection process; and failure of enough women to apply for job openings" (p. 2).

Employment discrimination in athletics has also taken on more subtle forms. When searching for coaches of women's teams, the administrator may only look at formal written applications. When looking for coaches of a men's team, the athletic director will solicit applicants or hire good coaches away from other programs. Worse yet, it is not unusual, when checking on the credentials or references of female coaching candidates, to hear concerns that the applicant may have homosexual inclinations or references to her physical attractiveness as being more masculine than feminine. In contrast, the reference checker seldom hears anything about the personal lives or appearance of male applicants. In practice, the double standard is obvious and difficult to confront. Homophobia is an equal opportunity employment issue that is a lot like communism; it is talked about behind the backs of applicants and almost impossible to combat. Likewise, descriptions of a candidate as a "feminist" are often used to imply that a job candidate is a "troublemaker." Uhlir (1987) observes:

> Despite the widespread belief that women have arrived in the sacrosant bastions of athletic power and privilege within the university, the reality is otherwise. In no area of higher education are women so noticeably absent from the most prestigious positions of decision making. A woman may even aspire more realistically to become a chief executive officer or a member of a governing board, than to become a director of athletics of an NCAA Division I institution. (P. 25)

The reduced numbers are not a problem if educators believe that young female athletes do not need female coaches as role models or that it is not important for women coaches to demonstrate to girls that adult women can be strong, decisive managers. Women who coach boys' and men's teams at high school and college levels are practically nonexistent (fewer than 1%). Why is no one expressing concern over the lack of female coaches in men's sports? "Women bring to sport many expressive qualities young males need to develop for optimal human functioning—compassion, nurture, care for others, and fostering human relationships. Women coaches can not only help boys develop such qualities, but can also demonstrate a women's ability to be a credible decision maker" (Schafer, 1987, p. 6). Isaac (1987) observes:

> This decline in the number of women sports leaders is causing the public to perceive women as invisible and powerless. Sports receives tremendous coverage in the mass media and rarely does the public glimpse a woman coach, official, or athletic director. . . . To millions of people, women are non-existent in positions of authority. If equity professionals ignore sex dis-

crimination in sports leadership, the public perception of women as powerless will continue and our young female athletes will be unable to dream of a career in sport. Positive intervention is needed. (P. 17)

The decline of women coaches cannot simply be coincidental to the occurrence of mergers of men's and women's athletics departments. Sanders conducted a 1985 study that investigated NCAA Division I women's programs not affiliated with men's programs or those having organizational structures where there was equal authority of men's and women's athletics directors. He reported that among fourteen of seventeen institutions responding (82.3%), only 29 of 102 (28.43%) of all head coaching positions of women's teams were occupied by males—almost half the national average. In addition, Sanders (1985) reported that 23 female head coaches had $25,000+ salaries compared to 11 males earning salaries over that level.

Has the merger of men's and women's programs into single department units submerged the development of women's programs and reduced employment opportunities for female coaches? Lopiano, in a 1983 study of women's sport programs ranked in the nation's top ten, found that 68% of separately administered departments had one or more sports in the nation's top ten and 34% had more than one. In merged departments, only 17% had one or more sports in the top ten and 5% had more than one (Lopiano, 1983, p. 14). The literature appears to indicate that more progress in providing employment opportunities and comparable salaries to female coaches has been made within administrative structures where the men's and women's athletics directors have equal authority.

The message is clear. Higher education officials must monitor carefully employment and program practices in intercollegiate athletics if women's sports are to grow into equal opportunity athletics programs, especially in merged administrative units. "In this new era, opportunities for women as leaders have diminished, sport options for women athletes have been reduced, and development programs for women athletes have been dismissed as beyond the role of college departments of athletics" (Uhlir, 1987, p. 28).

Issues Related to the Redistribution of Financial Resources

Recommended Policy: Gifts of cash and property, grants, gate receipts, patent royalties, income derived from classes taught, summer camps or a film on the University football team's wishbone offense are owned by the university—not by the individual faculty member or coach or the individual department. The president is responsible for creating and balancing a community of interests within the University by distributing revenues from all sources to finance the achievement of the institution's goals and purposes.

Program expansion and improvements in the quality of opportunities afforded female student-athletes will undoubtedly require a redistribution of existing financial resources available to intercollegiate athletics. If women's athletics must now receive a significant portion of the athletics financial pie, the probability exists for (1) a reduction in numbers of opportunities for male athletes, (2) an adjustment in the traditional "standard of living" of men's athletics programs, and/or (3) across-the-board reductions in benefits or the elimination or decrease of costly athletic program practices in men's and women's athletics in order to maximize sport participation opportunities for both sexes.

USE AND OWNERSHIP OF REVENUES

There is an inherent danger in permitting any part of the university from earning and spending its own revenues without restraint. It is even more problematic for any university unit to believe that the revenues derived from its programs are not the property of the university. Yet, such beliefs abound in intercollegiate athletics. From immediately following the development of the Title IX regulations to the present, athletics administrators have lamented over having to share their men's athletics earned funds with women's athletics. Taking revenues derived from athletic programs and assuring they are used to provide equal opportunity for male and female athletes is a very different notion from taking men's athletics money and giving it to women's athletics.

Gifts of cash and property, grants, gate receipts, patent royalties, income derived from classes taught and summer camps are owned by the university rather than by individual faculty members or coaches or any single department unit. The president is responsible for creating and balancing a community of interests with careful distribution of income from all sources. Liberal arts is as important as business administration despite the fact it does not produce the full-time-equivalent units or revenues of the latter. That principle should also be applicable among men's and women's sports in the athletics program (Lopiano, 1988).

Cost Containment on the National Level

It would be foolish to suggest that universities need not be careful to protect the quality or revenue-producing capabilities of its athletics programs in addition to remedying inequities in opportunities for male and female athletes. Often, these revenues are the primary source of funding equal opportunity programs. Thus, it is important for higher education administrators to recognize that revenue production is a function of successful teams and competitive success is not simply a matter of institutional effort.

The success of a sport program is largely dependent on the effort of the institution vis-à-vis the efforts of institutions with which it competes. The notion of competitive equity is lost if one institution is permitted to expend resources to gain a competitive advantage and the other does not (that is, if one institution offers 100 scholarships in football and another offers 20, chances are the former institution will field more successful teams). Thus, maintenance of competitive equity in intercollegiate athletics is accomplished through the voluntary affiliation of institutions within a national athletics governance structure (for example, NCAA, NAIA, NJCAA) for the purpose of agreeing on common rules and limitations.

Likewise, no single institution can take unilateral cost-cutting measures without damaging its competition equity vis-à-vis other institutions. Thus, if cost reductions are necessary to free up funds to finance the development of women's athletics, chief executive officers must tenaciously pursue national legislation to reduce the costs of intercollegiate athletics among all institutions. If we are to bring fiscal sanity back to athletics, we will attack recruiting first. We will put our coaches back on our campuses and keep them off expensive roads and airways in their ancillary capacity as recruiters (Lopiano, 1988). National athletic governance organizations are also able to orchestrate strategies to revise federal legislation that has an impact on athletic program expenses. For instance, there is a need to reform the new tax laws that require student trainers and managers to be paid wages for their work instead of scholarship stipends. In many institutions these tax laws have doubled and tripled the cost of such student assistance. The only practical alternative of failure to reduce costs is simply to cut opportunities for male athletes. There simply are not enough new revenue sources available to athletics programs to double athletics budgets in order to provide mirror programs for women.

COST CONTAINMENT ON THE INSTITUTIONAL LEVEL

Few would argue that there is no fat in intercollegiate athletics programs at the institutional level. However, finding that fat is another matter. When asked to produce cuts in expenditures, athletics departments typically respond by cutting the bone from minor men's sports and women's programs and leaving the fat in revenue-producing men's sport programs. The justification for such actions is usually the necessity to protect the "goose that lays the golden egg." Such approaches to cost containment will doom most equity efforts to failure.

How does the chief executive officer know when cost-cutting is bone versus fat in intercollegiate athletics? In nonathletic programs, when institutions are faced with having to cut costs, there are a number of items that are central to the achievement of learning and research excellence that should be the last to go: among them, faculty salaries, student-teacher ratios, competitive scholarships to attract the most talented students. The first thing to go is foreign travel and out-of-state travel unrelated to teaching and research. Athletics is no different. The acquisition and retention of quality coaches, athletics scholarships, and team travel budgets are essential to the maintenance of program quality (Lopiano, 1988).

On most college campuses, athletics administrators, like their academic counterparts, will offer significant resistance to cost-cutting requests. Sex discriminatory practices may be entrenched and the majority of existing funds already committed to men's programs. Efforts to cut fat in intercollegiate athletics may require the assignment of an objective member of an institution's central administration to analyze expenditures as they relate to competitive success. While this suggestion sounds simple, the fact of the matter is that intercollegiate athletics budgets are complicated and convoluted in nature (Atwell, Grimes, & Lopiano, 1980). These programs have, for the most part, not been developed by professional managers. Thus, cost/benefit analyses are almost nonexistent. When 40,000 football programs are produced, removing several four-color pages may provide cost savings equivalent to a full athletics scholarship without any negative impact on the success of the football team.

Lopiano (1980) has suggested several approaches to cost containment that deserve consideration. Athletic program management and accounting practices should be carefully monitored. Administrators should demand a cost-benefit relationship for any proposed expense related to "keeping up with the Joneses" in order to maintain competitive status of a program. Higher education should conservatively approach proposals to expand athletics facilities during the next five years. Commitments to large debt service in light of predictions of rising costs and continued athletics program deficits may be fiscally irresponsible. Many athletics programs are already carrying debt service commitments that are disproportionate to their total budgets. While major investments in the people who produce quality athletic programs (coaches) need to be maintained, the productivity of clerical and other support personnel involved in large ticket offices, concessions, and game management operations should be carefully examined. Transportation and travel arrangements should be evaluated for cost effective practices. The number of day teams are spending on the road related to the number of days of competition should be examined and the entire travel package for all sports team should be put out on bid to a travel agent.

DEVELOPING WOMEN'S SPORTS AS REVENUE-PRODUCERS

There has been considerable debate as to whether women's athletics will ever be able to pay for itself. The real point is whether institutions are making every effort to insure that men's and women's sports are doing all they can to produce any revenues that can contribute to defraying program expenses. There are Division I women's basketball programs that produce gate receipts in excess of $350,000 annually. Yet, many institutions have made no commitment to developing quality women's programs that can contribute to the income column of intercollegiate athletics. Developing a revenue-producing women's basketball program (or any sport program) requires a major investment in those areas essential to the development of a quality program (for example, head coach salary, scholarships, team travel, and recruiting) as well as a commitment to promotions and marketing support and a realization that product development does not happen overnight. Redistribution of revenues can also mean making investments to insure revenue production.

For many athletics programs, the combination of student fees, men's football and basketball gate receipts, and television income combined with modest, unsophisticated fund-raising efforts have produced revenues adequate to support athletics programs. The financial needs created by women's programs have created increased need for revenues. Institutions should consider investing in professional fund-raising and other promotions expertise in order to maximize the revenue production of athletics.

Summary

Struggling with the demands of developing women's programs may create the need to reassess what many have considered to be excessive athletics program practices. Breaking the vicious cycle of increasing athletics program costs in the name of eliminating sex discrimination prohibited under federal law may prove to be an extremely worthwhile activity (Lopiano, 1975). Reopening the doors of employment and professional advancement to female coaches and administrators in a proactive way may save countless dollars in litigation costs and the time of numerous staff members who would have to be involved in OCR investigation procedures. Rather than presenting a burden to institutions of higher education, Title IX and the demand to provide equal opportunities for female student-athletes may very well prove to be the salvation of intercollegiate athletics.

4

Race on the College Campus

RICHARD E. LAPCHICK

Colleges and universities are supposed to be, along with parents and religious organizations, the guardians of our nation's moral values. When discrimination is part of the hiring system, when exploitation is part of the recruiting process, when athletes do not get an education, our nation's institutions of higher education have forfeited that guardianship.

When two men with closed minds help a nation learn more about itself, then we begin to realize that the nation's mind had been closed all along. We were poised to celebrate the fortieth anniversary of Jackie Robinson's break into the majors in 1987—a celebration of how far sports have helped us come to overcome racial problems. Then chance appearances on television by Al Campanis and Jimmy "the Greek" Snyder helped to change all that forever. Campanis asserted that blacks do not have the "necessities" to be field managers. Jimmy "the Greek" Snyder went beyond Campanis with a genetic explanation of black athletic prowess. Both Campanis's and Snyder's remarks were seemingly focused on pro sports.

In the post-Campanis climate, the racism evident in hiring statistics is staggering. Racism at pro level is now well documented. Yet the racial factor at the college level has barely begun to be addressed, reaching a new peak with the debate over NCAA Proposition 42 in early 1989.

A scandalously low 1.56% of America's 470,673 university faculty positions are held by blacks. The dismal hiring figures for black faculty at colleges and universities have been predicated on the grounds that not enough blacks have "credentials," an argument that sounds sadly like Campanis's remark. Hiring practices in college sport are even worse than in pro sport and nearly as bad as in higher education overall.

Professional Sport: The Summer Palace of Campanis

First it is important to examine why these gross inequities were submerged by what was going on in pro sport, where certain illusions had the look of reality. Major league baseball is 25% black; the NFL is 60% black; and the NBA is 75% black. Blacks and whites in each sport are earning $1 million a year or more. A few earn $2 million or more. Blacks have been the highest-paid players in baseball (Ozzie Smith, $2,340,000), basketball (Magic Johnson, $2,500,000), and football (Bo Jackson, $1,391,750). With *average* salaries of more than $500,000 in the NBA and in the major leagues and $200,000 in the NFL, pros are rich; racial discrimination seems at an end; the fame of the black athlete seems secure. Blacks are coaching in the NBA, college basketball, and college football; Frank Robinson cracked the ranks in baseball once again early in the 1988 season. Blacks are obtaining college educations as a result of sport. Black Olympic superstars are recognized as representatives of their country.

Before Al Campanis, many were ready to see in these numbers the proof of sport as the great equalizer. Finally, we thought, there was a sector of the economy where talent told the story. But Campanis's remarks led some of us finally to look below the surface. The reality we discovered was very discomfiting.

Major League Baseball

Baseball was neither the worst nor the best racially. The first black pro player in the modern era played baseball. Three of the top six highest earners of 1988 in team sport (Smith, Jim Rice, and Eddie Murray) were black baseball players. Nevertheless, the racial factor is alive and well in major league baseball.

When the Campanis story broke, only 17 out of 879 baseball front office jobs were held by blacks. Everyone suddenly began to ask, "If 25% of the players are black, then how can 1.9% of the management personnel be black?" The hiring of Harry Edwards and Clifford Alexander were dramatic statements by Commissioner Peter Ueberoth, but positions at the top remained almost exclusively white. The question heard over and over again was this: If blacks are accepted as players, then why not as managers and front office personnel?

Positional Segregation

An analysis of what positions blacks play on the field may provide an answer to the question just asked. A similar study has never been done for college players. However, if college athletic department hiring practices are any guide, then it is safe to assume that the statistics do not differ significantly.

When a study was conducted of what characteristics managers at the college and pro levels were seeking in players at different positions, the managers came up with the following qualifications for the positions of pitcher and catcher, second base, short stop, and third base: the ability to think, to make decisions, and to be team leaders. Now look at what percentage of each American-born racial group played these positions in 1988:

	White	Black American	Latin
Pitcher	90	6	4
Catcher	90	4	6
Second base	74	18	8
Short stop	68	29	3
Third base	85	15	4

The "thinking positions" central to the game itself were all dominated by whites. Only at second base did blacks match their percentage in the majors.

The same managers and coaches described the characteristics they were looking for in outfielders and first basemen as speed and reactive ability. A staggering 78% of all blacks playing offensive positions in the majors played either first base or outfield. Only 42% of all whites played in those spots. It may be that blacks are excluded from decision-making office jobs because the experience they bring from the field is primarily in non-decision-making positions.

Blacks have charged that the standards for survival are higher for them than for whites. Marginal blacks are not likely to become veterans. According to the 1987 team rosters and statistics, the charges hold up. In 1988, 53% of black baseball players had career averages greater than .270, versus only 35% of whites. On the other hand, 19% of whites had career averages below .241 versus 12% of blacks. It was even worse on the pitchers' mound, where few blacks compete. By percentage, 19% of black pitchers had earned run averages (ERAs) below 3.00, versus 9% of white pitchers. You simply had to be better to stay around if you were black.

Jimmy "the Greek" and Black Dominance in Sport

It was not enough that we kept black players around a shorter length of time and allowed them to play only select positions. Some of us still had to come up with a comforting rationalization concerning why blacks dominate certain sports. With Doug Williams leading the Washington Redskins on their 1988 championship charge, Jimmy "the Greek" Snyder was supposed to tell us how important it was to have the first black quarterback in the Superbowl. Instead he wanted to discuss thigh size. In the post–Jimmy "the Greek" atmosphere, a shocking number of respected people have seemingly agreed with a physical explanation of why blacks excel in sport. Whites can explain away that success with racist theories about genetics. Yet there were never any theories of white sport dominance in the 1930s with reference to white *physical* characteristics.

Many today are surprised to learn that Jewish players dominated basketball in the 1920s and 1930s. Contemporary writers did not talk about thigh size; they discussed mental skills and attitude. Ed Sullivan, later to be America's first famous television variety hour host, was a sport columnist for the *New York Daily News*. In a 1933 column he wrote, under the banner "Jews are Star Players":

> Holman, Jewish star of the Celtics, is a marvelous player. He has always reminded me of Benny Leonard. Both are of the same alertness and general make-up. Jewish players seem to take naturally to the game. Perhaps this is because the Jew is a natural gambler and will take chances. Perhaps it is because he devotes himself more closely to a problem than others will. Whatever the reason, the fact remains that some of the greatest stars of today are Jewish players.

But in time all-black teams began to beat all-white teams. The Rens took the Celtics in basketball. According to John Holway, author of *Voices from the Great Black Baseball Leagues*, teams from the Negro baseball leagues beat white major league teams in over 60% of their 445 games before Jackie Robinson broke the color bar in 1948. Joe Louis became a hero after he beat Max Schmeling; Jesse Owens was an acceptable black star after he won big for America in Berlin. Suddenly we had genetic theories. Yet, unlike those mental capacities theorized for Jewish basketball players, we had physical explanations for why blacks could run fast for short but not long distances, why they could jump higher than whites; and, later, why they could run faster in long-distance races, why they could not swim, and so on. Just an example will suffice from a college coach writing not long after Ed Sullivan's column appeared. Dean Cromwell coached Owens in Berlin. Later, as the University of Southern California's track coach, he wrote *Championship Technique in Track and Field*. In it he said: "The Negro excels in the events he does because he is closer to the primitive than the white man. It was not that long ago that his ability to spring and jump was a life and death matter to him." That book was published in 1941.

Things were more serious when blacks were not only playing but actually dominating sport in the 1970s. M. Kane's

1971 assessment in *Sports Illustrated*, entitled "Black Is Best," brought nods of agreement from whites and outrage from blacks. Blacks had more tendon and less muscle, giving them an advantage in "double-jointedness and general looseness of joints," Kane claimed. Also, blacks "have superior capacity to relax under pressure." Kane said, "Perhaps because of a physical inheritance, no black has ever been a swimming champion."

Whites have conceded the physical superiority of blacks because it fits the image: whites still have the brains. "All the racial upheaval of the 1960's had taught *Sports Illustrated* was that it's okay to be racist as long as you try to sound like a doctor," Bill Russell countered. His theory of blacks' success: "I worked at basketball up to eight hours a day for twenty years—straining, learning, sweating, studying." Russell knew there were social, economic, and political factors involved. Kareem Abdul-Jabbar told *Sports Illustrated:*

> Yes, I was just like the rest of those black athletes you've read about, the ones that put all their waking energies into learning the moves. That might be a sad commentary on America in general, but that's the way it's going to be until black people can flow without prejudice into any occupation they can master. For now it's still pretty much music and sports for us.

If there was an acceptance of genetic explanations for why blacks dominated some sports, if blacks' stays were shorter, and if positional segregation kept them out of decision-making positions, then chances of blacks' advancing through management were slimmer.

Post-Campanis Hiring in Pro Sport

An absence of blacks in management was the prevailing situation in major league baseball at the time of Campanis's Nightline interview. In that year, although 25% of the players were black, the black achievement included no managers, 12 of 134 coaches (9%), no general managers, a total of five key executives, and 1.9% of all front office personnel. Two years later, there was one black manager (hired at the helm of what was arguably baseball's worst team) and still no general managers.

According to the Commissioner's Office, 33% of the 542 front-office and on-the-field hires made since Al Campanis were minorities. While credit should be given, there have been questions about the numbers. A club-by-club survey by the *Kansas City Times* showed that only 133—less than half of the 288 minority workers employed—were black, 6.1% of the total of 2,005 front-office and on-the-field positions in 1988. That was up from 72 blacks (3.8%) out of 1,914 jobs the year before, but is far less than the ratio in baseball.

The second and perhaps bigger problem is that the commissioner's data do not specify which positions blacks were hired to fill. It was suggested that they were clerical workers in the office and groundskeepers on the field. All we know is they were not hired as general managers or, with the single exception of Frank Robinson, as managers.

However, the naming of Bill White as President of the National League was certainly a sign that things may change faster and more substantially under Commissioner Bart Giamatti. White instantly became the highest-ranking black sports administrator in history.

Football was at the rear of the parade. Some 60% of the sixteen hundred players were black, and, although the NFL did nearly as well as the NBA or MLB with assistant coaches (47 of 220 or 18%), as of January 1989 there had never been a black head coach or general manager in the modern era of the NFL.

Cleve Bryant, who left the New England Patriots to take the Ohio University job in 1985, is one of four black head coaches at the Division IA level. He told *Sport:* "At one point the NFL was saying that there were no black coaches with head coaching experience. Now they tell me I have to win more games. Someone has to tell me a different line. I've shown leadership, I've had experience. I've done everything everyone else has done and my phone hasn't rung." A survey done after the 1989 Super Bowl indicated that 5% of NFL front office personnel were black.

The NBA was, by far, the most progressive. But then, with 75% of its players black, this record might be expected. As the 1988–89 season closed, blacks accounted for 21%

(five) of all head coaches in the NBA; 22% of all assistants; the only two general managers in pro sport; the highest-ranking executives in any league office; and nearly 11% of front office personnel around the league. The NBA has created the best model in pro sport.

College Sport: A Bastion of Racism?

If we accept that pro sport is a commercial venture, then it might be expected that sport at the university level would be a harbinger for future progress, for we are accustomed to thinking that universities are the keepers of our ideals.

John Thompson was our 1988 Olympic coach. His Georgetown team has won the national championship; is a perennial power in the Big East Conference; has one of the highest winning percentages of any active or retired college coach; and was recently the president of the basketball coaches' association. On top of that, Georgetown is considered to be one of the outstanding programs in the country—a country plagued by academic and athletic recruiting scandals. Thompson's players graduate at a rate of nearly 90% when, as has been cited in other chapters, only 27% of Division I players graduate nationally. If John Thompson were an example of what is happening at American colleges and universities, then we would have a model for pro leagues. Unfortunately, Thompson is hardly the norm.

Illinois State had hired Will Robinson as the first black head coach at a predominantly white Division I school one year before Thompson went to Georgetown. As of May 1989, there were only twenty-five black head coaches at predominantly white universities (9.09%), while 57% of all the players at this level were black. When the 1988–89 season ended, four black coaches were fired. Rudy Washington, director of the Black Coaches Association, told *Sport* magazine: "Blacks get jobs because of crisis situations like Memphis State and Minnesota, or because they are jobs nobody else wanted like the Georgetown job. There's been a definite reason every time black coaches get jobs. If they hire on qualifications alone, it's seldom a black hire."

The story for women's basketball is no better: nine blacks were coaching the 263 Division I women's, predominantly white, college teams. That makes only 3.4% of the total. NCAA Division I basketball was actually far behind the NBA where there were five black coaches (21%) among the twenty-three teams in the 1987–88 season. That number does not speak well for the colleges.

College football will not provide too many candidates for the long-awaited first black head NFL coach. As Cleve Bryant said, college experience does not seem to matter if you are black. Even if it did, colleges are not yielding that opportunity to blacks. Willie Jeffries, later Howard's coach, was the first black to coach a Division IA program when he took over Wichita State in 1979. As of early 1989 there were only four: Bryant, Wayne Nunnely (University of Nevada, Las Vegas), Francis Peay (Northwestern) and Dennis Green (Stanford). Like their basketball counterparts, each took jobs in losing programs. At UNLV, Nunnely would live in the shadow of Jerry Tarkanian, their legendary basketball coach. Peay took over a program in the Big Ten, where he had no chance to move into the elite of the conference. Green was hired when Jack Elway was fired at the end of the 1988 season. These programs seemed doomed to failure prior to the arrival of these coaches. None has so far had a dramatic reversal of fate.

Beyond the revenue sports, black athletes compete heavily in college track and, to a lesser extent, baseball. In 1988–89 there were five black track coaches (4.5%) at the 109 Division IA schools and not a single black baseball coach at a Division IA school.

BLACK HEAD COACHES AT PREDOMINANTLY WHITE DIVISION I, IA, AND IAA UNIVERSITIES, May 1989

	Total No. of Schools	Black Coaches	
		No.	%
Basketball			
Men	275	25	9.1%
Women	263	9	3.4%
Football	175	4	2.3%
Baseball	252	0	0%
Track (Men's)	200	5	2.5%
Total	1,165	43	3.6%

Of the 1,165 head coaching positions available in those sports in Divisions I, IA, and IAA, 43 were held by blacks as of May 1989. That 3.6% of the pie represents fewer than half of the total (7.8%) of black head coaches in professional sport—by which are meant not all sports, but only the five sports that blacks compete in most in college.

Considering that these are the sports wherein the black athletes play, we could at least expect better coaching representation at the level of assistant, if not at the level of head coach. The most extensive survey of assistant coaches was compiled by Clarence Underwood in The Student Athlete: Eligibility and Academic Integrity. Underwood is assistant commissioner of the Big Ten Conference. In 1983, he canvased America's thirteen biggest conferences, representing 278 schools. Sport by sport, blacks served as assistant coaches as follows:

Basketball   72   (an average of 1 for every 4 Div. I programs)
Football   97   (an average of 1 for every 2 Div. IA & IAA programs)
Track   21   (an average of 1 for every 5 Div. IA programs)
Baseball   2   (an average of 1 for every 130 Div. IA programs)

Thus, while blacks held approximately 18% of the assistant coaching positions in the pros, they held only 192 (4.8%) out of more than 4,000 assistant coaching positions in the colleges. While these figures may have improved (the Black Coaches' Association has three hundred members, some from other NCAA divisions) since Underwood's survey of 1983, the BCA says it is no more than 5% today.

Critics of the college system point out that where blacks were assistants, their primary role was to recruit black athletes. Even so, they can perform an important role for black athletes on the team as role models.

Playing for White Coaches

With the percentage of black coaches in college sport so low, more than 95% of the teams that black athletes will be playing on will be coached by whites. Their assumptions about black people will determine how they treat the black player. The coach becomes the black student-athlete's main white contact at our nation's predominantly white schools. According to surveys, the black athlete feels he is discriminated against by his coaches—and counseled differently from whites by his academic advisors. This may reflect the racism he experiences from them or it may reflect a general distrust of whites. Even well-intentioned acts can be interpreted by blacks as being racially motivated. The same phenomenon, of course, can work the other way.

Over the years, black student-athletes have continued to make the same complaints: subtle racism such as different treatment during recruitment, poor academic advisement, harsh discipline, positional segregation on the playing field, and social segregation away from it. Then there are the complaints of overt racism, namely: racial abuse; blacks benched in games more quickly than whites; marginal whites kept on the team bench while only actively playing blacks are retained; extra money for white players; summer jobs for whites and good jobs for their wives.

To say that most white coaches are racist is a great exaggeration. But most coaches, racist or not, have been raised in the prevalent white culture. The norm for them is the white society's norm. Inseparable from this inevitable fact are images—albeit invariably false images—of what black society is and what kind of men it produces. The white coach who accepts these "black characteristics" (and surveys show that most white Americans do accept them), may believe that blacks are less motivated, less disciplined, less intelligent, more physically gifted; and that they are raised in a culture wherein drugs and violence are common, they are more comfortable with other blacks, and they have other black athletes as role models. The white coach who believes some or all of these characteristics may believe that they are pejorative and can be changed—or simply that such is the way God chose to make things. He may think of himself as being racially prejudiced—but more than likely, he views himself as a coach with a mission to "uplift" black values. In either case, he acts on these images and his black players are victimized. If the coach believes that blacks are less highly motivated and less disciplined, he will lean heavily on them in practice and in games. He will make the black athlete who complains of injury learn to push himself harder, to endure more and more pain. In the worst case for the black player, the white coach, well intentioned or hateful, might just let him play without guidance.

John Thompson once told *Sports Illustrated* why he wants his predominantly black teams to be known as disciplined. "Undisciplined, that means nigger . . . they can't play as a team and they choke under pressure. It's the idea that a black man doesn't have the intelligence . . . to practice self-control."

The white coach who believes that blacks are less intelligent may choose a certain academic path for them and may suggest less demanding courses to reduce the pressure. In the 1989 NCAA study on the black athlete, only 31% of black athletes felt their coaches encouraged them academically. Coaches naturally think of their profession as a role-model for black athletes. How many black doctors, lawyers, accountants, or psychoanalysts are white coaches apt to know? But these coaches do know who John Thompson, George Raveling, and John Chaney are. Thus, it is not surprising that too many black athletes major in physical education or athletic administration. For too many coaches, on the other hand, the main concern is keeping blacks—and whites, too—eligible. Admission standards are bent, and cheating runs rampant. But it is the value system, placing sport success above academic success, that is at fault here. If they graduate, how will they apply those studies, since blacks are largely shut out of this job market? *If* they graduate: this is key, since only 20% of black Division I basketball and IA football players reportedly graduate. Eight out of ten do not graduate; fewer than 1% play in the pros. Where do the rest go? Like many white athletes who face similar—if less frequent—exploitation, they appear in the sport pages as former stars in trouble with the law. More than 250 athletes were in such trouble in 1988! In the end, the effects of some actions of white coaches on black athletes can have devastating consequences. Study after study has shown that as long as the act is *perceived* as being racially motivated—even if it is a well-intentioned act—the end result is the same.

So what should black athletes do? If they think they should play at a school with a black coach, they will be dramatically narrowing their choices. So, with few exceptions, black athletes will have to attend predominantly white schools with white coaches. The NCAA study showed some of the results. Academically, many blacks enter these colleges at a disadvantage. This may be artificially maintained by a series of academically inferior courses. They are unlikely to get a degree because once their eligibility expires, so may the school's interest in them. Memphis State went twelve years without graduating a single black basketball player. Athletically, they will have to be the best—because otherwise they would not be there. Still, with prevailing stereotyping, many coaches will make assumptions about these athletes that they would never make about whites. Socially, the study showed blacks feel isolated on campus. They may be segregated in student housing and off-campus housing, on road trips and in bed. They face subtle and overt racism from white students. As we have seen all around the country, from the University of Massachusetts to the Citadel, overt acts of racism are on the rise on college campuses.

If all or even some of this description applies, then why should black athletes subject themselves to such painful circumstances in the first place? The answer is simple. They have been told by the media, guidance counselors, and coaches that sport is their path to success. According to the 1989 NCAA study, 44% of black football and basketball players believe they will play in the pros. They see Kareem and Magic. For a few of them, the Moses that ought to lead them to the promised land is Malone, who skipped college altogether. It will be hard for such athletes to take their professors as role models when they know that Kareem, Magic, and Moses all earn more than a professor's annual salary each night they play.

Sport has always been promoted as the hope of black people. But too often this is an empty, blighted hope. If you are good, you can play until you are eighteen. If you are very good, you can beat the 100-to-1 odds and keep going until you are twenty-two. If you are great, maybe the 10,000-

to-1 odds against making the pros can be beaten. But if you put your studies aside while challenging those nearly insurmountable odds, then you will have surrendered the once-in-a-lifetime chance at an education.

Forty years ago Jackie Robinson broke the color line in baseball. Twenty years later, Jack Olsen wrote his famous series for *Sports Illustrated*. He concluded: "At most, sports has led a few thousand Negroes into a better life while substituting a meaningless dream for hundreds of thousands of other Negroes. It has helped perpetuate an oppressive system." The only difference today is that more blacks are chasing that dream, which has become even more elusive.

College Sport Administration

If there is to be a more promising future for the black athlete, then more black coaches and assistants will have to be hired. Just as some argue that hiring practices in pro sport will change significantly only when blacks own a franchise, it is argued as well that more blacks must become college presidents and athletic directors at schools that have major programs. It is ironic that there were more black presidents (five) than athletic directors (two) in the 1987–88 year.

Gayle Sayers became the first black athletic director when he got the job at Southern Illinois in 1973. McKinley Boston became the third black athletic director at a Division I school when he was hired by the University of Rhode Island in 1989. Gene Smith is AD at Eastern Michigan and Charles Harris is AD at Arizona State. Harris told *Sport*: "There's no feeder system for athletic departments. An athletic department is so small that there aren't enough positions to really work your way up and cultivate new and young managers. The whole system is self-fulfilling."

Based on Underwood's survey, Harris's complaint would seem to be a major understatement. In this survey of 277 schools, fourteen of more than eleven hundred (1.2%) assistant and associate athletic directors were black; fourteen of more than eleven hundred business and ticket managers, sport information directors, and trainers were black (1.2%). That is not even up to the 8% of pro front office personnel who were black. Thus, it is certainly no cause for encouragement that 266 of a possible 7,738 jobs from coach to trainer surveyed were held by blacks.

The Future of the Black Athlete

We do see black athletes on every campus in the country. Blacks in the revenue sports carry the nonrevenue sports, in which few blacks compete. Yet, according to Harry Edwards, only 10% of scholarships go to black athletes, and those are almost exclusively in football and basketball, the sports we see on television. The television exposure leaves the general public believing that blacks dominate college sport, whereas they actually receive fewer athletic scholarships than their proportionate number in the population.

Both the NAACP and Jesse Jackson have indicated that they will take a hard look at college athletic departments. Logic suggests this. There are seventy-seven pro teams in the NBA, the NFL, and major league baseball. If each has an average of 100 employees, then the potential job pool is approximately 7,700. However, there are 1,853 NCAA, NAIA, and NJCAA schools with athletic programs that field an estimated 19,839 teams needing 19,839 head coaches. The 800 NCAA schools average 2 assistants per team, the 503 NAIA schools average 1.5, and the 550 NJCAA teams average 1 assistant per team. That means there are approximately 34,166 assistant coaching positions. If each athletic department had 10 staff positions, that would be another 10,000 jobs. Thus, there are potentially more than 40,000 jobs in college sport wherein minorities could be employed.

Colleges and universities are supposed to be, along with parents and religious organizations, the guardians of our nation's moral values. When discrimination is part of the hiring system, when exploitation is part of the recruiting process, when athletes do not get an education, our nation's institutions of higher education have forfeited that guardianship.

Unlike professional sports, colleges now have the opportunity to take the moral high road. The NCAA has appointed a task force to address this issue. Nonetheless, it will take action by the individual university presidents to bring about necessary changes. They can bring former student-athletes and former students who are minorities back to the athletic department with meaningful employment. If they do not act on the opportunity, the heat in college sport of the future might not be only on the gridiron or on the court.

Recruiting

ARE IMPROPER BENEFITS REALLY IMPROPER?

ALLEN L. SACK

While the myth of amateurism may be consistent with the values and interests of universities and their largely middle- and upper-class constituencies, it is far less likely to be embraced by working- and lower-class athletes, who constitute an important source of labor for the college sport industry.

Society's response to Prohibition illustrates what happens when laws are passed without due regard for the mores of the population they are meant to guide. Within a year of passing the Eighteenth Amendment, it was clear that Americans had simply not stopped drinking. Violations of the law were so rampant that resources available to the first Prohibition commissioner proved to be ludicrously insufficient.[1] The fifteen hundred agents hired to enforce the law were overwhelmed. Once legitimate businesses could no longer manufacture alcoholic beverages, organized crime lost little

71

time filling the void. By passing a law that large segments of the United States population did not support, the government actually spawned corruption and precipitated a national scandal.[2]

Anyone who follows developments in college sport is aware that certain NCAA regulations, especially those regarding illegal payments to athletes, are violated on a fairly regular basis. In 1982, Digger Phelps, Notre Dame's basketball coach, charged in a nationally televised interview that many universities had slush funds that funneled substantial amounts of money to college athletes. More recently, the media have been filled with reports of athletes' receiving illegal benefits like low-interest loans, money for travel, profits from the sale of game tickets, jobs for parents and relatives, the use of expensive cars and motel rooms, and in some instances, enough money from boosters and agents to be considered salaried employees.[3] The NCAA has tried to enforce its rules by expanding its staff of investigators, but to no avail. Like the Eighteenth Amendment to the United States Constitution prohibiting the sale of alcohol, the NCAA's amateur code appears increasingly difficult to enforce, and the corruption associated with college sport has become a national scandal.[4]

In light of these cautionary remarks, one major purpose of this chapter is to determine the degree to which college athletes actually view NCAA rules regarding amateurism as legitimate. It may be the case that much of the alleged corruption associated with college sport is the result of rules that are out of line with the mores and values of many athletes recruited to play in the college sport industry. Because the United States is a pluralistic society, one is unlikely to find unanimous support for any one set of moral principles, including those regarding amateurism. Thus, the second purpose of the study is to examine a number of factors that may influence support or lack of support for the amateur ethos among athletes themselves.

This is essentially a descriptive study. However, no analysis of data is ever totally inductive. Throughout this chapter, a number of general hypotheses (these are hunches rather than formal hypotheses) have provided a broad orientation to the data. The first is that athletes from lower socioeconomic backgrounds will be least likely to recognize the moral legitimacy of the NCAA's amateur code. Many athletes may find it difficult to understand why universities, television networks, coaches, and many other people can make millions from college sport while athletes themselves are routinely sanctioned for rule infractions like selling game tickets for expense money. But it is poor and working-class athletes who are most likely to feel the direct economic impact of NCAA policies. An athletic scholarship covers room, board, tuition, and fees. It does not cover travel to and from school and other expenses incurred by the average college student. Athletes from less affluent backgrounds may view amateurism as a luxury they simply cannot afford.

The second hypothesis is that black athletes, given their status as the poorest of the poor, are likely to find amateurism to be a particularly exploitative concept. Over 30% of all black Americans live in poverty, and blacks have median incomes that are only half those of whites.[5] For many black Americans, sport is viewed as one of the few avenues open for achieving financial success. Under these circumstances, it may be unrealistic to expect blacks to embrace a nineteenth-century aristocratic ideology that implies there is something morally suspect about accepting money for sport participation. It is also unrealistic to think that black athletes have not been aware that the dramatic increase in the proportion of black college athletes in recent years has parallelled college sport's ability to attract television revenue.[6] Black athletes may think it is only fair that they receive a share of the revenues they help to generate.

College sport for women has only recently taken on aspects of commercial entertainment. Throughout most of the nineteenth and twentieth centuries, women's programs have discouraged extreme competitiveness, fought against professionalism by refusing to offer athletic scholarships, and kept commercialism under control. In other words, women's collegiate sport has generally adhered fairly closely to the older aristocratic or British ideal of amateurism. This in part reflects the close correspondence between the amateur ideal, with its genteel and less competitive approach to sport, and

Victorian stereotypes concerning the inferior status of women in society. It may also reflect a commitment on the part of women to place the human and interpersonal needs of athletes above the commercial interests of sport as a business. Whatever the case, it will be hypothesized that woman athletes, even today, will be far more supportive of amateurism than men, and will be less likely than men to view sport as just another job.

To examine these hypotheses, a questionnaire was mailed to a sample of male and female basketball players from each NCAA Division.[7] The final sample size was 644. Some 45% of the athletes were from NCAA Division I schools; 30% were from Division II; and 25%, or 175 respondents, were from Division III. Respondents represented forty-seven schools and thirty-five conferences. A major strength of the survey is that it is the only one ever done that examines college athletes' attitudes concerning amateurism and employment issues in college sport. Another strength is that the sample, although not random, includes a variety of schools from the three NCAA divisions. Most studies of college athletes tend to be case studies of Division I schools.

How Amateurism Was Defined

A wide variety of definitions of amateurism have appeared over the years. For the purpose of this chapter, the NCAA's current definition should suffice: "An amateur athlete is one who engages in a particular sport for the educational, physical, mental, and social benefits derived therefrom and to whom participation in that sport is an avocation." Athletes are not allowed to take pay or to accept the promise of pay in any form. The NCAA has elaborate rules prohibiting what it defines as excessive or improper expenses, awards, or benefits. College athletes have been investigated by the NCAA for an action as seemingly innocent as having an athletic department cover travel expenses to the funeral of a teammate. Needless to say, cash payments from alumni are prohibited, as are various employee benefits normally received by professionals.

A number of questions in the survey focused on athlete's attitudes toward important facets of the NCAA's amateur code. For instance, athletes were asked if they think it is wrong for college athletes to accept money "under the table" for things such as traveling and living expenses. They were also asked whether college athletes deserve a share of the television revenue they generate for universities, whether college athletes have the right to the same kinds of benefits as other employees in the American work force (like workmen's compensation and disability insurance), and whether big-time college athletes should have a right to form labor unions. In addition, questions were also included that examined the athlete's primary motivations for playing college sports.

Attitudes toward Under-the-Table Payments

Overall, it was found that 43% of the athletes in the sample saw nothing wrong with accepting money under the table for things such as traveling and living expenses. A composite of five separate bivariate tables reveals that there are considerable differences in the responses to this question by race, gender, class, and scholarship status.[8] Blacks, males, lower-class athletes, and athletes whose financial aid is based on athletic ability were nearly twice as likely as others to view illegal payments as acceptable. The fact that 61% of blacks, 55% of males, 55% of lower-class athletes, and 51% of athletes on scholarship had lower regard for this important facet of the NCAA's amateur code may help to explain why so many athletes have accepted money from alumni and other sources when offered. It may be the case that many athletes actually do not think they are doing anything wrong when they accept such money.

Because 40% of the male athletes and only 9% of the female athletes in the sample are black, one could argue that gender differences in the survey results are actually a reflection of race or even social class differences. A bivariate analysis of race, class, and gender found all three variables to be related to each other. It was also found that race and scholarship status were closely related. Thus, a multivariate design was needed to examine the effects of each independent variable while holding the others constant. Because all of the variables in the study are categorical, it was possible to construct a series of multivariate tables that describe the joint effect of class, race, gender, and scholarship status on attitudes regarding amateurism. This type of tabular analysis is often referred to as the elaboration model. (Tables showing the precise results of the analyses in this chapter are in the Sources and Notes section in the back of the book.)[9]

The elaboration model indicates that males were more likely to approve illegal payments than females, regardless of race and class.[10] Although these gender differences were clearer among white athletes than among blacks, the general pattern holds up nonetheless. Likewise, race and class differences in responses to the under-the-table payment question appear to hold up, even when controls are introduced. What this suggests is that all three independent variables (race, class, and gender) have a direct influence on the dependent variable (whether or not the athletes took money). The model also suggests that the relationships are additive. For instance, a lower-class black male is much more likely to approve of under-the-table payments than an upper-class white female. A total of 67% of lower-class black males approved of such payments, by contrast with only 18% of upper-class white females.[11]

Attitudes Toward Sharing Television Revenues

Another measure of the commitment college athletes have to the NCAA's amateur code is the degree to which they perceive themselves to be employees with employee rights. One employee right that clearly separates amateurs from professionals is the right to share in the revenues generated by sport. In big-time college sport, these revenues run into millions of dollars. Although only 43% of the athletes in the total sample agreed that college athletes deserve a share of the television revenue they generate for universities, analysis of survey results reveals marked race differences in response to this question. Regardless of gender and social class, blacks were far more likely than whites to think they deserve a share of television revenue. It is perhaps noteworthy that 80% of lower-class black males think they deserve a share of the revenue by contrast with only 28% of upper-class white males. Responses to this question lend support to the argument that amateurism is more consistent with the values of the white upper class than with those of the working class and the poor.[12]

Attitudes toward Unionization and Employee Benefits

An examination of college athletes' attitudes toward whether they should have the right to unionize and receive other employee benefits reveals that race is again a good predictor of attitudes toward amateurism. Of all the black athletes surveyed, 58% agreed that college athletes deserve benefits like workmen's compensation and disability insurance, but only 34% of the white athletes agreed. Data analysis suggests that gender is not related and that class is only slightly related to attitudes toward employee benefits.[13] Athletes were also asked if they agreed that college athletes should have a right to form unions. That only 13% of the sample agreed is not surprising, given the anti-union sentiment in the nation as a whole. Nonetheless, 34% of the black male athletes, as opposed to only 8% of the white males, supported the right of college athletes to unionize. Gender and class did not have an appreciable effect.

Why Athletes Compete in College

One of the major purposes of the NCAA is to promote sport as a recreational activity. This would suggest that college sport should be pursued for its own sake and not for narrow utilitarian or financial motives. To assess the level of support for this amateur notion, athletes were asked to rank a number of factors as reasons for playing college sport. While 81% of Division III athletes rated "The sheer fun of playing" as their major reason for being involved in college sport, this was true of only 40% of athletes from Division I. Furthermore, regardless of division, blacks were less likely than whites to make that response. Only 23% of Division I blacks play for fun.

If athletes are not playing primarily for fun, the obvious question is, what are their motives? Many athletes chose the option "It pays for my education" as their primary motive for being involved in college sport. It is, of course, not surprising that almost no Division III athletes reported this as their primary motivation. Because they do not receive financial aid in return for their athletic services, their reasons for playing are more likely to emphasize intrinsic satisfaction than extrinsic rewards. The motives of Division I athletes, it would appear, are markedly different. Whereas only 4% of Division III athletes stated that their primary motivation for sport involvement was to pay for their education, this was the reason given by 45% of athletes in Division I. Blacks are far more likely to make that response than whites, regardless of division. Some 56% of Division I blacks play primarily to pay their way through school.[14]

Conclusions and Policy Implications

According to William Graham Sumner, any practice that becomes part of the mores takes on an almost sacred quality. The mores are not open to question or rational discourse; they are simply taken for granted.[15] For many Americans, the concept of amateurism has exactly this quality. Athletes who accept financial benefits in excess of what the NCAA allows are often placed in a category with prostitutes and others who are deemed morally unacceptable. Coaches and alumni who are caught providing such payments are denounced and severely sanctioned. Reformers who point to what they see as inconsistencies in the amateur code, or who have the temerity to suggest that college athletes be paid outright, are often ridiculed and vilified by leaders in the educational and sport establishment. Violations of the amateur code shock the deeply held sentiments of many influential people in the academic community.

One major conclusion of this study is that this moral indignation may not be shared by large numbers of college athletes. Sixty-one percent of blacks, 55% of males, and 55% of lower-class athletes in the sample see nothing wrong with accepting illegal payments. Eighty percent of lower-class black males feel they deserve a share of the television revenue they generate. This may, in part, help to explain the fact that no sooner has one school been sanctioned by the NCAA than another is being investigated. Many athletes may view amateurism as an exploitative ideology whose primary function is to keep labor costs at a minimum. The concept of ama-

teurism may be as alien to their world as Prohibition was to
the many Americans for whom alcohol was a normal and
perfectly acceptable part of daily life.

As is shown in several other chapters in this book, many
big-time athletic programs violate amateur principles by paying athletes for their services in one form or another. However, the amateur label persists because it performs a number
of important functions for universities. First, it allows the
college sport industry to avoid the labor costs of open professionalism. Second, the amateur label confers a special status
on college sport that renders it more compatible with the
"high culture" one associates with academic life. While the
myth of amateurism may be consistent with the values and
interests of universities and their largely middle- and upper-
class constituencies, it is far less likely to be embraced by
working- and lower-class athletes, who constitute an important source of labor for the college sport industry. The finding
that lower- and working-class athletes are far less likely than
others to see anything wrong with accepting under-the-table
money to pay living expenses lends empirical support to this
argument. The concept of amateurism, it can be argued, has
always served the interests of those who control athletics.

Although both class and race are related to an athlete's
attitudes regarding the morality of illegal payments, only race
was found to be related to whether athletes thought they
deserved a share of television revenue and other employee
benefits. It would appear that blacks, regardless of social
class background, have a far more instrumental view of college sport than do whites. Sport, it can be argued, has played
an especially important role in black culture. Even when
blacks have been barred from other areas of American life,
sport has offered a small opening through which they have
fought their way upward. Although sport participation may
be fun, black athletes have simply not had the luxury of
participating in sport merely for sport's sake. The black
athlete is likely to view college sport as a type of employment
in which athletic services are traded for room, board, tuition,
and other financial benefits. The fact that coaches, television
networks, and a wide variety of other persons and organizations share in the profits of college sport probably further

undermines any moral commitment blacks might have to the amateur concept.

Collegiate sport for women adhered to the older aristocratic ideal of amateurism right up until the late 1960s. Therefore, the expectation was that women athletes would be more committed to amateur regulations than men. When asked to make a moral judgment about the propriety of accepting money under the table, women were indeed far more likely than men to respond that it was wrong. Yet, on issues that did not require a moral judgment, but rather opinions about whether college athletes deserve a share of television revenue or other benefits, there were no significant gender differences. Men and women were also quite similar in the motives they gave for playing college sport.

One possible explanation for why women are more likely than men to say it is wrong to violate NCAA rules is that women's sport up until the early 1970s has, in fact, closely approximated the amateur ideal. Thus, women athletes are not as likely as males to have experienced the contradictions that emerge when amateur sport becomes highly commercialized. Another possibility is that women generally have a different sense of morality than men. According to Carole Gilligan, women often differ from men in their criteria for making moral judgments.[16] What accounts for these differences is open to a wide variety of interpretations. Other data from this survey revealed that female athletes were less likely than men to have cheated in schoolwork or to have had others do their work for them. The issue of gender differences in sport deviance deserves further attention.

The major policy implication of this study for current issues facing college sport is that efforts to prevent college athletes from receiving financial compensation in excess of what the rules allow are likely to fail unless college sport is limited to those of independent wealth. The very fact that a rule is widely ignored in practice is not in itself proof that the rule is a bad one. However, in the case of amateurism, these rule violations have been blatant and continuous for over a hundred years. During that period, young athletes like Jim Thorpe were stripped of their medals, denied eligibility, and labeled as misfits for accepting financial compensation that many could argue should have been theirs by right. Universities have continuously been held up to public ridicule for violating amateur rules and thus belying their station as defenders of ethical values. It can be argued that when the British approach to amateur sport was abandoned by most American universities, hypocrisy and exploitation were inevitable.

There are a number of alternatives to the present system that could help universities regain the moral high ground on compensation issues. A minimum change would be simply to increase the amount of expense money available to athletes. Offering athletes money for expenses and other incidentals would not upset the competitive balance in the college sport industry, and such payments would be no more a violation of the amateur ethos than the present practice of granting athletic scholarships based on athletic ability. A more ambitious proposal is for each university to create an academic endowment fund from television revenue that would help provide continuing scholarship aid for athletes who have finished four years of athletic eligibility but still need credits to graduate. Many big-time programs that are presently receiving the lion's share of television revenue already make such aid available to their athletes.[17] An academic endowment fund, overseen by the NCAA, could help athletes at those schools whose programs are not as financially successful as others'. The NCAA's new program is an important first step in this direction, as is the policy of the consortium of more than thirty-five universities started by Northeastern University's Center for the Study of Sport in Society.

Both of the above proposals would help to counter some of the cynicism that was discovered among athletes in this study. Athletes see coaches driving big cars, endorsing products on television, and making $100,000 incomes. They must also see the windfall profits generated by a bowl victory or by an appearance in the NCAA's Final Four. Efforts to show that some of that revenue comes back to athletes, especially if it is in the form of educational benefits, would be a clear statement to athletes and to the public at large that college sport has the interests of student-athletes uppermost in mind. On the other hand, if schools continue to make substantial profits from college sport and at the same time impose even stricter sanctions on athletes who accept small sums of money to meet basic living expenses, more and more athletes are bound to start questioning the moral legitimacy of the NCAA. Again, the example of Prohibition should be instructive.

A more far-reaching proposal for increasing the share of revenues that athletes can derive from the college sport industry is to follow the model of the International Olympic Committee. In Olympic sport, the rules now permit athletes to accept living and training grants, endorsement fees, and in some cases, prize money, as long as these funds are administered by their sport governing bodies. Some Olympic athletes, like Carl Lewis, can put money earned from athletic competition into trust funds and use money from these funds to pay expenses. All of the money can be drawn out of the trust fund when amateur competition has ended. It may be in the best interests of higher education for the NCAA to follow the lead of the IOC and begin giving serious consideration to mechanisms for allowing athletes to receive financial benefits more in line with the valuable services they render to universities and to the public at large. It is probably unrealistic, at this point in history, to expect schools to opt for a less commercialized and professionalized model of sport. It makes good sense, therefore, to reexamine the way that college athletes are compensated.

Drug Abuse

THE STUDENT-ATHLETE AND HIGH-PERFORMANCE SPORT

JOHN M. HOBERMAN

> *The All-American way is not the way of international track
> & field. . . . I'm very fortunate that I never had to do it,
> whereas now I would. If I were going back to compete in
> the Olympics, I would blood dope. If you're an American
> athlete now you've got to do it.*
> FRANK SHORTER, 1972 OLYMPIC MARATHON CHAMPION

While much attention has been paid over the past two decades
to the abuse of so-called recreational drugs such as marijuana
and cocaine by American college and university students, the
abuse of performance-enhancing drugs is emerging as a second
substance-abuse problem on many campuses. The essay that
follows is intended as a survey of the issues and problems
associated with the testing of student-athletes for allegedly
performance-enhancing drugs.

The first part of this chapter briefly examines some efforts
over the past decade to describe and control substance abuse

by student-athletes involving both "recreational" and allegedly ergogenic substances; the principal enforcement program in this area has been administered by NCAA. A related question addressed in this section is whether the student-athlete's relationship to proscribed substances is typical or atypical within the student population as a whole.

The second part describes two recent court decisions that take contrary positions regarding the drug testing of student-athletes. An examination of these decisions shows how the status of the student-athlete both resembles and is different from that of government employees who are required to undergo drug testing.

The third part describes the world of high-performance sport in which accomplished student-athletes are participants. It is argued that the world of Olympic-level sport includes a substance-abusing subculture that will affect world-class sport for the foreseeable future. A related issue is whether universities can or should prepare student-athletes for the world of "scientific" sport.

Substance Abuse and the Student-Athlete

The drug-testing program of the National Collegiate Athletic Association (NCAA), which was authorized in January 1986 and went into effect on August 1, 1986, is proceeding despite the many legal challenges it has faced since its inception. Student-athletes who compete in NCAA championship events, including post-season football bowl games, are subject to random testing for a total of eighty-six prohibited drugs: a variety of stimulants (for example, amphetamines and superdoses of caffeine); "recreational" drugs like marijuana, heroin, and cocaine; anabolic steroids (widely believed to increase muscle mass and tolerance for heavy training); and diuretics (which increase urine flow and may wash prescribed drugs out of the body prior to drug testing). The rules call for an athlete who tests positive to be removed from posteason events and suspended from athletic competition for a minimum of ninety days.

Although the vote at the NCAA's eightieth convention was overwhelmingly in favor of drug testing, the measure was opposed by proponents of programs administered by universities. Southern Methodist University voted against testing "on principle," according to its faculty adviser for athletics. "Drug testing should be under institutional control," he stated. "And this legislation does not satisfactorily provide rehabilitation efforts. We at S.M.U. already have a drug testing program under way." The University of Michigan's athletic director offered the following rationale for institutional control: "Every college will now test for drugs itself because it won't want to send a team to a championship and be embarrassed by having one of its stars kicked off of the team because of drugs."[1]

It could be argued, however, that institutional control opens the door still farther to the corruption and suspicion that now affect large areas of elite international sport (see the final third of this chapter—"The Brave New World of High-Performance Sport"). For example, in March 1988 the president of the University of South Carolina announced that a committee studying the university's drug-testing program had found that it had not been functioning for many months; in addition, the committee stated that a football player who had tested positive for drug use three times had not been dismissed from the team in accordance with the rules.[2] In summary, the temptation to falsify results at the administrative level should not be underestimated.

The smaller National Association of Intercollegiate Athletics (NAIA) requires member institutions to formulate and put into effect drug education plans for student-athletes. In February 1988 the NAIA temporarily suspended two colleges and two universities for failing to submit acceptable programs by the January 1, 1988, deadline.[3]

The NCAA testing program resulted in widely publicized suspensions of prominent college football players during the 1986–87 and 1987–88 seasons. In January 1987, Brian Bosworth of the University of Oklahoma was prevented from playing in a bowl game after he tested positive for anabolic steroids. In December 1987, George Mira, Jr., of the University of Miami was suspended by the NCAA after Lasix, a banned diuretic, was detected in his urine sample. In 1987 the NCAA banned 24 football players (of 1,452 tested) from post-season competition after they tested positive for banned substances, 8 fewer players than were barred in 1986. But Frank D. Uryasz, the NCAA's assistant director of research and sports medicine, pointed out that test results do not necessarily reflect actual drug use by athletes. "We know that the use of banned substances is higher than what these numbers would represent."[4]

In October 1987 the NCAA drug-testing committee made it known that it did not take its test results at face value and proposed a plan (a voluntary form of which was adopted in January 1988) to test for steroids during the football off-season. This proposal was, as one journalist noted, "an admission that, in that first year, many athletes circumvented the screening by merely ending their steroid use in time to avert a positive reading at the end of the season." One member of the drug-testing committee stated that the purpose of the plan was "to send out a message that we're aware that was the process being used by athletes and needs to be eliminated." Dr. James C. Puffer, chief of the Division of Family Medicine at the University of California, Los Angeles, and physician to the football team, estimated that between 35% and 40% of Division IA football players use steroids.[5]

The arguments offered by George Mira's attorney contesting the suspension illustrate the potential complexities of these cases. He contended that Mira's family had a history of medical problems requiring the use of diuretics; that the NCAA had failed to inform athletes that Lasix—the trade name for furosemide—was a banned substance; that, contrary to medical opinion,[6] furosemide "does not mask another chemical compound." He concluded: "It is not a performance-enhancing drug, it is not a drug deleterious to George Jr.'s health in the moderate amount he consumed."[7]

The NCAA drug-testing program, as this comment suggests, comprises two distinct classes of substances: (1) performance-enhancing drugs and (2) so-called recreational drugs. The diuretic Lasix, like the banned drug probenecid, may be classified as a "masking" agent for performance-enhancing steroids. The status of cocaine is somewhat ambiguous. "This powerful stimulant can produce feelings of euphoria and is capable of improving some aspects of performance through prolonged endurance. However, larger doses produce muscle spasms and convulsions."[8] In addition, the "stimulating effect of cocaine may mask an athlete's sense of fatigue, which can lead to injury."[9] In summary, the value of cocaine as a performance-enhancing drug, especially over the longer term, is very doubtful.

Studies conducted at universities have indicated that student-athletes do not differ from the general student population regarding the use of "recreational" drugs. A study published in 1978 concerning drug use among athletes at Arizona State University, Pennsylvania State University, Northern Colorado University, the State University of New York at Geneseo, and the University of Tennessee concluded: "Athletes do not represent a special subpopulation within our society with respect to drug use and the athlete is as much a part of the culturization that has taken place with respect to drug use as any other individual in the university population." Another study published in 1981 "showed no significant differences between athletes and nonathletes in their use of the most common mood-altering drugs." Comparison of a 1982 survey by the National Institute on Drug Abuse (NIDA) and a 1983 NCAA study "shows that with the probable exception of anabolic steroids (for which the NIDA did not collect data), college athletes are less likely to use drugs than are their peers in the general population."[10]

This essay, however, focuses on performance-enhancing substances that are generally not used by nonathletes (bodybuilders being the exception to this rule). In this regard, collegiate student-athletes occupy a developmental stage between high school athletes and elite (and generally older) post-collegiate performers. It is now recognized that steroid abuse is widespread among high school students in the United States.[11] "In some cases, parents of high school athletes have asked doctors to prescribe the drugs to help their youngsters excel in competitions or win college scholarships." Both the National High School Athletic Coaches' Association and the National Federation of State High School Associations organize seminars and workshops on the problem of drug abuse.[12]

The parent-child partnership is illustrated by the case of a college football player who took steroids to prepare for the annual physical tests administered by the National Football League. "I've been playing football since I was 8 years old," he said. "I've been dedicating my life to football. I wasn't going to lose out to someone who took steroids. I'm not going to fall behind." It is noteworthy that this athlete and his father, himself a former college player, read about steroids for five years and together visited several physicians in search of information about their use and risks, eventually obtaining "low-level doses."[13] Such parent-child collaborations are a part of the price our society pays for pressuring children to be "winners" even at an early age.

Legal and Ethical Aspects of Drug Testing

Universities and their student-athletes are now becoming entangled in the same web of legal and ethical issues as the federal government and the employees it wants to test, often against their will.

The fundamental importance of drug testing as a legal issue was illustrated in April 1988 when Attorney General Edwin Meese called for "zero tolerance of drugs in any place, any time." "I would like to see the day where every person arrested is subjected to a urine test," he said, indicating that the test could be used to determine whether that person would be granted pretrial release. "We need to have drug testing in most areas of work," the attorney general further stated, "because, as has been demonstrated, it cuts down on accidents and increases productivity as well as prevents people from disobeying the law." In response, Ira Glasser, executive director of the American Civil Liberties Union, criticized the broad scope of the proposed testing program.[14]

Only a few days prior to the Meese statement, Representative Charles Schumer (D-N.Y.) had argued during a House hearing for a very different approach to the problem, which would forbid private drug testing. "There are too many workers who are being subjected to bad tests, improper procedures and a profound lack of legal protection in the workplace," he stated. Companies that conduct testing in an improper manner can "ruin the lives of their employees." "An incorrect drug test with no chance for appeal can swiftly destroy a career and a family." Representative Schumer described most urine tests as "cheap and wildly inaccurate."[15]

The drug-testing issue is fast becoming one of the classic legal dilemmas of our time. On one side is an impressive series of objections to the testing of large groups of people, whether it is carried out in a random fashion or scheduled in advance. On the other side is the concern that public safety not be endangered by drug-abusing personnel in a variety of critical positions, and that fair competition in sports not be endangered by performance-enhancing drugs.

One important argument against testing is the privacy issue. The program the government has proposed for the Customs Service requires urinating into a cup while a government agent waits nearby to appropriate the sample. The National Treasury Employees Union calls this a "demeaning, humiliating and offensive" procedure; similarly, a federal district court judge has called it "degrading."[16] A second argument is that testing procedures can be circumvented or "beaten" by scheming employees; or that test results are subject to errors that could cause serious injustices, such as a loss of employment or undeserved notoriety as a drug abuser. A third argument holds that mass testing implies a presumption of guilt that is cast unfairly over a great majority of innocent people. In February, 1988, for this reason, a federal appellate court in California stated that there must be some basis for a "particularized suspicion" of a train crew member to justify testing him for drugs.

On the other side there is the argument that drug use presents a "clear and present danger" to public safety. It is claimed that certain employment categories require testing. "Drug use by officials involved in enforcing drug smuggling laws is simply intolerable," the Justice Department argued in the Customs Service case, referring to the possibility of "bribery or blackmail." This urgent situation requires in turn a diminished right to privacy in the traditional sense. In 1987 a judge on the United States Court of Appeals for the Fifth Circuit, while conceding the "personal or private" nature of passing urine, wrote that "strong government interest" in employing reliable personnel justified "the limited intrusiveness" of urine testing.[17]

These contrary positions on the issue of drug testing are represented by two important court decisions regarding the testing of student-athletes. An examination of these decisions shows how the status of the student-athlete both resembles and is different from that of a government employee. It should be pointed out that the NCAA, as a private organization is less bound by Constitutional guarantees regarding individual privacy than is the government. This interpretation was confirmed by the Supreme Court in the Tarkanian case in 1988. This decision has been widely interpreted as confirming the NCAA's authority to carry on with its mandatory drug testing program.

The first decision, by Judge Conrad L. Rushing, a California superior court judge sitting in San Jose, was handed down in November 1987 in response to a case brought by two Stanford University athletes who had argued that testing violated their constitutional right to privacy. Opposing the NCAA program, Judge Rushing invoked all three anti-testing arguments: the right to privacy, the likelihood of inaccurate tests, and the overbroad presumption of guilt. In addition, he challenged the notion of a "clear and present danger" by arguing that the NCAA program is unconstitutional "in that there is no evidence of a 'compelling need.' "[18]

On the privacy issue, Judge Rushing held that the NCAA had not demonstrated a need for testing "so compelling that it justifies massive intrusion into plaintiffs' privacy rights."[19]

The scientific accuracy of the drug tests in question was another contested issue:

> Experts testifying for the students [plaintiffs] challenged the scientific validity of the NCAA urine tests. Randall Baselt, PhD, director of the Chemical Toxicology Institute in Foster City, California, testified that NCAA laboratories may fail to detect as many as 50 recently developed, more water-soluble steroids. Baselt also said that the chemical similarity between steroids and natural substances in the body can lead to false positive results (San Jose Mercury News, October 15, 1987).

Opposing this testimony, Robert Dugal, Ph.D., director of the National Institute for Scientific Research-Health in Pointe-Claire, Quebec, one of three laboratories approved by the International Olympic Committee that does drug testing for the NCAA, argued that false positive tests are not a problem. He conceded that some commercial laboratories might not produce reliable test results.[20]

Judge Rushing offered a strikingly broad argument in favor of the plaintiffs regarding the relationship between drug testing and the presumption of guilt. "As a group," he wrote, "United States student athletes are the furthest thing from sociopaths and criminals. The paradox of this testing program is that a criminal accused of the most serious crimes is afforded more rights than our athletic heroes."[21] This statement raises the question of how much Judge Rushing actually knew at this time about drug use among college athletes.

Finally, as we have seen, Judge Rushing did not find the "compelling need" to test that, for example, the Justice Department found in the Customs Service case. In fact, it is interesting to speculate on how the "clear and present danger" standard might be applied to college sport.

At the same time, Judge Rushing did permit the continuation of restricted drug testing of Stanford football and basketball players, suggesting that some sort of "compelling need" for testing did exist. John Scanlan, associate professor of law at Indiana University; commented as follows: "Mandatory drug testing has usually required proof that the social consequences of drug use are likely to be so immediate that the public health and safety are threatened, as with railroad operators or air-traffic controllers. Nothing that the court offers as the N.C.A.A.'s reasons for drug testing suggests there is that level of urgency about testing."[22] This aspect of Judge Rushing's decision suggests his implicit acknowledgement of "urgent" interests in the integrity of college sport programs.

A more explicit description of these interests is developed in a second decision handed down in August 1988. In August 1988, broadening his injunction of November 1987, Judge Rushing issued a 28-page ruling exempting all Stanford athletes from the NCAA's mandatory drug-testing program. Judge Rushing now argued that "It appears the evidence is wholly insufficient to support the NCAA program of drug testing in any sport." He cited a need to maintain the privacy of medical records, the student's right to urinate without being observed, and "the athletes' right to treat themselves with appropriate over-the-counter medications as other students do." Significantly, Judge Rushing continued to maintain that college athletes do not abuse drugs more than their peers.[23]

Another decision, handed down in Seattle in March 1988 by U.S. district court Judge Walter T. McGovern, ruled that the NCAA's program of random, mandatory drug tests is constitutionally sound. Judge McGovern found a "diminished" right of privacy "in the context of collegiate athletics." The observing of an athlete as he or she urinates is acceptable, he reasoned, in that "there is an element of communal undress that is not present in other university contexts."[24]

The McGovern decision, which resulted from an action brought by a runner against the University of Washington, is interesting for two reasons. First, the "clear and present danger" justification for testing does not appear credible when applied to student-athletes. The best Judge McGovern could do in this regard was to point to the public's right to fair competition. It should be noted that this argument raises the question of whether student-athletes should forfeit a right to privacy on account of a public demand for their fair performances.

The judge is more persuasive when he argues, like Frank D. Uryasz, the NCAA's director of sport sciences, that the *athlete* has a right to fair competition. "Student-athletes as a whole have been supportive of the program," Uryasz says. "Those who reach NCAA championships want to be assured that the competition is clean and equitable." It should be emphasized here that these athletes may well favor testing for performance-enhancing drugs, but not for "recreational" drugs such as marijuana and cocaine. They argue that they should be treated on an equal basis with other student groups in this regard. In April 1988 the University of Montana revised its drug-testing program in conformity with this viewpoint. It decided to continue to conduct random, mandatory tests for drugs considered to be performance-enhancing, but not test for "recreational" drugs like heroin or marijuana.[25]

It should be pointed out that the relationship of drug testing to "clean and equitable" athletic competition can be presented differently in the course of legal argument. Judge McGovern and the NCAA see a causal relationship between testing and fair competition, on the assumption that drugs can provide athletes with an unfair advantage. But the plaintiffs in the Stanford case challenged the very premise of this argument. "The whole reason for the program," said an attorney for the two Stanford students, "is to ensure fair competition, but there's no evidence that steroids or any other drug enhance athletic ability."[26] Similarly, an expert witness for the Stanford plaintiffs "testified that the NCAA drug tests appear to be based on popular misconceptions about the power of drugs to enhance performance."[27] Unfortunately, this Gordian-knot solution to the drug-testing issue is untenable, since it is based on outmoded scientific opinion.[28] Responsible policy-making in this area will have to take into account the widely acknowledged efficacy of certain prohibited drugs, primarily anabolic steroids.

The second aspect of the McGovern decision concerns the custodial role of the university "in protecting the health of student-athletes . . . and educating about and deterring drug abuse in sports competition." (Taking this hygienic argument to its logical conclusion would, of course, mean mandatory drug testing for all students and, above all, a ban on smoking.) At stake here is the scope of the university's custodial role. As an attorney for the plaintiff pointed out: "The notion that the Fourth Amendment should be relaxed when we're looking after your own best interests smacks of the most profound attitude of *in loco parentis*."[29]

It is also worth asking whether the health of student athletes is always the first priority of campus drug-testing proponents. In some cases the health issue may serve as a pretext for putting in place a testing procedure that gives college coaches and athletic administrators more control over the lives of student athletes. In other cases, as in that of the University of South Carolina already referred to, the testing program may simply be ignored by athletic personnel.

These cautionary observations are prompted by the troublesome fact that academic university administrators and athletic personnel do not necessarily view the student-athlete in the same way. In the wake of Judge Rushing's ruling,

Donald Kennedy, president of Stanford University, said: "We are naturally pleased by the decision because we think it vindicates Stanford's belief that student athletes should be treated like other students."[30] But many athletic personnel are motivated to treat student athletes as a breed apart; and it is for this reason that institutional control—which may mean athletic department control—of drug testing presents special hazards.

Finally, Dr. Kennedy's statement suggests that the university should serve as a bastion of civil rights within society at large; in this case, as an oasis within which the individual (student) is protected from unwarranted intrusions into his or her privacy. It should be noted that Stanford, in a most untypical action, actually sided with those student-athletes who resisted the NCAA. At the conclusion of this chapter, I shall suggest how the university might prepare the student-athlete for the drug-ridden world of high-performance sport.

The Brave New World of High-Performance Sport

Student-athletes in some major sports are already integrated to some degree into high-performance sport cultures. Football, basketball, and baseball players may anticipate professional careers and prepare themselves accordingly. If they are planning to enter the NFL, their preparation may well involve the use of anabolic steroids to increase size and strength in advance of testing by team scouts. What is more, the ethos of professional sport can affect amateur athletes' attitudes toward drugs in a more general sense. In an address to the general assembly of International Sports Federations in October 1987, Robert O. Voy, M.D., director of Sports Medicine and Sports Science at the United States Olympic Committee, pointed out this interrelationship. "National drug control programs in amateur sport are often thwarted by what goes on in professional sport," Dr. Voy noted. Some professional sport subcultures "operate with the assumption that drugs are legal, including anabolic steroid use," and this affects the attitudes of younger athletes.[31]

In recent years elite track and field athletes have found that they, too, have a professional option, although only a handful of the most gifted athletes will find it as remunerative as the professional team sports. The more important point is that the mores of this high-performance community have had an impact on American student-athletes involved in track and field who compete internationally and on those who aspire to do so. I shall describe some of the dynamics of this international subculture and the role that prohibited drugs have come to play in it—a frightening warning for the future of college sport.

Modern high-performance sport is to an increasing degree a global monoculture whose values derive from the sphere of technology. It is my view that the technologizing of high-performance sport contains, and in some ways conceals, an agenda for human development for which high-performance athletes serve as ideal models. High-performance sport has become an exercise in human engineering that aims at producing not simply an athletic type but a human type as well. For this reason alone, high-performance sport offers an important challenge to humanistic scholarship. For a variety of reasons, the nature of this challenge is better understood, and more frequently acknowledged, by European observers.

On November 16, 1985, the president of the Federal Republic of Germany, Richard von Weizsäcker, addressed a meeting of the West German National Olympic Committee on the subject of modern sport. Mr. von Weizsäcker's long and carefully reasoned presentation offers a penetrating analysis of a high-performance subculture in which drug abuse ("doping") has become a way of life for many athletes and a constant preoccupation even for those who abstain. For this reason, I will cite some of its key passages below.

The problem, says Mr. von Weizsäcker, is that whereas science and technology can be progressively transformed, the human body cannot be. The temptation to treat the human body as if it were a machine comes into conflict with our most cherished ideas of what a human being is and should be, and the result of this conflict is a reckoning with the idea of human limits. "That the specific limits which have been set by nature itself should not be exceeded is beyond all doubt," he states. "What remains in question is precisely how these limits are to be defined." We do know, however, that in some circles the temptation to exceed these limits has become overwhelming. "The danger that specific body-types will be developed for specific sport disciplines is no longer a matter of science fiction; for this reason we can already see on the horizon the danger that specific athletic types will be bred by means of more or less concealed chemical or even genetic manipulations."

Mr. von Weizsäcker's prescription for this difficult situation is what he calls "a clear and binding ethics of sport" resulting from a kind of self-interrogation. Sport, he says,

> will be able to preserve its humanizing influence and contribute to human dignity only if, as it develops, it resists this pressure, if it recognizes its own inner laws, if it sees and accepts these limits. . . . Its worldwide success does not release sport from the obligation to examine its own deepest premises. On the contrary, it is precisely this almost limitless success which forces sport to reflect on both its premises and its limits."[32]

This analysis of the predicament of modern sport is essentially conservative, in that it assumes that sport's "deepest premises" include both a refusal to bring about certain physical transformations of the human body and a renunciation of certain performance-enhancing techniques, including drugs.

The current crisis in international track and field has developed precisely because many elite athletes do not share this "conservative" premise, or because they feel driven to stay on a technical par with substance-abusing athletes.

One example of such peer-group pressure concerns the technique of blood doping, which involves removing about two pints of blood from an athlete and freezing it for eight to twelve weeks. By this time the athlete's hemoglobin level will have returned to normal. The blood, or the red blood cell fraction, is then infused back into the athlete during the week before competition. The theory behind blood doping, which is considered scientifically sound, is that increasing the number of red blood cells increases the flow of oxygen to the muscles, thereby increasing endurance. It should be noted that many rumors about alleged blood-doping practices have circulated among long-distance runners and skiers during the past fifteen years.[33]

In these circumstances, the principled athlete may feel himself to be at a hopeless disadvantage. "The U.S. is putting pressure on its doctors not to blood dope our athletes," commented Frank Shorter, the 1972 Olympic marathon champion, in January 1988. "That is what's going to show in the Olympics this year. I think the All-American way is hurting us because the All-American way is not the way of international track & field or many other Olympic sports. I'm saddened and upset by its use, but I also feel that I'm very fortunate that I never had to do it, whereas now I would. If I were going back to compete in the Olympics, I would blood dope. If you're an American athlete now you've got to do it."[34]

Such developments have produced widespread cynicism among elite athletes. In 1984 Dr. Wildor Hollmann, head of the Institute for Sport Medicine and Circulatory Research in Cologne and the current president of the International Federation for Sports Medicine, stated:

> No one trusts anyone any more. Every athlete asks himself what the other one crouching next to him in the starting blocks is doing, what kinds of things he has been taking in the course of his training in order to win. And if the athlete who asks himself this stands there completely clean and loses, then he may later call himself a fool for having behaved that way."[35]

What is more, this is a permanent state of affairs. "Never again," Dr. Hollmann stated in 1985, "not even in the remote future, will we see a type of high-performance sport without doping problems."[36]

The age of scientific sport has also had a profound impact on the practice of sport medicine itself. The demands of high-performance athletes, including demands for steroid treatments, have forced many sport physicians into positions in which "one accommodates to pressures which have very little to do with health, ethics, and morality in the classical sense," as Dr. Hollmann puts it.[37]

Another problem is the integrity of the administrators who supervise drug testing procedures at both the national and international levels. "It is now time to admit that suppression of results by officials occurs," Dr. Voy pointed out in his October 1987 address. "Athletes must have the assurance that positive cases will be dealt with by all national sport organizations no matter what athlete . . . is involved."[38] But there are sizable financial incentives for organizers of international competitions to suppress positive test results. Daley Thompson, the British Olympic decathlon champion, has described this situation in the following terms: "There's too much money in the sport, which promotes the use and abuse of drugs and which leads to officials and everybody turning blind eyes because they want their meets to look good. They need the performances to bring all the people in. It's a vicious circle."[39] The Ben Johnson steroids scandal which marked the 1988 Seoul Olympic Games is only the most spectacular illustration of the widespread corruption that exists in certain Olympic sports.[40] Nor is it clear that real reform is possible at this time. As the more thoughtful athletes understand, reform will require a new relationship to the performance principle itself on the part of athletes, coaches, the press and the general public.[41]

What can universities do to prepare student-athletes for the world of high-performance sport and its drug problems? First, university officials who are independent of athletic departments must recognize the extent to which this world has become a corrupt environment and prepare an educational program for those student-athletes who wish enter it. Such materials and lectures must present a candid portrait of high-performance sport and the presumed motivations of those who benefit from its success.

The next step is to devise an innovative sport studies curriculum, aimed at the university as a whole, to describe how and why modern sport has become a deeply troubled— and important—subculture. As Dr. Hollmann has pointed out, the founders of the Olympic movement "unconsciously laid the foundation for a gigantic biological experiment on the human organism itself."[42] Among our social institutions, the university community is best suited to the task of assessing the implications of such momentous developments.

7

Agents on Campus

BOB WOOLF

*We live in troubled times, as times usually are. Some 3,000
sport contracts are drawn up each year, and there are 11,000
agents to negotiate them. Commercialism in sport today
is so strong that it distorts and threatens our educational
system.*

In the winter of 1966, Earl Wilson, a pitcher for the Detroit
Tigers, signed one of the first sport contracts ever negotiated
by an attorney or agent. I was that attorney (or agent),
consulting with Earl by phone from a hotel room a few blocks
away while my client met with the general manager of the
Tigers, alone, at his office.

In those days, third parties of the financial persuasion
were not welcome in the same room when teams were telling
their athletes how much they would be paid. When a problem
arose, Earl Wilson would excuse himself, hurry to a phone
outside the office, and call me.

He had won eighteen games that year, splitting the season
between Boston and the Tigers. We had decided what figure
he should seek and how he would ask for it. And now, in
that awkward and almost clandestine way, we won for Earl

the contract he deserved. In the process, we worked out an arrangement for deferred compensation that the Tigers use to this day with other players. The evolution of the player agent followed the evolution of money!

The field of sport agentry was a beautiful place to be in the mid-1960s—no conflicts of interest, no crisis of ethics, no huge pressures, no publicity, and no lawsuits. As near as I could tell, I was about the only one in it. I could not have envisioned—no one could—that I would pioneer a business that went from zero competition to an industry in which anyone with a telephone could find a niche.

The point ought to be made right here that, even twenty-five years ago, there was a certain stigma attached to being a sport agent—a spillover, no doubt, from the Hollywood or Broadway prototypes. Agents were not yet guilty of any sweeping excesses, lacking the influence or knowledge they would acquire later. But the teams still treated them as parasites.

Early on, I made an effort to define my role as that of a *sport attorney.* Frankly, I became less sensitive on the subject when the Watergate scandal came along and each day's headline told of another lawyer who was being led off to prison.

But, no, not in my wildest fantasy did I imagine a time when we would be negotiating $2-million-a-year contracts, endorsements, and fringe deals that would equal the budget of some third world countries. And contrary to dire prophecies of a few years ago, the end is not in sight. Either we have entered the age of emancipation for the athlete or the whole sport establishment has broken loose from its moorings.

Historically, the big money began raining down in the late 1960s and early 1970s. The American Football League had been judged a success after it merged with the older National Football League. Now new leagues began to be formed in basketball and hockey and, again, in pro football. Everywhere you turned a range war was in progress, with teams rustling each other's livestock. And as an offshoot of such competitiveness, the sport agent expanded his field of activity and began to look at what had been a protected area: the undergraduate. Agents enticed athletes to leave school early and, if necessary, to issue a legal challenge to the rules of leagues that had tried to respect the college programs. This was a practice I fought against for years, but one that would in time become acceptable.

Of course, there would never have been such a thing as a sport attorney if a need had not developed. The 1960s were a kind of golden era for sport, with television feeding enormous amounts of money into the machinery. The athletes of the sixties became far more sophisticated than their predecessors, and far more concerned with their future. Madison Avenue began to make opportunities available to them that were once the exclusive province of movie stars. The public responded instantly, assuming that actors were paid to say words as a way of life, athletes were not. Or, as Woody Allen put it, the mind is filled with delusions, while the body never lies.

This was a watershed time in sports. The pendulum had once swung wildly in favor of the owners. The athletes had few rights and fewer options, and if one was grossly underpaid his only recourse was to stay home and wait for his money to run out.

In issue after issue, the owners refused to compromise, instead watching the courts peel away the rules and practices that had, in another era, enabled them to build their teams and sports and survive until prosperity arrived. Unwilling to share that prosperity with the athletes, they were in danger of losing control of their own destinies.

At the center of this stalemate—a product of the boom years—was the sport agent. Athletes, faced with a situation previously unknown to them, turned more and more to professional help to negotiate on their behalf. In the mid-1960s, I was the only attorney known to be working with all of the four major sports. At the same time, the players were forming their own unions, but the need for help on the professional level was still there, and I knew my field would soon be getting crowded.

In the years when various leagues were warring, the draft became the primary battlefield. College athletes were the prize because the agents knew they were going to be making big money and they would be making it up front. So now these college stars, many of whom had never heard of an agent, were being chased by a whole new breed of them.

The competition was going to get fierce. The top collegians were not only a source of money but a magnet for publicity and recognition. Signing a Number 1 draft choice could assure an agent of seeing his name, even his picture, in print. Best of all, college athletes rarely knew what questions to ask, whereas the pros were growing jaded, accustomed to the way agents worked, and for the most part indifferent to their hype.

There was a time when I would attend the North-South All-Star game in Mobile, having heard from six to ten athletes. I would be the only agent there. Five years later, five hundred of them were roaming the hotels and the practice field, outnumbering the players by five to one.

In dealing with young athletes, it was painfully obvious that a huge potential existed for abusing their innocence. No one has a monopoly on integrity, and there is a risk that anyone writing about ethics will come off as self-serving or self-righteous. But I believe the record will show that I discouraged any athlete who asked me about quitting school to turn pro. Nor as a personal matter have I tolerated the refusal by a client of mine to honor a contract or the attempt to renegotiate one made in good faith. (This stand has, in the past, cost me a few clients, including Julius Erving.) I will do anything within reason to avoid a holdout, a practice I consider harmful to the player, the team, and the fans. Other agents disagree.

If there is one refrain I have heard from nearly all the young athletes who contact me, it is that they do not want to end up like Joe Louis. The great heavyweight champion had retired long before these young men were born, had, in fact, died before some of them were out of grade school. Yet his career, the wasting of his millions, and his long, losing battle with the Internal Revenue Service have become a part of the American legend.

Young athletes are prey to the get-rich-quick schemers and fly-by-night characters who chase after them. I found I spent more time preventing the exploitation of my clients than I did in generating funds for them. Consequently, I came early to my own set of standards and values and have tested them over many years of trials and occasional error. In the process, I arrived at what I think is a system that best serves my clients. I have found that for many athletes, the veteran as well as the rookie, it is best to have their paychecks sent directly from the team to my office. All their bills are paid from the office, and they are placed on a reasonable weekly allowance, after which I try to teach them good spending habits and good saving habits. Monthly accounting statements are sent to them, and all their expenditures are monitored to prevent excessive spending.

In addition, I prepare their wills, trusts, corporate structures, insurance programs, and tax returns, and I counsel their investments. I also negotiate their commercials, product endorsements, autobiographies, and movies, as well as their television/radio and personal appearances. A good representative lives through the injuries, the slumps, the trades, and the personal problems of each client.

At this time, in 1988, I would like to state that there are many agents who are doing a good job in giving responsible representation. You name the city, and I can tell you a number of people in that city who are doing a fine job for their clients. Unfortunately, it only takes one bad agent to reflect poorly on everyone. It only takes one bad police officer, judge, or district attorney to reflect poorly on the entire profession. We all get tarred by the same brush.

I still feel some anguish over what I consider the greatest mistake ever made by the ownership in sports: that is, the awarding of huge signing bonuses and contracts to athletes who had yet to prove themselves, instead of to the veterans whose value was already established. But the competition was for the rookie, and so an act of unfairness became institutional. It still makes no sense to pay an untested young man a million-dollar bonus, plus a huge guaranteed salary, based on his potential, rather than pay this to the perennial All-Star. In my view, the owners committed an irreversible error.

This, then, is the background for the deception and subterfuge and chicanery that soon were to be rampant on campuses across America. Agents and their helpers (so-called bird dogs) moved onto the campus—some respectable, some fly-by-night, some totally incapable. In terms of their football or business knowledge, many were but one phone call ahead of the athlete.

The athletes had no way of knowing who or what was really lurking out there, nor did the coach or the president of the university. The competition spawned all the abuses, the underhandedness, the petty (and not so petty) graft about which you have read and heard. Agents provided expensive watches, drugs, clothing, spending money, car loans, and acquiescent dates. These gratuities were almost never known to the coaches or athletic directors. Many were faulted for not being aware of what was going on, but unjustly, because they had no reason to be in contact with the agents.

By the late 1970s, agents unburdened by conscience had all but opened offices on the campuses of major football powers. How widespread was it? Three Heisman Trophy winners in a row, George Rogers of South Carolina, Charles White of Southern California, and Billy Sims of Oklahoma, admitted they had signed with agents before their eligibility had expired, subjecting their schools to investigations, possible suspensions, and the potential loss of millions in revenues.

A favorite tactic of some agents was to approach the player's family and offer money as a loan in return for a promise to represent their son. When the young man discovered that he should not have signed and that doing so was (1) a violation of the rules and (2) not in his best interest, the agent would then threaten to expose him, putting in jeopardy the team's record and possible championships.

Times have not changed in this regard. Once an agent has persuaded the prospect to accept a gift, a car, whatever— and, yes, persuasion is not always needed—the agent then controls a major chunk of his life. This is the unspoken objective. And when agents grow indiscriminate in their efforts to achieve it, when they toss money around wildly, a wonderful thing happens: they go broke. One agent went to trial on criminal charges in Atlanta in the early months of 1988. His business had collapsed, and his activities were exposed when he tried to sell to other agents the contracts he had obtained illegally.

In 1976, an attorney in Fort Lauderdale was convicted of soliciting illegal business after he had been caught trying to sign high school athletes to future service contracts, which would have kept them from competing in college sports.

Certainly, the athletes are not in most cases innocent parties and must bear their share of the blame. But they are the most vulnerable among us—a little naive, a little greedy, and conditioned by what they see around them. At every level, the athlete sees the coaches not honoring contracts, jumping from job to job. The coach is gone, and the players he recruited stay behind, feeling misused or worse. This is the example they can draw upon when *their* chance comes to take unfair advantage of an opportunity. Meanwhile, the agents teach them that it is dog-eat-dog out there, and you have to look out for Number One.

Once, the mother of a promising college athlete called and asked if I could help her son. He was $265,000 in debt! He owed not only his agent but an entire assortment of people, some of them total strangers to him, who were waiting to pounce when he became a pro. I was able to resolve the matter only because this young man really was good enough to attract a big contract and thereafter to settle those debts— but only, I must add, after multiple lawsuits had been filed.

I have known of agents who prowled the high schools and worked on the families of the star players, helping select the college that would, in their judgment, best showcase the boy's career. They would subsidize him for the next few years, then entice him to abandon his college education and turn pro—mainly for the aggrandizement of the agent, not the athlete.

Sadly, each callous act begets another. Even after they are committed, and have taken money and other gifts, many athletes go through the subterfuge of interviewing reputable people. Why? So they (1) can carry out a charade suggesting that they had obeyed the rules and (2) can say they turned down this person to stay with the one who sponsored them.

I would estimate that of the seniors each year, a substantial number are signed by agents before they have completed their eligibility. Many times, I would be asked to meet with a prospect, and when he reached to shake hands I would know by the Rolex watch on his wrist that he was taken. The meeting was purely for show.

This is the mentality of the young athlete on the take: I ran into one who had contacted me and wished him luck, saying that I heard he was going to be represented by a certain agent. "Naw," he quickly corrected me, "that's bull. I only made an oral agreement." That answer, of course, would have been funny if it had not cut so close to the bone. It happens that a person's word—an oral commitment— means a great deal to me. I feel fortunate that I have never felt the need to have a written contract with my clients. And on their behalf, I have negotiated over 2,000 contracts in twenty-five years.

Even wrestling with the question of agents and campus ethics can stamp you as a hopeless square. This I know: it is easy to get angry or depressed or spread the blame. But to cope with the problem—and reverse it—we have to understand the student-athlete. We need to feel his pressures and understand his perspective.

These secret and illicit agreements undermine the ethics of the player *and* the sport *and* the university. Of course, the athletes are partly at fault. They need to stop playing games, signing with four or five agents and pretending it was some kind of misunderstanding. As for the agents, they need to stop supplying the athletes with figures that are inflated and wrong and that, in effect, make the athlete a co-conspirator.

Keep in mind that anyone can be an agent, even if he is on his way to jail or coming out of it. There are no schools to train them and no tests to pass. To become an agent, all a fellow needs is one thing: a client who will hire him.

Agents and sport attorneys who care about these things have taken a few baby steps toward cleaning up the industry. Annually since 1985, an agent has been required to appear before the various players' associations to be accredited.

To restrain the agents and return a higher standard of conduct to the campus, I would propose these steps:

Step One: Establish a players' advisory committee. Every college or university should offer a committee, not unlike the one in the small town of Terre Haute, Indiana, that advised Larry Bird in his final year of college. It included the athletic director, the president of a bank, leading businessmen, attorneys, and accountants. I would add even a coach and a psychologist to a prospective committee. They would educate the athlete and his family about the people and situations and temptations they will encounter. The committee would be available to help him screen agents. If one contacted him, he would have a proper place to refer him.

Step Two: Pay players meaningful expense money. This is, I realize, a touchy issue and one certain to trigger an outcry from purists. However, the chapters in this book contributed by Dick Schultz and Allen Sack demonstrate that it is already an issue on today's agenda. With the monies that most schools derive from football, they should create a more livable environment for the players who provide these services. It seems to me this consideration is justified, and we simply try to flatter ourselves as intellectuals by ignoring it. Athletes are in a special situation. They generate vast sums for the university without being able to hold an outside job. Time and the dictates of the NCAA work against them. Among all other students, they alone are denied employment. By raising their monthly allowance to a more reasonable figure, the school makes it less tempting for them to get involved with unscrupulous people.

Step Three: Offer insurance. An insurance program should be provided by the schools. This is another enticement dangled by some agents. They have a powerful selling point: if you are crippled tomorrow, who will compensate you for the career you will never have? Do you know many nineteen- or twenty-year-olds who could resist if someone said, "Here's $10,000. Buy insurance. If you're injured tomorrow, at least you'll have this. I'll take the risk." What a persuasive argument *that* is.

An insurance system could be designed much on the order of a student loan.

Step Four: Require agents to be licensed. I have testified in Congress that anyone who represents athletes should be licensed, bonded, and supervised. Most states have enacted their own laws, but it is clumsy and unrealistic to think an agent will register with every state.

Step Five: Establish stricter rules in players' associations. The players' union should be much stricter in the supervision and monitoring of the actions of the agent. They now monitor the agents' contracts and even have established guidelines on how much an agent can charge. But we need more than that.

More enforcement is needed to limit how often an agent can contact a player and to penalize those who offer illegal inducements. If federal regulation in this area is to be avoided—and, frankly, I favor it—then there must be strong policy by each sport.

Step Six: Bar all agents from the campus. No agent should be allowed to visit a school for the purpose of recruiting a client until after the season has been completed. All agents should be forbidden from making a contact until the player has finished his eligibility. I found it heartening that Tim Brown, the brilliant wide receiver from Notre Dame, the 1987 Heisman Trophy winner, did not speak to an agent until late February of 1988.

In truth, it is not important for an athlete to be represented before the draft. Bad agents will tell him they can get him drafted higher; that is just not so. Having an agent may be helpful, in the sense that he can contact teams, assess their interest, even encourage those teams he is known to prefer. But, in twenty-five years, I have never been able to get anyone drafted at a notch higher. Very often I tell a prospective client to wait until after the draft before selecting a representative, for it may be in his best interest. Once he knows which team has selected him, he will be in a position to find someone in that city who can serve his needs best.

We live in troubled times, as times usually are. Some 3,000 sport contracts are drawn up each year, and there are 11,000 agents to negotiate them. Commercialism in sport today is so strong that it distorts and threatens our educational system. I hope we can change that. Up to now, I have never seen an agent on campus who did as well for an athlete as he did for himself.

Principals in the Equation

8

Still Out of Their League

WHO IS SPEAKING FOR THE ATHLETE?

DAVID MEGGYESY

We are living in a time when college athletics are honey-combed with falsehood, and when the professions of ama-teurism are usually hypocrisy. No college team ever meets another with actual faith in the other's eligibility
PRESIDENT WILLIAM FUNCE OF BROWN
UNIVERSITY, IN A SPEECH BEFORE THE
NATIONAL EDUCATION ASSOCIATION, 1904.

Big-time revenue-producing college and university sport pro-grams have again, during the past few years, revealed a frightening pattern of duplicity, hypocrisy, and unfair dealing in their treatment of scholarship athletes. The awful truth is, that in the revenue-producing sports, particularly football and basketball, a lust for profit and television exposure in

major university athletic departments and their parent universities has precipitated a pattern of moral, educational, and
economic exploitation of our country's finest athletes.

Among recent reforms that deal with the "problem of
college sport," few seem to be speaking for the athlete's
interests in a meaningful way. I write as a former athlete
from a perspective that has shown me positive and negative
aspects of the American sport system at the high school,
college, and professional levels. From my present perspective,
representing professional football players in their employment
relationship with the National Football League, it is obvious
that college athletes participating in major revenue-producing
programs are, in practical terms, athlete/employees.

The main question to be asked is this: is the athlete
receiving fair compensation for his four years of athletic
service? If we consider the amount of money generated by
many big-time revenue-producing athletic programs versus
the horrendously low graduation rates for football and basketball players, the answer is no. In the present system the
scholarship athlete gives far more than he receives.

Given the current crisis in college sport, as illustrated in
other chapters in this book, prospects for significant reform
emanating from the NCAA or its member schools seem
remote. Scholarship athletes and their parents may be forced
to look outside the present system to professional sport labor
unions, the courts, federal and state legislatures, enlightened
media, and athlete advocacy groups for pressure to initiate
reforms that will speak to the athlete's interests and aspirations. Without a voice that will speak for their interests,
athletes will continue to be exploited.

In this chapter I will confine my remarks to the major
revenue-producing programs at the 105 Division IA colleges
and universities. The Division IA institutions have the largest
athletic budgets, receive the most television exposure and
revenues, and perpetrate the most abuses. Typically at these
schools the athletic departments are more autonomous than
elsewhere and farther divorced from the college or university
academic structure; they exist as semi-autonomous sport entertainment adjuncts to the parent institution. This separa-
tion of athletic department and school causes many problems

of governance and control for university administrations. In the final analysis, the university's chief executive officer and board of trustees should be the ultimate responsible parties regarding the fate of the athlete. The athlete should not be solely in the hands of the athletic department. It is the university administration that sets in place policies and practices that will shape the athlete's career and determine the degree of equity at a particular school.

Clearly defining the relationship between major college sport programs and their scholarship athletes is an essential first step toward reform. It involves clarifying and changing public misperception about the athlete's role in big-time programs. The NCAA and its member schools have fostered and promoted an idealized characterization of the scholarship athlete as a student who receives an athletic scholarship and becomes a student-athlete. The university, it is suggested, has given the student-athlete an opportunity to obtain a college education, and the student-athlete is promoted as an amateur, participating in sport for the love of a particular game; the university, on the other hand, bestows a scholarship on the athlete that will allow for the continued development of the athlete's academic and athletic potential. However, this perception is greatly distorted. It ignores the commercial reality of revenue-producing programs and primarily serves public relations and economic needs of the universities and the NCAA.

We have seen the disquieting dropout statistics quoted in other chapters of this book. We have also read about athletes' attitudes in Allen Sack's chapter. In consideration of such evidence, a more realistic and truthful definition of revenue-producing athletes is that they have entered into an employment contract with the university. Their primary relationship to the university from the athletic department's perspective is as employees, not students. Athletes enter the collegiate sport system when they declare their commitment to a particular school by signing a letter of intent to receive a one-year employment contract, in the form of an athletic scholarship. Embodied in the athletic scholarship are tuition waivers, housing, meals, and books. The athletic scholarship or employment contract is offered on a yearly basis and can be terminated at any time, for any reason, by the university. Athletes desiring to change schools (employers) are barred from athletic competition for one year. Other athletic officials, coaches, and athletic directors are not bound by such constraints.

These athletes are further obligated to participate in all activities connected with their sport. These activities include practices, meetings, off-season training and conditioning programs, public relations duties, travel to road games with the team, and participation in scheduled contests. When required the athlete must forgo his Christmas and spring vacations for practice or participation in games. It is estimated by Professor Harry Edwards, who evaluated Pac-10 universities, that Pac-10 scholarship football players spend an average of forty hours per week, year round, fulfilling their athletic scholarship obligations. Time spent on football rises considerably during the season, up to eighty hours per week when the team plays on the road.

Present abysmal graduation rates are a reflection not of incapable or ignorant athletes but of an exploitive system that has little interest in scholarship athletes' receiving a meaningful college education and degree. Progress toward a degree, from many athletic departments' view, means maintaining the necessary grade point average to stay eligible for athletic competition. College athletes cannot be paid wages or salaries for their services, according to an agreed-upon set of rules created by the NCAA member schools. Incidentally, because scholarship athletes are not legally categorized as employees, they are not covered by state workers' compensation statutes.

Not properly delineating the relationship between the scholarship athlete and the university as employee/employer allows for a unrealistic analysis of the circumstances that face both athlete and university—circumstances that prevent the system from working as well for the athlete as it does for the schools.

In recent years five conditions have emerged in collegiate revenue-producing sport that have reinforced and created economic pressures on colleges and universities. Today's realities make the system even more unfair for the athletes. These conditions are: (1) the monopoly control of college sport by the NCAA, (2) increasing and uneven distribution of television revenues and the "winner-take-all" college sport marketplace, (3) the inability of college and university presidents to deal effectively with the NCAA and their own athletic departments and alumni, (4) increasing corporate involvement in post-season bowl games and post-season tournaments, and (5) the underground or black market economy for high school athletes. The overall effect of these five conditions has been to exert greater pressure to win in order to maintain economic viability. *The operating axiom for major college programs is, "You must spend to win and must win to spend."*

The consequence of this situation for athletes whose schools are caught in a spend-win/win-spend spiral is greater pressure to perform and to spend more time with their sport. This means longer and more frequent meetings and practice sessions, year-round weight-lifting and conditioning programs, playing in bowl games or post-season tournaments, and playing while injured. Athletes receive no extra compensation for the increased work load. In fact, the very thing they need, time to apply themselves to their academic work, is further diminished. Presently, scholarship athletes participating in revenue-producing sport understand that their primary reason for being at the school is to perform their job as athletes. Obligations to themselves as students are secondary.

In the world of big-time college sport, the only people who materially benefit from a winning program are the coaches. They can receive six-figure salaries, cars, houses, shoe contracts, and television shows. The university, with high national visibility, has received increased alumni support and new-found dollars for its general fund. In this jaded system, it is certainly important to remember that the athlete's performance is the primary reason why people come to see athletic events, and the athletes in the final analysis generate the revenues. In the rich-get-richer game of big-time college sport, too many scholarship athletes get poorer.

The Need for Change

A number of changes can be made in the revenue-producing programs that would make the system more equitable for the athlete. These changes range from making the existing athletic scholarships more workable for the athlete to radically changing the major college revenue-producing sport system into a professional sport structure where the athletes become "real" employees and receive monetary compensation for their services.

I would favor making the existing scholarship system work for the athlete by achieving significant modifications in that system. I would also favor the signing by athletes and their parents of contractual relationships with their particular schools. These employment contracts would spell out the obligations of each party prior to the athlete's signing a letter of intent, and they could embody the recommendations I set forth below.

I have serious reservations about significant reforms coming from within the existing structures of college sport. The actions of the NCAA and its member schools in response to the rash of recent scandals reflect only cosmetic changes. Their response so far has been to "band-aid the cancer" by placing more responsibility on the athlete. In the face of greater demands on athletes' time by coaches, athletes are told to study harder. When athletes who are forced to live in poverty by NCAA rules accept under-the-table money from an alumni sponsor, they are punished. They can lose their scholarship and be banned from athletic competition.

The present system works very well for the universities and their athletic departments and not so well for the athletes. Because athletes do not have a voice in the system, coupled with a strong institutional investment in the existing collegiate sport entertainment system, impetus for change that will address these more fundamental issues of fair compensation and just working conditions may come from outside the structure of college sport.

Governmental Action in College Sport

State governments, Congress, professional sport labor unions, and private groups have initiated efforts during the past few years to analyze, pass legislation on, and develop programs to deal with some of the most pressing problems facing college sport. In 1981, California enacted the first sport agent regulation law, which was sponsored by the National Football League Players' Association (AFL-CIO). During the past seven years, ten states have followed California in enacting sport agent regulation laws. In 1987 the NFLPA sponsored two bills in the California legislature that would mandate inclusion of college scholarship athletes in the California workers' compensation statutes and guarantee scholarship athletes an extra scholarship year to complete their college education. In 1988, Nebraska State Senator Ernest Chambers sponsored legislation that would mandate a small salary for University of Nebraska scholarship football players. Senator Bill Bradley and Congressman Tom McMillan have introduced legislation in Congress that will require colleges and universities receiving federal aid to make public to potential scholarship athletes graduation rates and other information regarding the academic performance of athletes in those schools.

The Center for the Study of Sport in Society at Northeastern University, with support from professional sport leagues and unions, has created the "bridge course" concept for professional athletes in conjunction with its consortium school network; these enable non-degreed former scholarship athletes to complete their degrees.

Impetus for this legislation and these programs flows from a dual understanding: (1) that a healthy, corruption-free intercollegiate sport program is good public policy and (2) that the colleges and the NCAA have not done enough to eliminate abuses and the exploitation of scholarship athletes. As big-time collegiate sport becomes even more economically profitable, professional sport unions, which view scholarship athletes as employees, will initiate organizing campaigns among athletes.

Proposed Changes in the College Sport System

A number of changes could be made in the existing structure that would make the athletic scholarship system more equitable for the athletes. These proposed changes would cost the universities little money, particularly when measured against the amount of revenues the major programs produce.

• Scholarship athletes should be allowed to retain their athletic scholarships, including housing, meals, and books, for a period of time after they complete their athletic eligibility. It is unrealistic to expect scholarship athletes, particularly those who participate in revenue-producing programs, to carry a full-course college course load. This is especially true during the season. If scholarship athletes are to have a legitimate opportunity to receive a college education, they need some period of time to pursue their education away from the demands of sport. Scholarships could be extended for three years and include all scholarship athletes, even those who are able to attend graduate school. Controls could be built in that require the athlete to take a specified number of course hours and maintain a certain grade point average. If the quid-pro-quo, four-year athletic service given in exchange for a college education and degree is to have value for the athlete, the school should make every attempt to provide a legitimate opportunity to the scholarship athlete to receive a college education. For 99% of scholarship athletes in revenue-producing sport, a college education is the primary value desired.

• Athletic scholarship recipients should be required to attend a six-week orientation program at their selected schools prior to their freshman year. This mandatory orientation program would allow academic and counseling evaluation of the educational needs of incoming scholarship athletes. Intensive workshops dealing with study skills, reading and writing skills, use of the library, and basic computer skills could be presented during this period. In consideration of the time demands placed on scholarship athletes, an intensive program integrating the student-athlete into the academic dimension of university life would allow the athlete an even chance in the classroom.

• Scholarship athletes should also be required to attend a course that explores the relationship between sport and society. In this course various aspects of big-time sport in contemporary American life, including the business of sport, sport and cultural values, racism in American sport, player-coach relations, drugs in sport, and the psychological dimensions of athletic performance could be presented. Sport, as it relates to many aspects of American life, offers a rich matrix for learning, particularly for those engaging in high-level athletic competition.

• Scholarship athletes' academic progress should be closely monitored by the school's academic advisors. These advisors should function as the athletes' ombudsmen and report directly to the school's chief academic officer.

• The one-year scholarship rule should be eliminated. Since the school demands a four-year commitment from the athlete and penalizes the athlete for leaving, the school should have a reciprocal obligation. Many athletes lose their scholarships if they are injured, clearly a deplorable practice made possible by the one-year scholarships. The NCAA-mandated change from the four-year grants to the one-year scholarships in 1974 has become the most blatant example of college sport's disregard for the scholarship athlete's education.

• Athletes should receive some compensation, including travel money to be used for going home on major holidays. To expect a scholarship athlete to receive no financial support in a college environment, given the revenue generated by his athletic performance, is untenable. Athletes coming from poor circumstances need some support in order to live with a measure of dignity in a college environment. Not paying athletes has spawned an under-the-table system of paying athletes. This underground economy has forced athletes to be cheaters and to engage in a pattern of corruption in order to survive financially—and when these payment schemes are discovered, the athlete suffers serious penalty.

What we need is a large measure of honesty and fairness in our college sport system. This system can work essentially in its present form if we, as a first step, cut through the obfuscations and distortions that profess big-time revenue-producing college athletes to be amateurs. In realistic terms, college athletes in major revenue-producing sport programs are employees, and the colleges and universities are their employers. The issues for the athletes are fair compensation and the opportunity to realize the value of that compensation.

The present system of procuring and compensating college athletes will not crumble by acknowledging the employer/employee relationship. It may allow reforms that create a reality of fair dealing for the athletes who, by their exceptional athletic gifts, produce the revenues. In any society the university is given the cultural mandate to express integrity, honesty, and a sense of fairness. The present pattern of unethical behavior in big-time college and university sport programs sullies that mandate. It is time for a change.

9

The Media's Responsibility in College Sport Coverage

SANDY PADWE

Gambling is illegal. Newspapers are not in the business of promoting illegal activities. Those who run odds say the readers want to know. They want to know how much the prostitutes are charging and the price of marijuana or the price of heroin, and we don't print that. What other place in the newspaper do you promote an illegal activity?

DAVE KINDRED

In March of 1987, Frederick C. Klein, the sport columnist of *The Wall Street Journal*, asked the key question facing every sport editor and sport director in this country. Klein directed his inquiry to *Sports Illustrated*, but it easily could have been asked of any media outlet that deals with college sport. How can a publication, he wondered, function as the supposed conscience of intercollegiate athletics, on one hand, while acting at the same time as "one of its main publicity engines?"

The answer is simple. It really cannot, for a good reason. Colleges need the media to sell their athletic products—for the most part Division 1A football and Division 1 basketball, the sports that generate the most revenue. These colleges spend a lot of money each year on their sport public relations budgets so they can gain free newspaper space and television time. That often translates into widespread interest, ticket revenues, and hopefully (if the teams are good and they have loyal fans willing to spend money to travel great distances) Bowl or NCAA basketball tournament bids. Newspapers, magazines, and television, meanwhile, need college sports because coverage of those sports help sell a lot of publications, newscasts, and advertisements. In turn, the reporters, columnists, writers, editors, and technicians who bring college athletics to the public need those sports just as much in order to earn a living.

It all makes for a comfortable little fraternity where ethical questions are seldom addressed, where the discouraging words and voices are far and away in the minority, where issue-oriented journalism is treated as if it were a mine field, and where the clichéd word and thought dominate to the point that the public often is left with a simplistic and distorted view of sport on the college level.

In general, I feel, the media have failed college sport and, because of this failure, are as much to blame for the moral and ethical wasteland intercollegiate athletics have become as the people who break the rules. Because the media have not applied the same journalistic standards to the athletic field that are applied to politics, the military, business, science, and medicine, and every other major field, dozens of amoral coaches, athletic directors, college presidents, boosters, athletes, agents, trainers, team doctors, and many others are free to ply us with their pieties, half-truths, and outright lies. They are free to extol "student-athletes," who are anything but; they are free to tell us they know nothing about all the fancy cars outside the posh athletic dorms where the "student-athletes" live apart from the main student body; they are free to tell us how virtuous it is to "play in pain" and sustain injuries that begin to cripple athletes when they are much too young; they are free to claim they know nothing about anabolic steroid, amphetamine, or cocaine use or about illicit payoffs from boosters and agents; they are free to preach the idea that the battles won on the friendly fields of athletic strife will someday lead us to victory in Grenada; or that the "character building" experienced in the Final Four or the Rose Bowl will eliminate insider trading on Wall Street.

And who are their conduits for this information in many— certainly not all—cases? The writer/columnist/broadcaster who has just had a nice free press room meal, paid for by the athletic department; who has received a pair of free tickets on the fifty-yard line or at half court for his wife and daughter; who gets a discount on his new car from the president of the booster club; who gets invited to private social gatherings with the local coaching legend himself and all of the town's movers and shakers, and who is always remembered at Christmas by the university athletic department with some bit of material or financial appreciation.

Given this comfortable climate, and the fact that most publishers, managing editors, and news directors simply view their sport pages and sport reports as a fair haven for tired escapists ("There is enough bad news on page one, right? Let's keep sport a happy place," they often reason), it should not be much of a surprise that journalistic vigilance is just a bit lax when it comes to college sport. Given the financial stakes involved for everyone, can we really expect a Brent Musburger or Billy Packer to look critically at the abuses in college basketball when CBS all but owns the NCAA basketball tournament? Can we expect a middle-aged sport columnist in a small college town with a top-ten football or basketball team to look into the questions of graduation rates, illegal recruiting, drug usage, the exploitation of black athletes, or the second-rate status of women's athletics?

As the influence of the electronic media grows and that of the print media wanes, what little life remains in investigative sport journalism will become even more crucial. Only a handful of newspapers and magazines actually have full-time investigative reporters or staffs in their sport departments now. So the gutsy editor or managing editor who starts caring about what is going on in sport often has to dip into the news department for help. During this decade, three Pulitzer Prizes have been awarded to papers for looking into various aspects of college sport: *The Arizona Daily Star* in Tucson for investigating the University of Arizona football program; *The Macon, Georgia, Telegraph and News* for an eighteen-part series on athletics at the University of Georgia and Georgia Tech (Jackie Crosby of the Macon team was a member of the sport department); and *The Lexington Herald-Leader* for examining the University of Kentucky basketball program.

In many towns the size of Lexington (population 204,165) and in smaller ones with major universities that play top-level sport, the college team is the focal point of the community and the backing for the teams borders on religion. Coaches have extraordinary and sometimes frightening power. Star athletes are treated like members of a royal family. Boosters and alumni form what seem like shadow governments, controlling purse strings and, in many cases, giving hear-no-evil, see-no-evil coaches, all their alibis—"Gee, fellas, how am I supposed to control what the boosters do?"—on those infrequent occasions when the NCAA enforcement staff, or some investigative reporter, catches up with the cheaters. All of this leads to an "us and them" mentality that can be stifling and completely dispiriting to any serious sport journalist. Unfortunately, it is a mentality that is widely tolerated in the offices of all too many publishers, editors, and news directors.

Mary Kress, the assistant managing editor for special coverage at the *Florida Times-Union*, delivered the most cynical, yet candid, explanation of this theory at the Gannett Center for Media Studies at Columbia University in the fall of 1987. Speaking at a conference on Media Economics and Sports Coverage, she said,

> In sports, we'd rather have an investigative reporter come in and do our tough reporting so that the sports beat reporter doesn't get in trouble with the coach or the players. The beat reporter gets a tip that could lead to a very good news story, but he doesn't pursue it. He passes it on to the investigative

reporter and he does it. The beat reporter goes back and covers the game and hobnobs with the players and hangs out in the locker room.

Kress then added, in reference to owners of media outlets, that [they do not]

expect the same of their sports departments as they do of their other news departments. Part of the problem may be that . . . readers want to know what happened at the game. And there's a lot of truth to that: The readers don't necessarily want to know all of the hard news stories that are there for the doing. But I don't think the readers really care about Chile or Tibet either, and we certainly don't have any lack of conscience in telling them about those things in our national and international news sections.

We are not demanding of our sports departments that they become better reporters, better journalists. If we've got an investigative reporter in the sports department, what are the rest of them? Are they just chroniclers of events? That means they're not reporting at all.

Joe Paterno is widely considered the most progressive football coach on the Division 1A level. Yet in discussing the coverage of the local town paper, *The Centre Daily Times*, with the Penn State student newspaper, he once said, "I think there's a little bit of an attitude . . . that they're not really enthusiastic; they don't want to be cheerleaders for the Penn State athletic program, which is what you don't see in the Omaha and Lincoln papers. There's more enthusiasm for the program in some other areas than what we have." Paterno then went on to say that he wasn't against "objective writers . . . I can't be critical of somebody who has certain principles."

The implication of what Paterno says is that life can be a lot easier in those areas where the press is part of the "team"—and it generally is. Paul Hornung (not the former Green Bay Packer star), who covered Ohio State football for thirty-eight years and who was the sport editor of the *Columbus* (Ohio) *Dispatch*, was keenly aware that some of his peers accused him of being a house man for the school and the late Ohio State football coach Woody Hayes. Hornung responded in a March 1979 *Philadelphia Inquirer* story by saying:

> I know I've been pegged [as Woody's] mouthpiece, but in the long run, I felt that our readers got a lot more because I was close to Woody, because I was close to Ohio State, had friends at Ohio State. The few items that I got and never used that would have made juicy gossip—well, our readers were far ahead of the game because I knew everything that was going on. It gave me an advantage . . . In my own heart I don't think our readers got cheated out of anything worthwhile.

When Hayes slugged a Clemson linebacker in the 1978 Gator Bowl game and was fired, Hornung said writing the story "was the hardest thing I ever had to do."

No doubt it was. So it was left to others, mostly in books and magazine articles, to strip away the myths about Hayes and portray him for what he was: a violent autocrat who equated football with war, loved General George S. Patton, and eventually disgraced himself and his university with his shocking display of undisciplined behavior in the Gator Bowl. Even after Hayes was fired, he continued to enjoy hero status in Columbus; it was almost as if what had happened in Jacksonville that December evening did not matter at all. In great part, he could thank the journalistic ethics of *The Columbus Dispatch* and Paul Hornung for that.

In those rare instances in university towns when the media complicate things for the athletic department by getting aggressive, the situation can get very nasty. Jeff Marx, one of the reporters from Lexington who won a Pulitzer Prize, knows how difficult it is to take on a powerful athletic program such as the one representing Kentucky basketball. He describes the reaction to a hard-hitting story:

> The day the story came out, the paper was prepared. We had extra security guards and extra people to answer the phones. The number of calls was uncountable. I think it was about 400 subscribers who canceled immediately. There was a bomb threat and we had to evacuate the building.
>
> The hardest part was not the anonymous hatred. That was expected and had to be accepted. But I didn't expect the type of personal abuse I received. Even my girl friend's family stopped talking to me for a while. I had to move out of my

apartment because my landlord told me, "people are looking for you." I stayed in a different place every night so no one would know where I was sleeping."

William Woestendiek, the executive editor of *The Arizona Daily Star*, told United Press International on the day his paper won the Pulitzer Prize in April of 1981, "Even the other news media opposed us. We were doing the unheard of thing, attacking a football coach [Tony Mason]. We also had the opposition of most of the community. A lot of influential people—many in the business community and alumni—constantly were trying to get us to kill the story. We were told frequently it was no story."

It is somewhat ironic, however, that after papers break a major story such as the ones in Tucson, Macon, and Lexington, pack journalism takes over, mainly because the initial legal risk has been taken by someone else. What happens next is a media circus complete with moralizing columnists deploring big-time college athletics, and the athletic department sycophants on papers and television stations attacking the bearers of the message.

"Inevitably, and ironically, these are the same sportswriters [and broadcasters] who lionized to the heavens (before the scandal broke) the now exposed athletes and programs," Anthony J. Maruca, vice president for student affairs at Princeton University, wrote in *The New York Times* on August 25, 1985. "Furthermore . . . many of them are also the most vocal critics of institutional leaders who try [to bring] reforms that are designed to control abuses, i.e., to 'de-emphasize' (a bad word in their lexicon) the competitive quality of play, as though that were the institution's highest priority if not its *raison d'etre*."

To de-emphasize would also mean curtailing the power and role of too many sportswriters and broadcasters. There is little journalistic glamor or money in women's field hockey or men's fencing. So the preoccupation with bigness grows and spirals out of control, aided and abetted by media folk whose community and economic stature would certainly decline if any form of athletic sanity were to prevail.

When it comes to the question of ethics in sport journalism, there is another area associated with "bigness" that must not only be addressed, but dealt with by the media. Too many in the business view it as trivial or a lost cause, simply attributing the dissemination of gambling information on college sport as a "service" to readers. Vince Doria, the sport editor of *The Boston Globe*, told the President's Commission on Organized Crime in June of 1985, "I think most newspapers have come to the conclusion that gamblers are readers, too. I think most of us believe that those readers need to be serviced." The other side of the argument is one advanced by Dave Kindred, now a columnist for *The Atlanta Journal and Constitution*. When he was with *The Washington Post* a few years before, he said:

> Gambling is illegal. Newspapers are not in the business of promoting illegal activities. Those who run odds say the readers want to know. They want to know how much the prostitutes are charging and the price of marijuana or the price of heroin and we don't print that. What other place in a newspaper do you promote an illegal activity. . . . The argument that if we don't run it, the other paper will or the odds will be made available somewhere else is morally baseless.

There have been two major point-shaving scandals (1951 and 1961) in college basketball and two other separate incidents involving Boston College and Tulane during this decade. The Tulane case in 1985 embarrassed the university into actually dropping its basketball program. After the Boston College and Tulane stories broke, there were—proving Anthony Maruca's theory—dozens of outraged commentaries in newspapers and on television. But if any newspaper or television station or network found what happened egregious enough to cause it to stop printing—or commenting on— point spreads, it is a well-kept secret.

There is one case in the newspaper business that is particularly sad but illuminating when it comes to the question of point spreads. It involves the fine paper based on Long Island, but which now serves New York City, too, *New York Newsday*. The sports editors of *New York Newsday* always resisted the idea of printing point spreads, but when the paper branched out to challenge the city's tabloid dailies, management decided that in spite of sport department opposition, it would put the paper in a more competitive position if it started to print the point spreads, and now it does.

The question of the point spreads does not stop with printing them or hearing about them. Many sportswriters bet on college games, sometimes with the knowledge of their editors, sometimes without. Some of these writers also have weekly columns in which they pick games according to the spread and I have seen and heard them discussing their bets in the press box and calling bookmakers from the press box. The writers often are privy to inside information because of their closeness to the teams they cover. When it comes to conflicts of interest, this is one of the biggest, yet it is almost impossible to stop, and the efforts to do so are lame at best.

If writers bet on games, how can they be expected to take the ethical question of point spreads seriously? And how can they be expected to be professional about their jobs, searching for stories that might involve gambling angles?

You could easily ask the same thing about the way today's generation of sportswriters and sportscasters view the drug issue. In 1986, Len Bias, the Maryland basketball star, and Don Rogers, a safetyman for the Cleveland Browns, died about a week apart. Both deaths were related to the use of cocaine and shocked the country. A short time later, I wrote an article in *The Nation*, bringing up the question of the way the press approached the issue of drugs and sport. In part, it said:

> There was no murkiness now for the sports news managers, no departmental generation gap to bridge. Most of the older editors and writers neither understood nor cared about drugs, while the younger generation had been exposed to drug use since college. But both were happy to ignore the warning signals around them. In fact, some young sportswriters had exchanged good weed and good coke during interviews with athletes. It proved the reporter was one of the guys and could be trusted not to write about sensitive subjects, just as the older guys had proved it for all those years by not writing about boozing and whoring. Why spoil a good thing and cut off a source by getting into the touchy stuff?

Press hypocrisy was never greater than in the days and weeks following the deaths of Bias and Rogers. Nobody, certainly no reporters, had written that either athlete had a problem. Were they looking in the first place? Not just at Bias and Rogers, but in general? Did they see enough to make them approach the athlete or a coach or a teammate or a family member so they could ferret out the story themselves? Vigilance and some honest reporting might have saved a life. Most reporters prefer to take sensitive information of this nature—whether the subject matter is drugs, alcohol, or sex—and gossip about it in press rooms all over the country. Time and time again I have heard reporters discussing all sorts of questionable situations involving sport figures (including some situations in which the reporter actually was present) only to be told that delving into these subjects was not relevant to sport journalism because reporters and editors get drunk, reporters and editors take drugs, and reporters and editors cheat on their spouses.

While all of these problems pose difficult ethical questions for the sporting press, there is another one that may be the most disturbing yet and involves the way the black college athlete is perceived, why he is perceived that way, and whether that perception will ever change. The trouble starts at the doors, not only of the sport editors and news directors, but at the doors of the publishers and owners. There are just not enough blacks in the sport media, and there are almost none in key editorial positions in newspaper and network sport departments. It is a problem that will take years to correct, and before it is corrected—if it ever really is—the public is going to continue to be misled and misinformed because the black point of view just is not seeing print or the television screen in an honest way. Instead the white sport press continues day after day, week after week, year after year, to present a stereotypical view of the black athlete to readers and viewers.

"What announcers and the media are teaching America is a two-tier system of perception," Derrick Jackson wrote in *New York Newsday* in June of 1987:

The "smart" players are white. The quick, leaping "athletes" who have unteachable abilities, are black . . . white players play as if they are reaching deep into their souls for their ability. They are gritty. They hustle. They practice. They think. The black men who sweat and hustle are locked in prisons of stereotyped perception. In those prisons, black men do not have grit; they have talent. They don't hustle; they have quick hands and great leaping ability. Teaching them is not necessary; they have instinct. In this two-tier system, black men don't think. A black basketball player is smart only if that happens to be his last name. . . .

Until [the networks] and America's newspapers break the shackles around their mindsets and headsets, it will be a long time before white Americans cease with the assumption that the masses of black [athletes] . . . come dribbling out of their mother's wombs. It will be even longer before a black player goes to the line and has it said about him—with the camera zooming in on his profuse, gleaming perspiration—"Is there a smarter player . . . than that man."

Very few white sport journalists could have written those lines or would even have cared to. Racism simply is not a priority in the sporting press. It only becomes one when the quotas—and they exist everywhere to keep the discrimination suits away—begin to slip and the famous "numbers" drop; then management begins to put out the calls for more minorities, usually blacks first, then women, then hispanics.

Roy S. Johnson, a former columnist and now Senior Editor at *Sports Illustrated*, serves as the sport co-chair of the National Association of Black Journalists. Johnson's group has compiled a list of more than 150 black sport journalists, but he says when editors of major papers are faced with making a minority hire, they automatically look for a "core group of five or six guys who work for high profile organizations":

When one of the five or six [Johnson was among them during his days at *The New York Times*] turns down a job at a big paper, the sports editor throws up his hands and tells the people he reports to, "We tried. What can I do?" When it comes to hiring blacks, editors seem to want only the next Pulitzer Prize winner. Very few editors will go to the trouble of searching for a black writer, hiring the person and then developing that person. That's why we developed the list, to give editors names of people who don't have high profiles but who are very good, even though they may be working for a smaller organization.

There has to be a change because what we have now in sports journalism is a crime of ignorance. There are all these

white reporters writing about people from a culture and background they don't understand. A lot of the white writers don't
even take the time to try and understand.

The problem does not end with writers or broadcasters.
There are virtually no blacks or women or hispanics in policy-
making positions in sport departments around the country,
and the record in the television industry—though a bit better
for blacks, Johnson says—is still critical. Yet it does not stop
the papers, magazines, and television announcers from moralizing about the lack of blacks in college coaching positions
or in administrative jobs in college athletic departments.

Solutions will not come quickly. Racism—and sexism—
in sport have been too ingrained over generations, and in
sport departments the problem is even worse because for
decades the question never came up. Only when black athletes began to have success in huge numbers did anyone begin
to notice the deep cultural and communication problems that
existed between these young men and women and the white
males whose job it was to cover their exploits.

There is nothing more cynical or depressing than to be
in a press box or a sport department filled with white sportswriters laughing and talking about black athletes in what
these whites perceive to be a black dialect. After all these
years, the derision is as malignant as it was fifty years ago
when the so-called Golden Age of sport journalism produced
a group of insensitive writers and editors who almost never
questioned why there were no blacks going from the colleges
to the professional leagues.

Their legacy is not the venerated—though often childish—
prose of their day. Their legacy is a lack of feeling, a lack
of caring, a lack of respect for what the profession of journalism is about. It encompasses more than the issue of blacks
and racism. It reaches into every corner of the sport world.
Too many of those "Golden Age" heroes looked the other
way too often on too many issues, and in doing so—because
of their stature and the hero-worship they were accorded by
generations of younger writers and editors—they set a moral
and ethical tone that has reached the 1980s and probably
will carry well into the next century.

What we have today in sport journalism is a new age, the Golden Age of Triviality. It is the age of *USA Today* sport lists and often lifeless statistical data ("When qualitative distinctions fade and lose their force, we turn to quantitative ones," writes Amherst professor and sport sociologist Allen Guttman); it is the age of twenty-four-hour sport call-in shows ("This is Joe from the Bronx. The Big East is better than the Big Eight"); it is the age of Brent Musburger, Billy Packer, and Dick Vitale and the endless, shameless television hype for "March Madness"; it is the age of the point spread and the lily-white, nearly all-male private club called the sport department.

With a few brave exceptions on a small number of publications and broadcast stations, this is not an age for questioning on the major issues or talking about ethics in sport. It is the age of the big snooze, an age that could easily steal the slogan "Toys R Us" and put it up over the entrance to the sport department.

10

The Coaching Responsibility

JACK BICKNELL

If I were fired for doing something illegal, immoral, or unethical, then I certainly would hang my head in shame. If I were fired for not winning enough games, this would not be the end of the world for me.

When Walter Byers, the long-time executive director of NCAA, estimated that 30% of major college programs are involved in illegal activities, it underlined how far those of us in college sport have to go in order to make a bad situation better.

As other contributors to this book have demonstrated, serious problems exist in college sport. As a head coach, I know that I can keep my program problem-free. However, I fully recognize that it is my responsibility to do so. I believe that the overwhelming majority of my fellow coaches also take this responsibility seriously.

I joined the profession of coaching because of the satisfaction of being involved with young people at a very im-

portant time in their lives in a sport that I truly believe in
and enjoy. I look upon myself as a teacher and educator in
the true sense of both words. I try to treat each member of
my squad the way I would want my own son treated. I want
them to enjoy their collegiate experience thoroughly both on
and off the field.

If a university hires a quality person as head coach, he
will work with the school's and player's best interests in
mind. Everything else then is likely to work out all right.

The head coach of any major intercollegiate athletic program is directly responsible for the entire operation of his
program. Thus as a head coach of football I find myself
worrying about everything and everybody. The group that
needs my attention above all is the players. Each player who
participates in football is the direct responsibility of the head
coach, and so is every assistant coach, graduate assistant,
volunteer assistant, manager, and office secretary. The head
coach even has to worry about the actions of some of the
school's most well-intentioned alumni and friends. I also
have to worry about things outside my control, problems in
society such as racism and drugs.

The American Football Coaches' Association adopted a
code of ethics that was approved on August 15, 1952. This
code is easy for coaches to understand and should not be
that difficult to follow:

> The distinguishing characteristic of a profession is that its
> members are dedicated to rendering a service to humanity.
> Personal gain must be of lesser consideration. Those who select
> football coaching must understand the justification for football
> is that it provides spiritual and physical values for those who
> play it, and the game belongs, essentially, to the players.
>
> The welfare of the game depends on how the coaches live
> up to the spirit and letter of ethical conduct and how coaches
> remain ever mindful of the high trust and confidence placed
> in them by their players and by the public.
>
> Coaches unwilling or unable to comply with the principles
> of the Code of Ethics have no place in the profession.

I use two basic rules to help me insure that my program
is run responsibly. First I must know my own values and
those of my university. I honestly believe that if there is no

contradiction in my value system, making the proper decisions is one of the easier aspects of the job.

My second rule is to hire quality people who accept these values. Working with quality people eliminates a large percentage of potential problems.

The Pressure to Win

I certainly cannot pretend to have all of the answers, but there is one fact that is constant at all levels. Unless you win you will eventually be fired. How you handle this basic fact of life is very important to your future in coaching.

If I were fired for doing something illegal, immoral, or unethical, then I certainly would hang my head in shame. If I were fired for not winning enough games, this would not be the end of the world for me.

Boston College wants to win and there is pressure on me to perform my duties in a professional manner. Yet there is a great deal more pressure on me to conduct my program in an honest and ethical way. My contract stipulates that if I violate NCAA rules or fail to work within the guidelines set forth by our school, my contract can be immediately terminated.

As pointed out by John Slaughter and Doug Single elsewhere in this book, a strong president and an athletic director with whom you can truly communicate are critical to the success of any athletic program. Certainly, the time when a head coach really needs a strong president and athletic director is when a wealthy contributor to the athletic program or to the general fund threatens to withdraw support unless the coach is fired, or demands that recruiting procedures be altered from existing regulations in order to attract certain players, or illegally offers to support those already in school.

Sadly, we have seen the consequences of such actions in some programs in the Southwest Conference. Southern Methodist University had to shut down its football program for a couple of seasons and now must begin at square one. Every coach who has been through the rebuilding of a program knows the painful process that awaits the school that must start over, perhaps doubly painful since it really has so little base from which to begin. At SMU, there is little doubt that had the administration of the school and the athletic administration resisted the pressures of wealthy and influential alumni, this terrible situation would not have occurred. This serves as the most stark example of what can happen whenever school and athletic administrations cannot say "No!" Coaches must recognize that they can be placed at the mercy of a school administration that does not resist such illegal contributions.

The ideal situation is to work for a president who is not afraid to tell the wealthy contributor that he is willing to forgo his contributions in preference to alienating the coach who is doing a good job.

Yet, there comes a time when every coach's career hits the down curve. If the curve deepens to any degree, the resulting pressures on the coach, the assistant coaches, and the players begin to build from the outside. There are always impatient supporters used to success; there are always potshotting media people who do not take the time to explore reasons for poor performance and present reasonable explanations. Each coach must deal with these pressures in ways that work best personally.

Recruiting

Rule compliance at Boston College is a very simple issue. It starts with the president and his policies. It is carried out through the athletic director, and ultimately it is my responsibility to see that we do things properly. I have never been able to comprehend how some schools have problems understanding something this simple.

Every year our staff and I sit down with our athletic director and go over the recruiting rules and regulations. Our athletic director encourages each coach to come to him if there is any question about what he can or cannot do. He then makes it clear: "If you cheat you are gone." All of my coaches understand his feelings completely. It is not really all that complicated. Obey the rules and there will be no problems. If the rule states you can visit a high school only once a week, go only once a week. If the rule is not realistic, work to get it changed.

I then talk to my coaches about how I want them to recruit. From my background as a high school coach I know the way other high school coaches wish to be treated—honestly and in such a way that they know exactly what you are thinking. I have never gotten in trouble with an honest, early evaluation.

My only other discussion with my coaches centers on positive recruitment. I want them going into the homes of our prospects extolling the virtues of Boston College; what an education at B.C. can do for them; what studying, living, and playing in the Boston area can mean to them culturally and socially; and what advantages and opportunities our program presents for them as student-athletes.

I do not want our coaches tearing down other institutions. I know there are coaches who tack up all the negative press clippings they can get about schools or about areas where rival institutions are located and then make sure that a recruit sees all of that while he is listening to the pitch. I believe that, essentially, the ethical way of recruiting also makes the most sense. I want kids who think positively and who are not susceptible to being convinced by someone else's negative approach.

We spend a great deal of time trying to find out what kind of individual we are dealing with. Are his priorities in order? Is his education important to him? We need great players like everyone else, but I have found that "good kids" solve most of the potential problems. I don't like selfish people. When I visit a home I obviously am trying to impress the parents and the player, but I am evaluating them also. Is this young man a team-oriented individual? The player's attitude can be as important to me as how highly recruited he was. We all have seen a number of top players who were not that highly recruited—and yet they have become top players.

It is also vital to make alumni completely aware of the recruiting regulations, because this is where many schools have problems. Unfortunately, the alumni have been taken out of the recruiting picture entirely. Though I understand why the rules were changed, I do not approve, because many of our alumni helped portray the excellent job opportunities available after graduation, as I am sure they did at many other schools as well.

It is difficult to legislate integrity; but if a young man is found guilty of accepting an illegal inducement from a coach or athletic representative, that athlete should become immediately ineligible for the duration of his college career. I would recommend that he keep his scholarship but that he not be allowed ever to play in college again. These young people must learn the rules and should not be allowed to break them without consequence. We may lose some players with our low-key approach—but we do not get saddled with "head cases" that will hurt us in the long run.

A coach cannot be treated any differently. A coach involved in a major violation should be banned from coaching at an NCAA school forever. Get these people out of the coaching profession. There is no excuse for flagrant disregard of the rules.

The Freshman Athlete

When new student-athletes first arrive at Boston College, I want them to get adjusted socially and become thoroughly acclimated academically before I worry about football. It has been my experience that if student-athletes enjoy school and are on top of things academically, they come to practice in a good frame of mind and ready to work.

We level with high-school athletes in recruiting and make it a point to tell them they should not count on playing as freshmen. The result is not having to deal with students who are disillusioned at the outset of their college careers; the further result is a happier athlete who gets into the spirit of the team and the school as his career proceeds. This translates itself into a happy locker room, athletes motivated to succeed, and a greater chance of success for them—and for their coach!

In our program, if a freshman cracks the lineup it is simply because we have determined that he can handle the challenge physically, mentally, and emotionally. In every instance, we measure the player's role with those yardsticks. However, it is still a rare occurrence for us to let a freshman play much.

Many years ago, I read an article in which former Nebraska head coach, and now athletic director, Bob Devaney, pointed out that the biggest changes in a young person's life occur during the college years. Coach Devaney was then leading the fight against the freshman eligibility rule. What he said at the time brought me up short: that a student comes into college as a teenager just out of high school and leaves as an adult; that the biggest emotional and physical changes in life occur during this time; and that it is patently unfair to put an eighteen-year-old kid, just three or four months out of high school, against a twenty-two- or twenty-three-year-old man who has spent four or five years developing in those key areas.

I can live with the idea that freshmen should be ineligible—if everyone else did the same thing. However, I believe that if college presidents and the NCAA decided to make them ineligible officially, we would have to increase the number of athletic scholarships. Frankly, I wonder if many schools could handle that burden financially.

Academics and Athletics

Working at Boston College means working in an atmosphere where there is great emphasis on academics. Our athletes must be able to compete in the classroom as well as on the playing field. The athlete and nonathlete alike must have a green light from the admissions people before they can come to the school. In recent years, the school has underscored this fact, with the result that we often must bypass a superior prospect who simply is not equipped to handle our school academically.

The benefits, of course, include getting other good athletes who also are reasonably intelligent. This is a combination that makes our teaching and coaching jobs easier; that forestalls morale problems because intelligent kids inevitably are more receptive to good coaching and understand their roles in a team concept better; and that establishes a continuity of players through four years of varsity competition— and the head coach need not accumulate more gray hairs than necessary worrying whether his key players can stay in school.

Once the young man is recruited and on the campus, it is extremely important to have academic support services available. Academic advisement, tutors, and just somebody to talk to away from an athletic environment is critical, and this is becoming common practice at most schools, for athlete and nonathlete alike.

I take it as my responsibility to make sure this student is going to class. There is no excuse for poor class attendance; and a head coach can get the message across better than anyone on his staff. If the problem continues, the best way to solve it is to suspend game participation. If a head coach attacks poor class attendance or noncompliance with academic responsibilities early in an athlete's career, many academic problems will cease to exist.

Success in graduation starts in the freshman year. It is crucial that student-athletes be on time academically at the end of their first year, including summer school. If they are still on time after their sophomore and junior years and enter their senior year with eight or nine courses to go, they will be in position to have a normal senior year and to graduate without a great deal of pressure.

It is important to note that coaches, academic advisors, and tutors cannot do the players' work. This is why it is critical that only people with a burning desire to succeed in school be recruited.

With all the added pressures of football, not every young man can graduate in four years. The possibility of a fifth year allows some flexibility in course selection. There is no reason why a hardworking individual cannot succeed in five years. The school has a responsibility to see that the young man graduates.

The Racial Factor on College Campuses

The racial factor in coaching need not be the mine field that many like to portray if a coach has only one commandment: thou shalt be fair and consistent.

Of course, coaches know that consistency, more than any other personality trait, is the most important key to long-lasting success, but it is especially important in dealing with the various racial, ethnic, and religious components of a team. I attempt to build an environment on our football team that is conducive to mutual respect and understanding. That means that I, as head coach, must set the example with my assistants and, in turn, demand that all of us carry it on to the players.

Racism, as a problem, most often comes to us in the form of an individual player whose previous environment spawned those ugly feelings. We try, during our recruiting procedures, to uncover as much about personality and personal habits as we can. This includes talking to the athlete's high school coaches about how well he gets along with his fellow players, regardless of their ethnic background. Obviously, if we find a prospect has a problem, or has been a problem in the matter of team harmony, then we must reconsider just how much we really want that individual.

The coach enters a real mine field when, after getting a player, he discovers that the new recruit has serious problems. This can become like a cancer that will eat its way through a team and tear it apart if not cut out at the first discovery. This means direct action by the head coach to the point of demanding that either attitudes be changed or the player will no longer be welcome as a member of the team, regardless of his status!

I do not want racial cliques on my football team. I want our players to join with each other and become a team in the true meaning of the word. We encourage athletes to do things together, to join each other at meals or in social times. Our rooming list on the road is made up without regard to whether blacks room with blacks or hispanics with hispanics. In short, I want the young men on our team liking each other and willing to sacrifice to help each other. When it is fourth and goal on the one-yard line, and the game is on the line, a player is more apt to get the job done if he is doing it for someone he likes than if he is doing it for someone he barely knows or for whom he has little respect.

Athletes should know that they have their coaches to talk to in difficult times, and this will mean so much more if they respect their coaches' feelings for the particular problems that may be bothering them.

When they are away from the team, minority athletes must manage their own interpersonal relationships with the student body in general. How they do it strictly is up to them, but if they have already seen a healthy environment around their team, then they have something on which to build.

Most universities have established centers and programs for minority students where they can bond with others of their origin if they feel the need. Serving a purpose of identification and allowing an outlet for such areas as tradition, common interest, and heritage, such programs become a part of the undergraduate experience.

As coaches, we must provide the proper environment for racial harmony and then insist that it be maintained.

Drugs and Alcohol on Campus

Education about drugs and alcohol is vital. In 1981 we began a drug and alcohol program under the auspices of our health services department. This program was well received, but I did not relax until 1985, when we established a testing program. Now that we have a full-scale university-funded drug testing program, I can speak with confidence and certitude about the general absence of steroids and drug involvement on our team.

On the question of steroids, I used to worry about their use because of misinformation and conflicting statements that on one hand praised steroids for solving the problem of getting players bigger and stronger, and on the other hand portrayed the terrible future effects they could have on a young man's physical being. It bothered me that a young man at thirty-five, with serious health problems, would look back and wonder why his college coach, who well might have known the dire effects that lay ahead, did not become more involved in policing these drugs.

Now we know for certain that there are dire effects, and our drug program seeks to head them off before they can begin. In the case where athletes come to us already on steroids, we can stop the usage.

Our program to detect marijuana, cocaine, heroin, crack, and the other instruments of degredation and potential death is designed as a deterrent to drug abuse. We are not trying to catch anyone, but we are trying to help any of our players who might develop a problem.

Drugs are available at every level of society, but so too is information about their terrible effects. No longer can any young person plead ignorance of what can happen to him if he or she uses drugs. High schools have drug education/ prevention programs; so do grammar schools; and there is a blizzard of public service announcements on television every day of the year. This means the young no longer can say, "I didn't realize . . ."; and with the help of the drug-testing program as an added weapon, I can sleep a little better at night knowing we are on top of this problem.

My chief concern however, is alcohol abuse. Anytime a disciplinary problem comes across my desk from a campus incident—and I get a written report anytime one of our players is involved—I can be almost positive it will be alcohol related, even before I delve into the reasons. I have talked to campus authorities, and they tell me that alcohol is the main cause for most of their problems. But I do not excuse our young people just because "it happens to everyone else." I deal with each case individually, and I spare no one's feelings.

We try to shortstep all of these problems with one basic rule for our athletes: avoid doing anything that would embarrass your parents and your team. If you don't care for either of them, then you must face me and suffer the consequences of your actions.

The Right Relationship with Media

Relations with the media really are a matter of experience, like anything else in coaching. My relationships with the media who cover our football team have, for the most part, been positive. Of course, we also have had more winning seasons than losing seasons; and we have been to four post-season Bowls during my tenure at Boston College. So there really has not been a great deal of a negative nature on which the media can dwell. I believe that every coach who has had similar successful seasons has found the same environment.

The media has a job to do, and that is to report the news. At the same time, I have a job to do, and that is to coach a football team and safeguard the best interests of that team, my school, and our overall football program. Since my school is paying me, then everything associated with its best interests must come first. I need not be the media's best friend in times when our program is under seige.

The first rule in dealing with the media is to be totally honest in all that you say. Don't lie or make excuses. If they delve into areas wherein you feel the interests of the team or the school will be adversely affected, simply refrain from any but the necessary comments. But do not lie, because sooner or later, someone is apt to find the truth, and then the problem will be ten times worse than before—to the point of perhaps costing you a job.

Second, be accessible—no matter how much it may hurt, or how you may feel toward a particular member of the media who has become a harpoon marksman. Openness shows you have nothing to hide.

Now I realize that every coach has a different way of meeting and treating people, simply because personalities are different. But I have found that making myself accessible to the media has enabled me to get to know them better—and has enabled them to get to know me better. For the most part, we have established a measure of respect, tinged with some degree of friendship. There have been instances when this rapport has turned some finely honed media swords into plowshares, at least temporarily until we have been able to solve some of our problems and get things turned around.

The only issue in which I flatly refuse to cooperate with the media is discussing potential recruits during recruiting season, and that has become the biggest media problem that I have faced. Speculative talk simply fuels the fires that already may be raging in alumni who are trying to get you to recruit this player or that player. It also puts pressure on the school for going after the so-called "top one hundred" regardless of their merit or qualifications; on the kids themselves to commit to a program that may not really interest them too much; and of course, on the coach to land the prospects that have been discussed.

In a word, exactly whom we are after is no one's business but our own, the young man's, and the young man's parents. The public will find out who he is after he has made his commitment, but in the meantime, I want this very delicate process to remain just as we have always kept it—private.

Agents

The problem of agents has become one of the most difficult confronting college athletics today, as the chapter contributed to this book by Bob Woolf explains in detail. Simply stated, there are NCAA rules stipulating most emphatically that a college athlete cannot sign an agreement or accept payments of any nature from an agent while he still has eligibility remaining. If he does, he loses his eligibility.

There are two groups of agents: a group who totally disregard the rule and get a prospect to do the same thing; and another group who abide by the rule and, while they may contact a professional prospect during eligibility time, make no move to bind an agreement. The latter group then handles all of the negotiations once the athlete's college career has ended.

As in recruiting violations, it takes "two to tango"; and though we instruct our players as to the precise nature of the rules in this regard, no coach can absolutely control what will happen. The rule is not ambiguous, so there can never be the excuse "I didn't really understand what I was doing." There cannot be any recourse: if a player is found out to have signed then I will not hesitate to let him go.

As I noted, there is no way that I or any other coach can absolutely control the problem, but there are means by which we can lessen the consequences. One is by recruiting players of good character and trusting that they will follow the rules in regard to acquiring an agent. The second would be legislative help in the way of laws forbidding agents to contact athletes with eligibility remaining. We have already seen this enforced in a case in Georgia, and, as coaches, we should make such legislation a priority because it will protect our players and our programs from these unscrupulous practices.

Barring—and even abetting—legal relief in these matters, the real answer to this complex problem is for the reputable people in the field of athletic representation to clean up their own industry.

Conclusion

Without oversimplifying a very complex issue, I may say I really believe that the entire situation of ethics in college athletics starts with the president of each institution. If he or she clearly defines what the aims and objectives are in regard to the athletic program, the coach knows immediately where he or she stands. When the president, athletic director, and coach work closely together, serious problems should not exist.

Unfortunately, the public perception of "big-time" athletics is sometimes negative. A vast majority of the schools work within the rules, but unfortunately the ones that flout the rules get much of the publicity.

I have not always won, so I know what to do when you end up the year three-to-eight. That type of season puts football in perspective, so in that respect I have been fortunate. We are playing a game. We are not solving the Mideast crisis nor are we working on a cure for cancer.

The most important aspect of this job is that we are working with young people, between the ages of eighteen and twenty-two, who need understanding, discipline, and better-experienced people who care about their future.

This is the greatest profession in the world. Weed out the crooks and develop hardworking athletes, and good things will come to your program. I am very fortunate to be a head coach at a Division I school, and I enjoy every aspect of my job.

11

The Role of Directors of Athletics in Restoring Integrity to Intercollegiate Sport

DOUG SINGLE

The services provided to student-athletes by both the athletic department and other university departments should work toward integrating student-athletes into the academic life of the university rather than furthering their isolation as a subculture outside the university mainstream.

The profession of director of athletics is indeed an odd one. Consider, for example, the fact that, although being a director of athletics is the avocation of many men, it is no child's aspiration. Although no little girl or little boy (including my son), when asked the question "What do you want to be

151

when you grow up," ever responds "A director of athletics," stadiums, athletic banquets, dining rooms, and offices are filled with people who would love to be directors of their own athletic programs. This generational difference in fantasies reflects certain powerful realities about both the nature of college sports and the problems and possibilities inherent in being a director of athletics in the United States.

Americans love sports with a passion that has elevated athletics from a national pastime to a national ritual. Nowhere is the significance of athletics as a social institution and a social problem more evident than in college sport. Intercollegiate athletics, especially at the Division I level, represents the "big time," not simply in terms of media exposure and revenues but, more importantly, in terms of the social power, values, traditions, and symbols embodied in intercollegiate athletics.

At many levels, Americans' passion for intercollegiate athletics reflects the larger social significance of sports in American culture. College athletes and coaches, for example, share with their professional colleagues a unique role as symbols of many of the most cherished values in American life: the desire to win and succeed and the belief in achieving excellence through individual perseverance, dedication, self-discipline, teamwork, and competition. The athlete as hero, therefore, reflects the importance of athletics as a community ritual in which Americans celebrate and reaffirm many common values and experiences. In this context it is easy to understand why children dream of being star athletes rather than athletic administrators, and many adults are envious of anyone who participates in the athletic enterprise.

The fact that many Americans would love to work in athletics does not repudiate an equally important truth: namely, that the role and responsibilities of a director of athletics are exceedingly more complex and difficult in real life than they are in the idealized world of the average fan's imagination.

The growth of big-time athletics has radically redefined the role and responsibilities of intercollegiate athletic administrators. As intercollegiate athletics itself has been transformed from an extracurricular activity embedded in the traditions of liberal education into a full-fledged business, the professional duties of directors of athletics have changed accordingly. In fact, contemporary directors of athletics more closely resemble corporate executives than ex-jocks or academic administrators.

The qualifications, skills, and talents necessary for a successful director of athletics are extensive. Given the range of programs offered by an intercollegiate athletics department, a director of athletics must have technical expertise in sports ranging from football to field hockey to swimming. He or she must also have training in marketing, sales, licensing, fund-raising, finance, and facilities. In addition to mastering these areas of technical knowledge, a director of athletics at the Division I level must also be an effective manager of human, financial, and physical resources. Finally and perhaps most importantly, a qualified director of athletics must be an educator.

When we examine the state of intercollegiate athletics today, we are immediately confronted with two interrelated realities. On the one hand, directors of athletics have succeeded in expanding the role of intercollegiate athletics within the university and throughout society. On the other hand, we have failed to preserve integrity within intercollegiate athletics because we have abdicated our role as educators. The central issue to confront, therefore, is what type of leadership directors of athletics must exercise to restore integrity. Before we can fully appreciate what the present and future role and responsibilities of directors of athletics should be, we need to examine the role directors of athletics have played in creating the current ethical crisis.

Decline of Integrity in Intercollegiate Athletics

Individuals within and outside of athletics have lamented the decline of integrity in college athletics since the mid-1970s. Until recently, however, far too many members of the athletic community have denied and/or ignored the obvious fact that a crisis of ethics not only exists, but that it also represents the most serious problem within intercollegiate athletics. At the heart of this crisis is the disturbing truth that many directors of athletics have actively participated in the creation, development, and perpetuation of a set of values, activities, and practices that has undermined the ethical foundations of both college athletics and higher education itself.

As college athletics entered the big time, many directors of athletics lost sight of the fundamental values, principles, and activities that should define the purpose of an athletic program within a university. We have allowed television, NFL and NBA expectations, media interests, boosterism, and our own selfishness to get out of control. As a result of these developments, the role of athletics within the university has come to be defined on the basis of misplaced priorities and justified with a unique blend of tortured logic and self-serving rationalization:

- Commitment to the student-athlete concept is "proven" with graduation rates built upon soft curricula, majors in eligibility, and other academic hocus-pocus;
- "Support for student-athletes" is equated with providing separate luxurious dormitories, treating athletes as a privileged class, and exempting student-athletes from meeting the same responsibilities and standards as other students;
- The admission of student-athletes without the necessary skills or abilities to succeed academically at a given university has become transformed from exploitation into a "legitimate contribution" to the expansion of educational opportunities for disadvantaged individuals and groups.

Given the powers invested in the office of the director of athletics, it is not surprising that the scandals and concerns rocking the ethical foundations of intercollegiate athletics have revealed a paucity of enlightened and courageous leadership. Such a revelation is not intended to repudiate the obvious fact that many past and present directors of athletics have shown solid and principled leadership. My point here is simply to emphasize that the crisis in ethics is first and foremost a crisis of leadership. We have failed as leaders simply because we have helped to create the very crisis we now must confront. Therefore, we have not only the opportunity but also the responsibility for taking steps to re-establish integrity in intercollegiate athletics.

Imperative Agendas for Athletic Directors

There are three immediate tasks directors of athletics must execute properly if the current movement for reform is to succeed. First, we must reexamine the goals, values, and priorities of our own programs and intercollegiate athletics nationally, and reaffirm a proper role for athletics within university life. In this regard, we must be able to develop a philosophy and model of intercollegiate athletics, especially at the Division I level, that will restore integrity through actions as well as words. The commitment to integrity must extend beyond good public relations and banquet speeches and into the nuts and bolts of our day-to-day activities as athletic administrators.

The second task is to implement policies and procedures to ensure that coaches and staff conduct their responsibilities in ways that reflect a shared commitment to the student-athlete concept and to compliance with NCAA rules and regulations. Finally, directors of athletics must take strong, immediate action to alleviate discrimination and foster equity within intercollegiate athletics.

Despite all claims to the contrary, big-time athletics has clearly demonstrated its power to distort the values of college life. Although intercollegiate athletics can benefit an academic institution, by no means should it be the top priority. Research and teaching, faculty and students, and the process of education itself are far more important.

Unfortunately, few institutions have developed as their goal the one common denominator that each should choose in intercollegiate athletics—the positive experience of the student-athlete. This means we must emphasize the *student* in student-athlete—not only regarding class attendance and graduation rates but also the *quality* of the educational experience. This process begins by developing recruiting procedures to ensure that prospective student-athletes have a legitimate chance to graduate from our institutions. Student-athletes must also be encouraged to value education, not simply eligibility. The values embedded in the student-athlete concept are prostituted whenever athletic expediency takes precedence over academic integrity.

It is imperative that we recognize and reaffirm the fact that the single most important reason for providing college students with an opportunity to participate in intercollegiate athletics is to enhance their educational experience. The existence of intercollegiate athletics derives its only intrinsic value from its potential to enhance the educational and personal growth of its participants. When an intercollegiate program exists primarily for the purposes of embellishing the profits, prestige, and reputations of institutions and coaches, or of providing a training program for a career in professional athletics, then it automatically relegates the educational development of student-athletes to a secondary role. When this occurs, it is contradictory for an athletic program to claim it contributes positively to the essential purpose of a university.

Athletic Academic-Assistance Programs

As the difficulties involved in integrating the goals and values of big-time athletics with the academic well-being of student-athletes became increasingly apparent, one of the most important responses from directors of athletics was the creation of athletic academic-assistance programs. When properly conceived and managed, these programs serve to ensure that athletic success does not result in academic failure.

The goal of any academic-assistance program for student-athletes should be the integration of academics and athletics at both the individual and institutional levels. At the individual level, academic-assistance programs ensure that participants in Division I intercollegiate athletics are students as well as athletes. Postsecondary institutions are obligated ethically to establish services that provide student-athletes with the opportunity to receive an education.

There is no question that student-athletes in Division I institutions have certain unique needs in comparison to non-athlete students. The time and emotional demands of athletics, combined with the distinctive culture that exists within organized athletics as a social institution, clearly separate the experiences of student-athletes from other college students. Our recognition of these differences is critical if we are to successfully meet the individual and institutional goals of integrating academics and athletics. This is not to say that student-athletes should receive special—that is, preferential—treatment. Rather, the issue at hand is simply that student-athletes, like other subcultures within a diverse university community, have needs and experiences that are not common to all students.

The unique needs of student-athletes, however, should never be viewed as a justification for preferential treatment. The services provided to student-athletes by both the athletics department and other university departments should work toward integrating student-athletes into the academic life of the university rather than furthering their isolation as a subculture outside the university mainstream.

Unfortunately, far too often Division I athletic programs have created and maintained academic-assistance programs for student-athletes for the sole, if not always overt, purpose of separating student-athletes from the academic life of the university. Far too many directors of athletics have fostered the growth of autonomous academic-assistance programs for student-athletes as a way of managing rather than solving academic problems. While such programs have had some success in advancing the educational progress of student-athletes, for the most part these programs have further exacerbated the schism between academics and athletics. Far too often, even the most successful of these programs operate under the assumption that athletic departments should have exclusive responsibility for and control of the academic lives of student-athletes.

Academic-assistance programs centered solely in athletic departments have failed not because there is no legitimate need for the services they provide, but because of the ways in which these services have been conceptualized, implemented, and justified. Such programs are inherently driven toward maintaining eligibility rather than fostering education and toward "protecting" student-athletes from academic standards, faculty, and deans rather than assisting and educating student-athletes to take advantage of the available resources. At the heart of this model of academic-assistance programming for student-athletes lies the goal of creating an integrated system of services that encompasses both the resources available to all students and a set of services, based in the athletic department, designed to supplement those resources.

When academic assistance is defined as the mutual responsibility of the faculty, the undergraduate dean's office, and the designated academic advisers within the athletic department, the university combines its resources to meet the institutional and individual goal of integrating academics and athletics. Within this structure, athletic academic advisers would be required to ensure that student-athletes consult faculty advisers on a regular basis while also working with both the student and his or her faculty adviser to monitor the student-athlete's progress toward a degree.

How to Win the Right Way

Fostering commitment to the student-athlete concept and establishing a proper role for athletics within the academy also requires that directors of athletics set realistic expectations for coaches and their programs. If we as athletic directors place a higher value on winning than on the total experience of the student-athlete, we are telling coaches all the wrong things. The challenge involved in combining athletic competitiveness with academic excellence may be difficult, but it is the only challenge worth undertaking as either an athletic administrator, a coach, or a student-athlete.

Winning in athletics enhances an institution's prestige only if it occurs in the context of the university's central concerns. What we can, and should, demand of our coaches and their programs is the following: that student-athletes reach their optimum levels athletically, academically, and personally; that our teams rarely lose to a weaker team; that all involved draw satisfaction from the activity itself; and that, within that context, we operate programs with fiscal accountability and moderation.

Compliance

The issues involved in compliance, like those embodied in debates over the proper role of athletics within a university,

illustrate the very nature of the ethical crisis within intercollegiate athletics today. Since 1970, several trends in compliance indicate individually and collectively that the ethical
foundations of intercollegiate athletics are gradually eroding
from within. Beyond disturbing increases in the number and
seriousness of rule violations since 1970, we have also wit-
nessed the persistent growth of attitudes that have transformed compliance into a necessary evil rather than a positive
good. For example, far too many directors of athletics, coaches,
and other individuals within intercollegiate athletics have
adopted the attitude that "It is all right to cheat because
everyone else does." An equally widespread corollary to this
view is the belief that "You have to cheat to win." In this
perspective, ethical conduct is measured by expediency rather
than principles, and "what works" becomes more important
than "what is right."

In whatever manifestation, this permissive environment
regarding illegal and unethical activities is unacceptable. No
institution or community can maintain any real degree of
ethical conduct unless its members are willing to respect and
abide by agreed-upon rules. Although the law cannot legislate
integrity or morality, integrity and morality cannot exist
without law. The importance of compliance with NCAA and
conference rules and regulations is therefore a matter of
ethics; the degree to which an intercollegiate athletic program
is committed to compliance stands in direct proportion to
its commitment to institutional integrity.

In compliance matters, directors of athletics occupy the
most important leadership position within intercollegiate athletics. Although the NCAA national office plays a significant
role in both compliance and enforcement, institutional integrity and accountability cannot be imposed from the top
down. Individual member institutions must take *primary*
responsibility for compliance. Compliance is not an "NCAA
problem"; it is an institutional responsibility. Accordingly,
responsibility and accountability for compliance begin and
end with directors of athletics.

The quality of direction a director of athletics provides
in compliance is intimately tied to his or her ability to devise
and implement an institutional compliance program. Running a clean athletics program requires a director who not

only believes in scrupulous adherence to NCAA/Conference rules but also creates and enforces a system of compliance within the programs.

The director's role is radically simple: to insist that the right way is the only way. Commitment to integrity through compliance is not a matter of altruism or elitism, but rather of intent and context. If we intend to do our jobs with honesty and integrity, then we must recognize that the rules governing our conduct define the context of our work. To implement this philosophy is difficult—compliance is a knotty and complex administrative task—but it is also, by definition, the quid pro quo of athletic administration.

Equity

The third critical task directors of athletics must undertake to restore integrity in athletics is to establish equity within intercollegiate athletics. The failure of intercollegiate athletics to establish fairness in opportunities and treatment of women, as well as blacks and other minorities, is an ethical disaster. Directors of athletics must take strong, immediate action to eradicate discrimination and provide women and minorities with legitimate opportunities as student-athletes, coaches, and administrators. One of the greatest strengths of athletics is that it can and should transcend racial, sexual, religious, and political barriers. As a result, no individual or group should be denied the opportunity to work or play in intercollegiate athletics simply because of race, gender, sexual orientation, religion, or ethnic background. If our philosophies and practices within intercollegiate athletics remain exclusive rather than inclusive, then the battle to restore integrity will never be won.

12

The Role of the National Collegiate Athletic Association

RICHARD SCHULTZ

The NCAA can continue its attempt to legislate integrity: we can add more rules, complicate the rule book even more, and triple the size of the enforcement staff. But unless each institution is ready to commit itself to complete integrity, we are never going to achieve it.

In an era of controversy regarding the integrity of college sport, one of the important functions of the NCAA is legislation. This legislation establishes the regulations for the governance of intercollegiate athletics. Over the years this process, at best, has become very cumbersome, complicated, and frustrating. In the area of legislation and structure, it is very important that the NCAA provide leadership to its members and see that quality reform is brought into the legislative and structuring process.

Integrity

When we discuss the legislative process and the quality of legislation, we are naturally led to the issue of integrity, the basis for much of the NCAA's legislation. Unfortunately, it is virtually impossible to legislate integrity, and one reason the NCAA finds itself entangled in legislative snarls today is the fact that for more than fifty years it has tried to do just that.

The NCAA can continue its attempt to legislate integrity: we can add more rules, complicate the rule book even more, and triple the size of the enforcement staff. But unless each institution is ready to commit itself to complete integrity, we are never going to achieve it.

The solution to total integrity in intercollegiate athletics is very simple. Each individual institution, from the governing board to the chief executive officer to the director of athletics to the individual coach, needs to make a total commitment to integrity in their programs, with proper institutional guidelines for compliance. If that commitment is made to the NCAA, we will have instant credibility and the majority of our problems dealing with integrity will be eliminated. The commitment to integrity is more than just running legitimate recruiting programs within the guidelines established by the membership. It also includes the recruiting of bona fide student-athletes, athletes who are well equipped to be college students, who will graduate at a rate equal to, if not substantially higher than, the rest of the student body during the same time period; and it includes assurance that the academic programs will be legitimate ones, with a good spread of major studies throughout the entire academic range.

Governing boards of member institutions have the major responsibility of guaranteeing integrity. In most cases, when there are serious problems in an athletics program, it is for one of two reasons. Individual coaches can become powerful enough to circumvent the chain of command and appeal directly to board members to accomplish their programs. Or, in some cases, the reverse happens. Governing board members become so interested in intercollegiate athletics and the success of its programs that they try to assume full command of the athletics department and allow violations of NCAA rules. Because of this, governing boards have to give strong support to chief executive officers and delegate to them the full authority for integrity in those programs. The governing board also needs to be strong and supportive when alumni and friends exert intense pressure that creates an unfavorable atmosphere or compromises the university's principles, as well as NCAA rules.

Once this authority and support are granted to the chief executive officer by the governing board, it then becomes his or her responsibility to hire, first of all, an athletic director with a strong commitment to integrity. The athletic director, in turn, must hire coaches with the same strength of character and interest in having a program steeped in integrity. Athletic directors and coaches need to understand clearly that their first responsibility is to the institution and that their jobs will be swiftly terminated if they willfully violate association rules to gain a competitive advantage.

Public Perception

Hand in hand with the integrity issue in intercollegiate athletics is the perception that many persons have of college athletics. This perception is basically the result of the broad-brush theory, which has been exercised in this nation for a number of years, not only in college athletics but in the political arena and other highly visible areas as well. The broad-brush theory is a simple one: if an athlete at one institution has a problem, all athletes are guilty by association. The same is true for institutions: if one institution has a serious recruiting problem and is placed on probation, the general public and the media usually assume this is happening at all institutions. Because of this broad-brush theory, and the tremendous visibility of college athletics programs today, false impressions are created. While there may be some criticism of media coverage and negative reporting, one must realize that this coverage also has brought intercollegiate athletics to a high level of national popularity and interest.

The advent of television has changed the print media's methods of covering college sports. Prior to television, newspapers were the sole source for the scores and details of games. Since today the fan can obtain that information almost instantaneously through television, the print media have therefore concentrated more on in-depth feature stories about coaches, athletes, and programs. As a result, many coaches and athletes have been built into supercoaches and superstars, and the fall can be a long one if something goes wrong.

In addition to television, business and government scandals have created a special interest in investigative reporting. This originally was limited to the political arena, but in the past few years it has also spread to athletics, with many exposés of athletics programs. Some of the exposés are valid and some are pure sensationalism without much basis in fact. Regardless, they often project unfavorable perceptions. Let us look at what these perceptions are.

If you were to ask the average media person or the average fan his or her perception of college athletics, it would probably be something like this: colleges and universities are making millions of dollars from their athletics programs at the expense of the student-athlete; all coaches cheat; student-athletes don't graduate; and all student-athletes are drug addicts.

Examining the facts, one finds that the exact opposite is true. First of all, most universities are struggling to make ends meet. A handful of schools, those with 80,000- to 100,000-seat football stadiums, are selling out their games every Saturday and making a profit on their athletics programs, but these are the exceptions. In 1988 there were ten times as many NCAA schools operating in the red as those that finish in the black. The reason for this is simple. An athletics program is much more than a men's football or basketball program. In most cases, it is anywhere from fifteen to twenty-five other sports for men and/or women, with football and basketball in most cases being the only sports that generate revenue in excess of expenses. Some of the other programs will generate cash flow, but most of them will still operate individually at a loss. The funding of these programs is very expensive, and football and basketball players are being used to make money to sponsor programs for their fellow student-athletes. I do not think they mind being used in that way.

Second, all coaches do not cheat. In fact, only about 12% of the colleges and universities in the NCAA are under some type of investigation, and a good number of those are for self-reported secondary violations. Nationally there is a real interest in having good programs run according to the rules and regulations of the association and the respective conferences.

Third, the latest college graduation figures for student-athletes are encouraging. Athletes in all divisions (I, II, and III), as well as each division individually, are graduating at about an 8% higher rate than the rest of the student body in the same time period. The only area where athletes fall below the national average is in Division I-A football and Division I men's basketball. In those divisions, athletes are graduating at about a 2% lower rate than the rest of the student body. But that percentage is rising dramatically, and it appears that the new figures will put these sports at least on a par with the average student, if not several percentage points ahead. In most cases, when you look at the academic areas that the student-athletes are majoring in, you find a good spread across the majors offered at each individual university, which is very important. There is a major emphasis among the large universities on doing a better job of career counseling and academic advising to ensure that the athletes are bona fide students and will be well-prepared for life after college. Keep in mind that these graduation figures are pre–Proposition 48 students. It will be at least until the early 1990s before data will be available to determine the impact of Proposition 48, the NCAA legislation that set minimum academic standards for eligibility of incoming first-year students. When these athletes are included in the totals, the number should also increase substantially. Athletes are graduating, and universities are doing a good job of preparing their students.

Fourth, drug abuse, a major problem in this country, may be one of the most serious challenges that we have to deal with as a nation, but it does not appear to be a major problem with college athletes. The NCAA, has been testing athletes at championship events since 1987 as well as at postseason football games. During the first year, well over 3,000 student-athletes were tested, and only 2% tested positive for drugs and were declared ineligible. The vast majority of the positives were for anabolic steroids. Testing in the second year has not been completed, but it appears that there will be a decrease in that 2% level, which is very encouraging. I think it is safe to say that you could take any other segment of our society and test an equal number, and you probably would not come within 20–25% of the 2% achieved by athletes. Mandatory testing has been accompanied by a complete drug-education program. While some may not agree with testing, it certainly has been a deterrent, and the results that the association has seen are very encouraging.

Future Challenges

In the years ahead one of the major challenges for the NCAA will be to take the visibility that we mentioned earlier, which has created the unfavorable perceptions, and use it to emphasize the positives to change those perceptions. At the same time, if a commitment to integrity is made by individual institutions, these issues should dissolve over a reasonable period of time and the unfavorable perceptions along with them.

Another problem area is the way we view the welfare of the student-athlete. Often, the student-athlete has no input into the development of NCAA policy and the resultant legislation. One remedy for this might be the formation of student-athlete advisory committees in various parts of the country, who would make their concerns and needs known and reflected in new legislation. This idea is revolutionary but could be very effective.

We have discussed various changes, including legislative reform and perhaps a restructuring of the NCAA in the years ahead. Because of the National Forum conducted by the NCAA Presidents Commission, there has been much discussion about intercollegiate athletics and potential changes. Traveling around the country, one finds there is an interest in making changes in intercollegiate athletics as we know it today. Everyone talks about change, but when you ask what those changes should be, you get as many answers as there are people whom you ask.

This points up perhaps one of the NCAA's greatest problems: the tremendous amount of diversity. Everyone realizes that there is much diversity in Division I, where football already has been divided into two divisions within a division. Also, there are athletics programs in Division I with budgets ranging from $400,000 to $18,000,000, which makes for more diversity. But there is also a substantial amount of diversity between Divisions II and III, in both philosophy and modes of operation.

As we deal with this great diversity and try to decide what the changes should be, one concern should be uppermost. Over the years, colleges and universities have been protective of their institutional autonomy when it comes to academic affairs. It is very important as changes are discussed in athletics that these same institutions be just as protective of their athletics programs. Each institution should have an intercollegiate program that, first of all, fits the philosophy of the institution and, second, fits the resources available to the institution. Institutions with one philosophy should not try to force it on others that think differently and have different needs. If the various divisions could agree on greater federation—and this would not be possible unless the philosophical concerns were agreed upon first—there would be a good chance of accomplishing important change. One of the major stumbling blocks to reorganization over the years has been the fact that differences in institutional philosophies have not been resolved.

There are many other issues that the association needs to address in the years ahead. Part of its responsibility and role is to provide leadership to help individual institutions deal with current problems. We mentioned earlier the problem of better access for minorities and women. Another major issue is that of unscrupulous agents and their impact on college athletes and athletics programs, as well as the drafting by professional leagues of undergraduates who have not yet completed their academic work. It is very important that the association continue to assist and take a leadership role in helping colleges and universities deal with these problems. The primary function of a university is to give the student a good education, not to serve as a farm system for professional athletic leagues.

For years the association's members have been urged to retain a clear line of demarcation between college athletics and professional sports. With the current agent problems, this line has been even more difficult to maintain. In addition, there have been more calls for monthly stipends, not just to needy athletes but to all in attendance. The membership has tried to address this by providing more assistance through federal grants whose funds are directed entirely to those students with demonstrated need. Regardless, the pressure created by unscrupulous agents, coupled with statements by administrators and coaches that needy athletes are not able to live like other students because of a shortage of pocket money, will probably lead to long debates and legislative proposals from some members to provide a stipend.

In dealing with agents, there may be need for a basic alliance between the NCAA and the various professional sports associations to regulate what is now a serious problem for all groups. Not too many years ago, for example, a student-athlete who signed a professional baseball contract was totally professionalized as far as the NCAA was concerned. Today, an athlete can be a professional in one sport and an amateur in another, which shows that this line of demarcation has faded dramatically. In addition, the International Olympic Committee is now moving toward an open Olympics, one that would allow professionals to participate. This also would narrow the line of demarcation. It will be a real challenge for the NCAA and its members to walk the tightrope of providing adequate resources for athletes while, at the same time, maintaining strict amateur standards.

Yet, when you consider the small percentage of athletes who become successful professionals, you are again reminded how important it is that student-athletes be well-prepared academically to assume a meaningful role in society upon graduation. They cannot base their futures on hopes for a pro career.

All of these issues are important, and the NCAA needs to be involved in problem-solving. But most important, the NCAA must work with universities to ensure that their athletics programs are positive and are carried out in their proper role. The first responsibility is to guarantee that we have bona fide student-athletes who receive a good education and are well prepared for life. Second, we must return our university athletics programs, coaches, and athletes to their rightful positions as role models, not only for young people but for adults as well. Competitive athletics is very important to our nation. Both young and old have placed programs, institutions, coaches, and athletes on high pedestals, and when they slip, the fall is gigantic. Making sure that these slips do not take place and that we have complete integrity in our programs is a tremendous challenge, but it is a worthy one that must be assumed by all.

13

The Role of the Community-College President

ROSCOE C. BROWN, JR.

Most community colleges do not experience the economic and political pressures to provide a winning team . . . that some four-year institutions face. However, community colleges may be used by some four-year-college coaches and athletic directors to subvert academic regulations, such as Proposition 48.

As chair of the Interassociational Presidents Committee on Collegiate Athletics (IPCCA), a committee of college presidents and representatives of major college athletic associations formed under the auspices of the American Council on Education, I am convinced that the majority of community-college and four-year-college presidents are committed to well-balanced athletic programs that place a priority on educational outcomes. The following excerpts from a policy statement developed by the IPCCA (June 1984) highlight the importance that college presidents place on this concept:

> *Athletics as education* can be understood as a set of key contributions to the individual, to the institution, and to society at large. Among these contributions are the development of discipline, teamwork, and the self-confidence of individuals who participate in athletics; the improvement and sustenance of institutional reputations and morale; and the heightening of visibility that demonstrably aids in recruitment of students and financial contributions. Varsity athletics provide a stimulus to the development of broad based physical education and intramural athletic programs that contribute to the physical well-being of students. College athletics also have a public service role in satisfying the need or desire for spectator sports expressed by the general public in the stadiums and gymnasiums of colleges and universities across the nation.
>
> Presidents are urged to assume responsibility for athletics as they do other aspects of education. Each president should be certain the athletic programs of their campuses are conducted in accord with the highest *ethical* and *professional standards*. The IPCCA believes that presidents must spend more time in communicating with those who are involved with athletics, including trustees, alumni, and athletic directors about the educational outcomes of athletics. The result should be programs that bring pride to the college as an educational institution. Our society demands no less.* [emphasis added]

The specific nature of community colleges is such that a president can support an academically sound, student-oriented athletic program or else wink at practices that rank with the worst in the four-year colleges. Now enrolling more than 50% of all college freshmen, community colleges were created to provide open access to higher education for high school graduates, General Equivalency Diploma (GED) recipients, and those individuals who return to college to acquire skills for new careers. Most community colleges do not experience the economic and political pressures to provide a winning team and entertainment for the community that some four-year institutions face.

Blue Chip Athletes at Community Colleges

However, community colleges may be used by some four-year-college coaches and athletic directors to subvert academic regulations, such as Proposition 48, the National Collegiate Athletic Association (NCAA) rule that requires a 700 combined score on the Scholastic Achievement Test (SAT) or a 15 on the American College Test (ACT) and a 2.0 high school graduation average in a core curriculum to receive an athletic grant-in-aid. (More will be said about Proposition 48 later.) Some four-year-college coaches encourage athletes with poor high school achievement to attend a community college to improve their academic averages. Although laudatory in intent, this practice can also lead to a situation in which the athlete is given remedial and "gut" courses merely to raise his or her average. The two-year-college athletic association, NJCAA (National Junior College Athletic Association), has recognized this trend and has taken steps to strengthen its regulations for initial and continuing eligibility. Previously, regulations for continued eligibility required a student to complete only twelve hours by the end of the first term without attaining a specific grade point average (GPA). This has now been changed to require a 1.75 GPA for twelve semester hours by the end of the first term. The NJCAA has also increased the GPA for continuing into a second year of competition to 2.0. Actions such as these clearly indicate that the governing body of athletics for community and junior colleges is very committed to the principle that student-athletes in community colleges should perform academically in order to continue participation in varsity athletics.

Presidential Leadership

Presidents must exercise leadership in order to develop and maintain a "clean" athletic program. The president's first responsibility in meeting this obligation is *to know what's going on.* In too many instances, the president either does not investigate what is happening in the athletic program or is just kept in the dark. In some colleges communication between the president and those responsible for athletics is so informal that an athletic director can withhold information or distort undesirable practices to make them appear to be consistent with the principles of a sound athletic program.

The president must act, and act decisively, if undesirable practices are found. For example, in one situation with which I am familiar, a community-college coach was explicitly ordered not to use a star athlete whose average had fallen below the appropriate grade point level for eligibility. However, when the team went to another campus to compete, the coach allowed the ineligible player to participate. The athletic director learned of this from one of his peers and brought this matter to the attention of the president, who immediately removed the coach. This action sent shock waves through this particular campus, and it also sent a clear message to the other coaches that unethical behavior would not be tolerated. Since that time, there have been no further incidents on that campus. In still another case, an outstanding basketball player attempted to transfer from one institution to another, but the details of his unsatisfactory academic record were withheld. When the situation was brought to the attention of the president at the first institution, he contacted the president at the other institution, who initiated a full review of the student's record. As a result, the athlete was allowed to transfer but was not eligible for immediate participation. This kind of networking among presidents and athletic directors helps to prevent undesirable practices.

Since community colleges are open access institutions, there are opportunities for academic fraud and deceit if those in charge of the program want to pursue that course. Most community-college presidents recognize that community-college students tend to be older and to have other responsibilities, and when they participate in athletics it is primarily for the joy of sport and competition. The president of a community college should reinforce this philosophy by informing athletic directors, and others involved in student activities, of support for this philosophy. The president's attendance at formal ceremonies celebrating the accomplishments of men and women who have participated in sports, regardless of their won-loss records, sends a message to the college community regarding the importance that the president places on a sound athletic program.

Some Problems Specific to Community Colleges

• As a result of Proposition 48, some athletes who do not qualify for admission to four-year institutions are encouraged to attend two-year institutions to develop an acceptable academic record. In some instances they do not matriculate for a degree and, as a result, accumulate credits that are not applicable to a degree. Some two-year colleges are then criticized as places that nurture unqualified "jocks."

• In certain cases, two-year colleges have recruited student-athletes to participate in athletics during the season for a given sport and then have allowed them to drop out before completing course work during that semester. This practice results in a competitive advantage for those colleges but does little to link athletic participation with scholastic performance.

• Two-year-college athletes sometimes transfer to another two-year institution without informing their new college of past participation, thus attempting to increase the number of years of participation. Careful record-keeping and screening are needed to prevent this abuse.

• After studying the situation of the part-time student-athlete, two-year colleges have established stringent guidelines to monitor the progress of those students who wish to participate in athletics. Care must be taken that part-time student-athletes are not attending simply for athletic participation.

• Since two-year colleges are essentially open academic institutions, the importance of academic support for student-athletes should be examined. With increased pressure as a result of Proposition 48, two-year colleges must be certain that all athletes requiring remedial classes actually get them. According to the NCAA, in fall 1987 six-hundred athletes at NCAA Division I institutions failed to meet Proposition 48 standards. Of these, three-fourths failed to earn the minimum score on the standardized tests (SAT or ACT). Some four-year institutions sent nonqualifiers to two-year institutions so that they could become eligible through the transfer route. Care must be taken by two-year colleges to see that these athletes matriculate in a degree program and make satisfactory progress toward a degree before transferring.

As a member of the board of the American Council of Education when Proposition 48 was developed, I had, and still have, serious reservations about the use of standardized tests to establish eligibility for athletic grants-in-aid. Standardized tests, such as the SAT, have been shown to have a disparate effect on minority students (minorities score lower on these tests than whites). While I agree with the need for high school student-athletes to be motivated to achieve better in high school, I doubt that a 700 score on the SAT is a valid predictor of college success, particularly at academically competitive institutions. Indeed, the average SAT at some competitive institutions in which student-athletes matriculate is over 1100. Unless there is an extensive academic support program for an athlete with a 700 SAT score, the chances for success in those institutions are slim. Some institutions may have "bargain basement" academic tracks into which student-athletes with low SATs can be channeled, but this type of educational shenanigans can best be described as *pure exploitation.* Community colleges can and should provide the academic support and counseling necessary for students with poor high school records and low achievement levels to improve their academic performance. More institutions should consider using the community college to strengthen the academic preparation of college athletes before entering a four-year institution. Alternatively, four-year colleges might consider reinstating the freshman rule that prohibits freshman athletes from competing at the varsity level. During the freshman year, student-athletes could concentrate on developing the academic skills that would enable them to have a better chance of competing academically.

Community-college presidents should be knowledgeable about standards for appointment and reappointments of coaches, just as they are about the appointment and promotion of faculty members and members of the college's administration. Often, community-college coaches are hired as part-time employees, a fact that makes monitoring their performance more difficult. In those instances, the presidents must insist that the same ethical and professional standards required of full-time coaches are applied to part-time coaches. Cheating, unethical behavior, and disregard for the educational outcomes of student athletes are equally unacceptable, whether by a full-time or part-time coach. When unethical or unprofessional practices are found, those exhibiting such behavior should be discharged. The presidents should be careful, however, not to become involved in the details of such situations, and should insist that appropriate mechanisms are available to deal with unethical behaviors.

Another area of presidential responsibility is participation in the appropriate athletic governing organizations, such as the NCAA, NJCAA, and NAIA (National Association of Intercollegiate Athletics). Each of the major collegiate athletic associations has developed a mechanism for presidents to participate in governance, either through a presidents' council or appointment to the board of directors. Unfortunately, some presidents who have been appointed to these positions have not participated as actively as they should have. It is imperative that presidents not only be up-to-date on the various issues being discussed but also attend meetings where decisions are made. If a president sends a representative to athletic governing organizations, that person should be appropriately briefed, instructed about the president's wishes, and held accountable for representing the president's position. In too many instances presidential representatives have voted their own biases and beliefs rather than the position of their presidents.

A community-college president must formulate a philosophy of what constitutes a sound academic program for athletes. Ideally, athletes' educational programs should be no different from those of other students with the same academic needs and interests. That is, the educational program should involve appropriate remedial courses in mathematics, writing, reading comprehension, liberal arts, and career-oriented courses related to the students' academic goals. A problem arises when a highly skilled varsity athlete concentrates on athletics to such an extent that he or she is unable to pursue a sound educational program. Sometimes an athlete may be merely trying to attain a grade point average that will qualify him or her for a grant-in-aid at a four-year institution. Each institution should provide counseling for athletes so that they will focus on their educational goals. Community-college presidents should insist on procedures to monitor the educational progress of athletes.

A noteworthy example of presidential involvement in athletics is the community-college presidents' response to a change in eligibility regulations for community-college athletes that had been voted by the NJCAA. In 1986 the NJCAA approved a rule change by which freshman community-college athletes would be eligible for an entire year without having to achieve a specific grade point average provided they registered for twelve hours each term. Upon learning of this, the community-college presidents communicated their concern to the board of the AACJC (American Association of Community and Junior Colleges), which immediately established an ad hoc committee, on which the author served, to examine this regulation and to work with the members of NJCAA board to develop a more educationally sound rule. The outcome of these deliberations was the previously mentioned revision of the NJCAA regulation so that a 1.75 grade point average for eligibility is required at the end of the first term. In addition, the NJCAA revised its governance structure so that four presidents, selected by the AACJC, would serve on the board of NJCAA. This is a somewhat different approach than the establishment of a presidents' commission in the NCAA, in that the presidents are an integral part of the governance structure of the NJCAA rather than a separate commission. These initiatives, approved by an overwhelming majority of NJCAA board members, resulted in regulations and a much stronger governance structure. Indeed, the active involvement of community-college presidents improved the entire situation regarding community-college athletics. A headline such as the one that appeared recently in *The Chronicle of Higher Education*, "Sports-Governing Agency for 2-Year Colleges Votes to Tighten Academic Requirements for Athletes," indicates how the presidents' efforts were received by the higher education community.

In summary, while community colleges are ideally suited for development of athletic programs that reflect the philosophy of "athletics as education," there are also opportunities for abuse unless presidents accept responsibility for athletics and monitor athletic programs closely. I believe that an increasing number of community-college presidents are aware of this challenge and are working more closely with athletic directors and coaches to ensure that their athletic programs will be ethically sound.

14

Where Was the President?

A President's Responsibility for Change in Intercollegiate Athletics

JOHN BROOKS SLAUGHTER

In so many words, presidents and chancellors were being informed that they should mind their own business and stay out of those matters for which somebody else had the responsibility.

As a university president who loves intercollegiate athletics and who believes there is intrinsic merit in competing to win on the playing field or court, it is difficult for me to write a piece that is critical of college sports and those who participate or control them. But this self-criticism and introspection are essential, because improvements are needed.

As with any issue, there are many facets to be considered.

It is my view that reforms in intercollegiate athletics are required in many areas. Presidents cannot do it all, but they must be seen as proactive rather than passive participants in the process of change and reform. Similar charges could be given to athletic directors, governing boards, booster groups, coaches, and even student-athletes themselves. However, the purpose of this chapter is to shed some light on the past, present, and future roles of college and university chief executive officers (CEOs) in an effort to illuminate their responsibilities for this important aspect of American higher education.

If one were to list all the questions that have accompanied the long litany of problems and even scandals that have beset intercollegiate athletics in the recent past, there is one most often asked: where was the president or chancellor when all this was going on? As the chancellor of a major university campus that has had its own share of problems stemming from athletics, I have had that question directed to and about me. A more uncomfortable, even if appropriate, question can hardly be imagined.

Presidential leadership or, more accurately, the lack of presidential leadership is certainly one of the major issues associated with the perception that big-time college athletic programs are in trouble. While far more of these programs are conducted with integrity than are not, the ones that get press and media attention are those in which avarice, dishonesty, and the exploitation of athletes have replaced the high moral values and benefits of competition upon which intercollegiate athletics presumably were founded. Unfortunately, the list of those perpetrators of wrongdoing has grown inexorably long.

It is reasonable, therefore, to ask the question posed above about the involvement of presidents. The question certainly can be asked of and about the CEOs of those institutions guilty of NCAA infractions to ascertain why they were not more active in guarding against those practices that led ultimately to censure and/or penalties. But it can be put also to other presidents and chancellors to find out what they are doing to prevent a similar happenstance from occurring or to identify and implement reforms that truly integrate athletics into the academic community and strengthen the emphasis on the word student in the expression "student-athlete."

Background

Have presidents ever been in charge of athletic programs on their campuses? A cynical but perhaps accurate answer is no, and they probably never will be. During the latter part of the nineteenth century, when it all began, athletic teams were formed and controlled by students. Many of these student-athletes had little or no allegiance to the institution in which they were enrolled if, indeed, they were enrolled in school at all. It was common for a football player to compete in two or three different games for as many different collegiate teams over a weekend. Even Fielding H. Yost, a student at West Virginia University and later the celebrated coach of the University of Michigan, was hired by Lafayette College to play against Pennsylvania one weekend. After the game he is said to have "transferred" back to West Virginia (Lucas and Smith, 1978, p. 212). Students organized and coached the teams, and it was not until winning became more important than competing that professional coaches were hired. Faculties and administrators became involved only when college resources were sought to support the winning teams.

Some presidents resisted the involvement of their institutions in intercollegiate athletics, while others relished it. President Andrew D. White of Cornell, in response to a challenge issued by players from the University of Michigan in 1873, telegraphed: "I will not permit thirty men to travel four hundred miles to agitate a bag of wind." But another president, Ethelburt D. Warfield of Miami University of Ohio, all but required his faculty to join the football team and became the first, and hopefully only, president to ever incur an injury while competing for his college team (Rudolph, 1962, p. 374).

President William Rainey Harper of the University of Chicago was a trend-setter in using athletic success as a means of publicizing his institution and attracting students. When he hired former Yale All-American Amos Alonzo Stagg to coach his team, he did so with the charge "to develop teams which we can send around the country and knock out all the colleges. We will give them a palace car and a vacation too" (Lucas and Smith, 1978, p. 219). This attitude became the norm for many presidents of the era. Students were recruited by the presidents of Princeton, Trinity (now Duke University), California, Indiana, and other institutions by advertising the successes of their athletic programs. Alumni and public support was sought by invoking the victories that the college teams had achieved over rival institutions.

Few presidents were brave or foolish enough to buck this trend. One who did was President Charles W. Eliot, who headed Harvard from 1869 to 1909. Eliot started his tenure at Harvard by calling for excellence in athletics but later became discouraged by the excesses and the draining away of educational resources. Believing that overemphasis on athletics dissipated educational excellence, he fought a lonely public battle to keep athletics and academics in the proper perspective. Other presidents who felt the same way found it hard to publicly condemn athletics because of growing public interest and support and the possible negative effect on enrollment and philanthropy. In spite of their private feelings, they participated in recruiting and financing athletes, raising money for facilities and equipment, hiring coaches, and speaking in support of their winning teams.

Student control of athletics ebbed when faculties began to assume more responsibility for athletic programs. In 1895 the Intercollegiate Conference of Faculty Representatives (later the Big 10) was formed. The conference developed rules and regulations concerning such important matters as eligibility, recruiting practices, and payment of athletes. Other institutions followed suit, and conferences sprang up around the country based upon the Big 10 model.

Faculty control became a means of curbing some of the most egregious abuses but did not necessarily transform athletics into an educational experience for most of the participants. The situation at that time was not unlike the later circumstances the great sportswriter Red Smith described when writing about a former famous coach at Georgia Tech. Smith wrote:

Bill Alexander was a gallant gentleman and an intractable fighter for the football player's inalienable right to sign checks with an X. If a good defensive tackle wished to carry a book under his arm when he strolled the campus, Bill did not offer serious objections, although he disliked ostentation. He was, however, unalterably opposed to eyestrain.

The First Reform Effort

During the first three decades of the twentieth century, football captured the imagination of the American public. It was a dangerous, brutish game at the turn of the century, with permanent injury and even death becoming more and more commonplace. Formations were developed that were designed to destroy defenses. Eventually, an outcry to eliminate the brutality arose. President Theodore Roosevelt invited coaches of the major football teams to the White House in 1905 to suggest measures to remove the violence from football. Roosevelt put it in perspective by an interesting comparison: "Brutality and foul play should receive the same summary punishment given to a man who cheats at cards" (Rudolph, 1962, p. 376).

Some improvements did occur. The forward pass was introduced the next year, and injurious formations were outlawed. Some schools gave up football for rugby, but within a decade football was more prominent than ever. The problems were just beginning as more schools began to compete. The pressures to win, build, and fill increasingly larger stadiums and attract the best athletes continued to mount.

Shortly after Roosevelt's meeting with the leading football schools, the National Collegiate Athletics Association (NCAA) was born. In December 1906 the constitution of the fledgling organization was approved, and Article II of the document defined the mission of the association to be one of maintaining athletics "on an ethical plane in keeping with the dignity and high purpose of education" (NCAA Proceedings, 1906, p. 10). But the NCAA had difficulty in establishing and enforcing rules even regionally; therefore, so-called "home rule" policies were adopted, in which local customs and circumstances governed the actions of individual institutions.

Such was the backdrop for the first major effort to identify reform measures for intercollegiate athletics and to assign responsibilities for effecting them. This appeared in the form of a report prepared by the Carnegie Foundation for the

Advancement of Teaching culminating a three-year study of college sports. The report, released in October 1929, was titled *American College Athletics*. The preface to the report stated:

> The paid coach, the gate receipts, the special training tables, the costly sweaters and extensive journeys in special pullman cars, the recruiting from the high school, the demoralizing publicity showered on the players, the devotion of an undue proportion of time to training, the devices of putting a desirable athlete, but a weak scholar, across the hurdles of the examination—these ought to stop. . . .'' (Lucas and Smith, 1978, p. 319

The same observations still apply some sixty years later.

The preface contained two basic questions about the emphasis on athletic exploits that are being asked currently by educators concerned about the place of athletics in higher education. They were: (1) "What relation has this astonishing athletic display to the work of an intellectual agency like a university?" and (2) "How do students, devoted to study, find either the time or money to stage so costly a performance?" (Durso, 1975, p. 158).

The report attempted to answer these questions or, at least, to shed light on the issues inherent in the questions by addressing a number of topics. These included financing and commercialism; academic abuses; physical, ethical, and moral impact upon youthful participants; illegal recruiting and illicit payments; athletic scholarships; payments by alumni; misuse of complimentary ticket privileges; and the influence of the press and other media. Clearly, the same set of topics still occupies us today.

Perhaps the national preoccupation with the stock market crash, which coincidentally (perhaps) occurred on the same day the report was released, prevented much in the way of reform in college athletics. About the only noticeable effect that occurred was the buildup in intramural programs that provided an outlet for those persons not physically equipped or psychologically geared to varsity athletics. The goal of the report was to accomplish much more. Its primary purpose was to provide a challenge to college presidents to take control of their athletic programs and to overcome the cumulative effects of years of benign neglect and blind obeisance to the desires of students, alumni, trustees, and the public. The results of such inaction had been the creation of monstrous intercollegiate athletic programs that were threatening the continued existence of colleges and universities as educational institutions.

But presidents were no more desirous of accepting that challenge and the responsibilities associated with it than they have been in other periods of history. H. L. Mencken, the "Bard of Baltimore," wrote with perspicacity and accuracy that college presidents "are far too politic a class of men to take any really effective steps against an enterprise that brings in such large sums of money. . . ." (Lucas and Smith, 1978, p. 319). Thus, the first national effort at producing reform in intercollegiate athletics fizzled out, and college sports continued their unabated growth and popularity.

The Presidency: A Complex Task

The foregoing is not for the purpose of proving that presidential leadership in intercollegiate athletics has been missing completely. Some very courageous CEOs have risen to the occasion when necessary to correct problems that were engulfing their institutions as a result of athletic malpractice. Notable among these are Presidents Benjamin Ide Wheeler of the University of California–Berkeley and David Starr Jordon of Stanford, who led the early efforts to declare freshmen ineligible for intercollegiate track and football during the 1910–15 era. Presidents were central figures in dealing with the gambling crises in basketball during the 1950s, and some, like Southern Methodist University's Paul Hardin, San Francisco's Reverend John Lo Schiavo, and Tulane's Eamon Kelly have stood out as brave and principled leaders in more recent years.

It is clear from the foregoing that presidential involvement and leadership have never been consistent. The question that we ask now is whether they have become even less effective.

One can argue, correctly I believe, that leading a university is a much more complex and demanding task today than it was thirty or forty years ago. In those days it was easier for the CEO to be on top of everything that mattered on campus, and the authority of the president to decide issues and make policy rarely was questioned. However, beginning in the 1960s, presidents began to lose some of the tight grip they had on campus matters as faculty, students, and alumni began to demand to share the power. Governing boards, rather than following the lead of the president, inserted themselves increasingly into the daily life of campuses. These evolutions further diminished the authority of the president.

Presidential abdication of responsibility became commonplace, and increasingly more issues were decided without the involvement of the CEO. Presidents who heretofore had decided questions concerning curriculum, tuition, admissions, promotion and tenure, faculty salaries, and intercollegiate athletics found themselves petitioned by various constituencies to share the power and, in many cases, turn over the authority to someone else. As the magnitude and complexity of running the university increased, it was only natural that the need to delegate some of the decision-making increase as well. Although delegation is necessary and appropriate in a complex but well-managed organization, the delegator must ensure that proper accountability exists. When it does not, serious consequences can result.

Lack of sufficient oversight on the part of a president has occurred often and widely in intercollegiate athletics. As the pressure has grown to build winning teams, to appear on television, to fill the stadium, and to make money to pay coaches, scholarship bills, and the expenses of nonrevenue sports, the college president has come to realize that help is required to manage the enterprise. Enter highly paid athletic directors, large athletic department staffs, booster clubs, and even independent corporations with their own boards of directors to run all or a portion of the athletic program. Under these conditions the president can become a nonentity, a figurehead who is reduced to crowning the homecoming queen and entertaining basketball recruits who have to bow their heads in order to enter the president's office without sustaining serious and permanent injury. Add any of these ingredients to a situation in which an institutional governing board assumes hands-on responsibility for any part of the intercollegiate athletic program, and the president is on an irreversible path to major problems.

Unfortunately, such problems have been publicized enough over the past few years that we have learned to associate them with certain institutions. In each case, the president did not emerge from the fracas exuding an aura of being in charge or taking responsibility for restoring the institution's athletic program to a position of credibility and respect. This image of fecklessness, deserved or not, has been a major contributor to the clamor for more vigorous and more principled presidential leadership to stem the tide of disarray in intercollegiate athletics.

The NCAA Presidents Commission

In its annual convention of 1984, in response to leadership exhibited by the American Council on Education and the chief executives of a number of its member institutions, the NCAA voted to form a Presidents Commission that would participate actively in setting and managing the agenda of the association. The commission, composed of forty-four presidents/chancellors representing member institutions of the three divisions of the NCAA, has existed since then. Uneven in performance over that period, the Presidents Commission nevertheless has made its presence felt through its efforts to require increased academic performance by prospective athletes, to institute the death penalty for repeated violations of NCAA rules, and to initiate a series of national forums designed to inform the NCAA membership about the many issues related to athletic reform.

The Presidents Commission, in addressing change in intercollegiate athletics, has guided its work by asking itself three direct questions: (1) How can we maintain integrity in intercollegiate athletics? (2) How can we contain the costs of athletic programs and maintain a balance between athletic programs and other institutional programs? (3) What is the proper role of intercollegiate athletics in American higher education?

These questions emerged from the results of a commission-sponsored NCAA-wide survey of presidents and chancellors. The responses to the survey indicated clearly that CEOs were concerned not only with the answers to these questions but with the broader concern of how to control athletics on their respective campuses. This last issue, in the context of answering the three explicitly stated questions, has led to the frustrations and difficulties evidenced in controlling athletics on many campuses.

Agreeing to an answer to the question about integrity was a relatively easy one for presidents and the NCAA. No one wants to be seen publicly as opposing honesty and morality. By overwhelming votes, measure after measure designed to place a premium on honesty, self-discipline, and enforcement of rules was enacted by the membership at the 1985 special convention called by the Presidents Commission. It appeared to all that, after years of quiescence, presidential leadership had arrived and was here to stay.

Imbued with what later proved to be only a facade of power, the Presidents Commission focused its attention on the second question, pertaining to cost control, and the balance between athletics and academics. After being lulled into complacency and overconfidence by the tractability of the association electorate at the 1987 annual convention of the NCAA, the commission decided to call a special convention for that summer to deal with these troubling issues. Optimistic that the zeal for reform was universal and that the leadership of the commission was desired by all, the Presidents Commission, in its naiveté, failed to recognize that a backlash was building. That backlash to the reforms and changes being pushed by the "upstart" presidents, caused by the latent reactions of the more entrenched components of the American athletic enterprise both on and off the college campuses, prevented the passage of most of the commission's reform legislation. In so many words, presidents and chancellors were being informed that they should mind their own business and stay out of those matters for which somebody else had the responsibility.

And how did the Presidents Commission react to what occurred? It recognized that it had been finessed and vowed to continue its efforts. What frustration and anger were felt were self-directed because the commission recognized that it had been outsmarted and outworked. What had happened, in retrospect, was not surprising. There were strong differences of opinion, even within the commission, on many of the major issues debated on the floor of the convention. The only mitigating influence on the pall created by the legislative defeats was the initiation of the national forums that took place at the special convention.

The idea of the national forums was conceived by a subcommittee of the NCAA Presidents Commission. The subcommittee felt that issues such as freshman eligibility, need-based financial aid, and revenue-sharing were so complex and conflict-laden that special measures were needed for the NCAA membership to deal with them constructively. Chancellor Ira Michael Heyman of the University of California at Berkeley, the chairman of the subcommittee, wrote that the disagreements over such issues "are presently too vast to be bridged by legislative proposals, no matter how finely crafted. They can only be resolved by examining and debating first principles and basic premises." Chancellor Heyman realized that even presidents did not constitute a monolithic and homogeneous grouping that thought and acted alike and in synchronism. He realized that there were strong differences of opinion concerning the degree of emphasis that should be put on athletics, even among the CEOs of the major athletic conferences. He argued that disagreements existed about the importance of athletics to university life, how athletics should be funded and managed, and the extent to which the student-athlete should focus primary attention on academics as contrasted to athletic pursuits. The commission was convinced by the arguments of its subcommittee and committed itself to sponsoring a series of national forums whose overarching purpose would be to inform the debates that must take place before additional reform measures could be considered by the NCAA membership.

In conjunction with the forums, the Presidents Commission elected to initiate a series of comprehensive studies whose purpose it would be to give solid, broad, and persuasive evidence concerning the effects of participation in intercollegiate sports on the student-athlete and on colleges and universities. These studies, the commission members believed, would be of immense value to all presidents and chancellors interested in the impact of athletics on the lives of their students and on the institutions themselves.

The forums were completed at the January 1989 NCAA Convention when the discussion centered on the first study sponsored by the commission, a nationwide survey of college athletes. The report, a year-long survey of 4,100 athletes from 42 Division I colleges and universities, did not produce "any great surprises in the results," according to Martin A. Massengale, chancellor of the University of Nebraska, Lincoln and current chair of the Presidents Commission. But Massengale added that "they will provide data for us to use in considering policy issues for many years into the future." However, the ultimate impact of the forums and the studies on the reform movement is yet to be determined.

The Role of the Individual President

How can the individual president or chancellor take responsibility for the conduct of intercollegiate athletics and participate effectively in the movement for reform? This continues to be the basic question that plagues all CEOs, regardless of the emphasis placed on athletics at their respective campuses. One obvious answer is that the CEO should be involved at the national level (NCAA, NAIA, and so forth), at the regional or conference level, and at the campus or institutional level.

The importance of presidential involvement at all these levels is apparent if control of the fate of intercollegiate athletics is to be in the hands of presidents. All these levels are important but, from my perspective, the seminal activity must be the leadership exerted at the institutional level. If the president sends a strong and unambiguous signal to the athletic department, booster groups, the governing board, the faculty, and students that athletics will receive the same personal oversight as do all other critical activities of the college or university, many of the problems that have been experienced will disappear. An athletic director who reports directly to the campus head or who has a short reporting link to that person is then able to manage the day-to-day affairs of the athletic department within the policy guidelines that have been established.

No president or chancellor can afford to spend the vast amounts of time and energy required to watch over any one part of the campus operation on a constant basis. That is why there are directors and deans and provosts and vice presidents, who are better at what they do than any president or chancellor should be. But the CEO must set the direction for the enterprise, assigning responsibility for activities to be accomplished and holding those persons responsible for results. If this occurs, the question "Where was the president?" is not likely ever to be heard.

Conclusion

It is fitting and appropriate, I believe, to conclude this essay by repeating the passage used to conclude the Carnegie Foundation report of 1929. The concluding paragraph summarized the responsibilities of presidents for correcting the deficiencies noted in intercollegiate athletics. There are many things that need to be done by many segments of our society to address those deficiencies today, but the message for presidents has proven to be time-invariant.

> Experience has shown that, of all who are involved in those evils—administrative officers, teachers, directors of athletics, coaches, alumni, undergraduates, and townsmen—the man who is the most likely to succeed in uprooting the evils of recruiting and subsidizing is the college president. It is his duty to coordinate opinion and direct the progress of an institution. If neighboring presidents are like-minded, his task is a little lightened, but under no circumstances which we have been able to discover is it impossible even if he stands alone. It cannot be easy. But such are the position and the powers of the American college president that, once having informed himself of the facts, and being possessed of the requisite ability and courage, he will succeed. (Durso, 1975, p. 163)

FOUR

Policy Recommendations

I. Establishing a Philosophy to Address the Problem

There was broad agreement from all the authors in this book that institutional integrity and accountability cannot be imposed from the top down. While the NCAA can continue to attempt to influence integrity through legislation, unless each institution is ready to commit itself to complete integrity, we will never achieve it nationally. Therefore, individual NCAA member institutions must take *primary* responsibility for compliance.

The NCAA should work with the universities to ensure that their athletic programs are positive and are part of the educational process. The first responsibility is to guarantee that we have bona fide student-athletes who receive a good education and are well prepared for life after graduation. This emphasis on educating student-athletes ran throughout every article. This seemed to shift from the NCAA debates, where emphasis is on recruitment, cost containment, and other issues.

For such a complex problem, the solution to restoring integrity to intercollegiate athletics was cast in very simple terms. Each individual institution, from the governing board to the chief executive officer to the director of athletics to the individual coach, needs to make a total commitment to integrity in its programs. This was repeated time and again from Dick Schultz to John Slaughter to Doug Single to Jack Bicknell.

Moving toward the simple solution is much more difficult than stating what it is. Institutional governing boards, which ultimately must guarantee the integrity of their institutions, should give strong support to chief executive officers and delegate to them the full responsibility for integrity in athletics programs. The values of the colleges and universities must then be infused into the athletic department through the hiring of key people, such as the athletic director and coaches.

However, there are other factors involved in the solution, since we are playing sports in a society in which drugs,

195

commercialization, unbalanced media coverage, racism, and sexism complicate the pursuit of even the best intentions of the NCAA, governing boards, presidents, athletic departments, and coaches. Accordingly, experts and activists in these areas have been called upon for opinions and suggestions to help us advance toward that simple but historically elusive goal.

There was general agreement that the threat of sanctions is a deterrent and that the introduction of the so-called "death penalty" may be the most significant new weapon in stopping the illegalities. It was suggested in the preface that accrediting boards make the integrity of the athletic department one of the criteria it uses in assessing the standing of the institution.

It should be no surprise that additional programs and services will cost money. However, college sport is making more and more money. One possible source for financing could be an academic endowment fund created from television revenue. If the fund was overseen by the NCAA, it could help athletes at schools whose programs are not financially successful. Another likely source is the professional leagues, which could contribute some of their television revenues to help build the academic endowment fund. They could donate the equivalent of a four-year scholarship for each athlete who reaches the professional ranks. This money would be used exclusively to pay the continuing costs of education for athletes whose eligibility has expired but who have not made the professional teams.

This concluding chapter offers a series of policy recommendations that we believe can help move us toward that ultimate objective. Some are controversial, others are almost unanimously agreed upon by our authors. Attribution of ideas is indicated by the authors' initials. CSSS represents Northeastern University's Center for the Study of Sport in Society, while JF is Jim Frey, and CG is Christine Grant, long-time friends of the center who have some solid ideas for change that were not included in the text.

If and when the objective of total integrity is met, we will be able to return our university athletic programs, coaches, and athletes to their rightful positions as role models, not only for young people but for adults as well.

A. PRESIDENTIAL RESPONSIBILITY

1. *Presidents of all colleges and universities:*

• The president should be involved at the national level (NCAA, NAIA, NJCAA, and so forth), at the regional or conference level, and at the campus or institutional level.   *(JS, RB)*
• The NCAA Presidents Commission must continue to address change in intercollegiate athletics by asking itself three direct questions: (1) How can we reestablish and maintain integrity in intercollegiate athletics? (2) How can we contain the costs of athletic programs and maintain a balance between athletic programs and other institutional programs? (3) What is the proper role of intercollegiate athletics in American higher education?
• The president's first responsibility regarding athletics is *to know what's going on.   (RB, JS)*
• The president must monitor the academic progress of athletes.   *(RB, JS)*
• The president must act, and act decisively, if undesirable practices are found.   *(RB, JS)*
• The president must send a strong and unambiguous signal to the athletic department, booster groups, governing board, faculty, and students that athletics will receive the same personal oversight as do all other critical activities of the college or university.   *(JS)*
• The president must be seen as setting the direction for the enterprise, assigning responsibility for activities to be accomplished and holding those persons responsible for results.   *(RB, JS)*
• The athletic director should report directly to the president.
• The presence of a president at formal ceremonies celebrating accomplishments of men and women who have participated in sports, regardless of their won-lost records, sends a message to the college community regarding the importance that the president places on a sound athletic program.   *(RB)*

2. *Presidents of two-year colleges:*

• The president of a community college should reinforce this philosophy by informing athletic directors, and others involved in student activities, of support for the school's philosophy.
• There is a special presidential responsibility to be certain that all athletes requiring remedial classes actually get them. *(RB)*
• The president is responsible for ensuring that careful record-keeping and screening prevent two-year college athletes from transferring to other two-year institutions without informing their new college of past participation, thus attempting to increase the number of years of participation. *(RB)*
• The president should ascertain that part-time student-athletes are not attending just for athletic participation by establishing stringent guidelines to monitor the progress of those students who wish to participate in athletics. *(RB)*
• The president should be knowledgeable about standards for appointment and reappointment of coaches, just as he or she is about the appointment and promotion of faculty members and members of the college's administration. *(RB)*

B. THE ATHLETIC DEPARTMENT'S RESPONSIBILITY

If the current movement for reform within intercollegiate athletics is to succeed, athletic directors must first help develop a philosophy and model of intercollegiate athletics. This would include a reexamination of the goals, values, and priorities of institutional programs and intercollegiate athletics nationally and reaffirm a proper role for athletics within university life. *(DS)*

• Among the qualifications, skills, and talents necessary to be a successful member of the athletic department is that the employee be an educator. *(DS)*
• The athletic director should implement policies and procedures to ensure that coaches and staff conduct their responsibilities in ways that reflect a shared commitment to the student-athlete concept and to compliance with NCAA rules and regulations. *(DS)*

• The athletic director should demand of coaches and their programs that student-athletes reach their optimum levels athletically, academically, and personally; that our teams rarely lose to a weaker team; that all involved draw satisfaction from the activity itself; and that we operate programs with fiscal accountability and moderation. *(DS)*

• The athletic director should organize faculty-coach-athletic department communication forums to discuss the views of each in the contexts of their work. The goal is understanding through a dialogue designed to promote empathy between the groups. *(JF, CSSS)*

• The athletic director should take strong, immediate action to alleviate discrimination and foster equity within intercollegiate athletics. If our philosophies and practices within intercollegiate athletics remain exclusive rather than inclusive, then the battle to restore integrity will never be won. *(DS)*

In compliance matters, the athletic director occupies the most important leadership position within intercollegiate athletics. Therefore, he or she must create and enforce a system of compliance within athletic programs. *(DS)*

C. THE COACH'S RESPONSIBILITY

• The coach must be in tune with the values and philosophy of the school. *(JB)*

• If a coach violates NCAA rules or does not work within the guidelines set forth by the school, his or her contract should be terminated immediately. *(JS, RB, DS, JB)*

• A coach involved in a major violation should be banned from coaching at an NCAA school forever.

• The coach needs a strong president and an athletic director with whom he or she can truly communicate. This is critical to the success of any athletic program. The president must be able to stand up for a coach in the face of demands by wealthy contributors. *(JB)*

• Rule compliance is a simple issue: the coach must sit down with the athletic director and staff and go over the recruiting rules and regulations: if any member of the staff cheats, his or her contract is terminated. *(JB)*

II. Special Issues Within College Sport

A. WOMEN IN ATHLETICS

• No university policy or procedure shall conflict with applicable federal or state statutes prohibiting sex discrimination. *(DL, CZ)*

• No university policy or procedure shall limit access to or equitable participation of qualified individuals from any group of society (for example, women, ethnic or racial minorities, or the economically disadvantaged) in any higher education program or activity. *(DL, CZ)*

• Equal athletic participation opportunities shall be afforded male and female student-athletes. Institutional policies and procedures shall not discriminate on the basis of sex as they relate to the nature and extent of the sports programs offered, provision of athletic equipment and supplies, practice and competition schedules, provision of travel and per diem allowances, opportunity to receive coaching and academic tutoring, assignment and compensation of coaches and tutors, provision of locker rooms and practice and competitive facilities, provision of medical and training services, housing and dining facilities and services, publicity services, and scholarships. Athletic program expenditures need not be equal, but the pattern of expenditures must not result in a disparate effect on opportunity. *(DL, CZ)*

• All qualified persons should receive the opportunity to coach, and there should be more equitable compensation for coaches. *(DL, CZ)*

• Gifts of cash and property, grants, gate receipts, patent royalties, and income derived from classes taught, summer camps, and films of a university football team's offense patterns are owned by the university—not by the individual faculty member or coach or the individual department. The president is responsible for creating and balancing a community of interests within the university by distributing revenues from all sources to finance the achievement of the institution's goals and purposes. *(DL, CZ)*

• Cost containment on the national level and on the institutional level must not take a disproportionate bite out of the budget for women's athletics. *(DL, CZ)*

• Universities and colleges should allow every effort to be made to develop women's sports as revenue-producers. *(DL, CZ)*
• The number of women reporters, editors, and executives in media should be increased. *(SP)*
• Levels of sensitivity to negative images of women portrayed in the media should be increased. *(CSSS)*

B. RACE

A great deal of emphasis has been placed on racial discrimination in professional sport, especially the hiring practices of professional franchises. However, a look at the numbers of positions that could be available in colleges and universities shows us that there are far more problems as well as far more possibilities there than in professional sport. There are at least one thousand colleges with athletic programs. There are an average of fifteen teams at each (many Division I and IA schools have more.) Blacks make up a meager 2% of athletic departments. The NCAA has appointed a task force to address this issue. Nonetheless, more must be done.

1. Hiring:

• More blacks must become college presidents and athletic directors at schools with major programs. *(RL)*
• Head coaches need to be hired for *all* sports, not just "black sports." *(RL)*
• More assistant coaches should be hired, and their primary role in recruiting black athletes should be expanded. *(RL)*
• The NCAA vita bank for minorities and women needs to be strengthened. *(RS)*
• Sports information directors must be more sensitive to media stereotypes of minorities.

2. Academic advisement:

• Admissions standards should no longer be distorted to accommodate the black athlete. Bases for admissions must be realistic. The admissions office must advise coaches if student-athletes have a real chance to graduate and what academic help, if any, they may require. *(CSSS)*
• All players should have equal academic access and advisement. *(CSSS)*

• Better career counseling must be offered to black athletes, who have been told by the media, guidance counselors, and coaches that sport is the way to fame and fortune. These student-athletes must take legitimate majors in order to change the huge percentage of black student-athletes who now major in physical education, speech communications, and sports administration. If they graduate, how will they apply those studies if blacks are shut out of these job markets? *(CSSS)*

3. *Social environment:*

• Coaches should be models to both the community and to players in hiring and social relations. *(JB)*
• Players' backgrounds should be checked so that racist players are not recruited. Family visits are imperative. *(JB)*
• Scholarships should be given out in all sports, since now only 10% of scholarships go to black athletes and those are almost exclusively in football and basketball. *(CSSS)*
• Team housing, road trips, and meals should be integrated. *(JB)*
• Minority athletes should be encouraged to deal with their own interpersonal relationships with the student body when they are away from the team. *(JB)*

4. *Athletic performance:*

• Positional segregation must be ended. *(CSSS)*
• Blacks must be coached more; do not assume they are "naturals." *(CSSS)*
• Minorities should be encouraged in sports other than football, basketball and track and field. *(CSSS)*

5. *Media:*

• There should be more honest portrayals of chances to make the professional teams. *(CSSS)*
• More minority writers, editors, executives, and on-air people should be hired. *(SP)*
• The media should be sensitized to the negative ways in which they have portrayed minorities. *(CSSS)*

C. THE COACH AND THE RECRUITING PROCESS

• The coach should develop recruiting procedures to ensure that prospective student-athletes brought to campus have a legitimate chance to graduate from our institutions. *(DS)*

• The coach should consult with the admissions office—can the athlete make it?—and get a real evaluation of the academic potential of the recruit. If the recruit is borderline, will sufficient assistance be available? If the recruit's prospects are doubtful, he or she should not be recruited. *(JB)*

• The coach should recruit openly regarding the school's academics, discussing graduation rates, what previous players are doing after graduation, and a recruit's academic potential. *(CSSS)*

• The coach should inform the players regarding academic and public expectations of them. *(JB)*

• The coach should recruit positively by extolling the virtues of the school and not by tearing down other institutions. *(JB)*

• The coach should find out what kind of individual is being recruited to be sure the athlete will fit in at the school. It is important to meet the parents. *(JB)*

• The coach should make alumni completely aware of the recruiting regulations, because this is where many schools have problems. *(JB)*

• The coach should inform recruits that any athlete found guilty of accepting an illegal inducement from a coach or athletic representative will become immediately ineligible for the duration of his college career. *(JB)*

• Athletes and their parents could enter into contractual relationships with particular schools. These contracts would spell out the obligations of each party before the athlete signed a letter of intent. *(DM)*

• The institution should eliminate the one-year-scholarship rule. The system demands a four-year commitment from the athlete and penalizes him or her for leaving. The school should have the same obligation. *(DM, CSSS)*

• Student-athletes could receive some compensation, including money to travel home for major holidays. *(AS, DM, BW)*

• The institution should revise the amateur code in the manner of the International Olympic Committee. In olympic sports, the rules now permit athletes to accept living and training grants, endorsement fees, and, in some cases, prize money as long as these funds are administered by their sports governing bodies. *(AS)*

D. ACADEMICS

The overall message to the players must be that the school will provide special attention to its student-athletes to ensure their academic preparation; however, in exchange for this it will be expected that student-athletes fulfill the same academic requirements as all students.

University and College Level

1. *Current college athletes:*

• Philosophically, the school must emphasize the *student* in student-athlete—not only class attendance and graduation rates, but also the *quality* of the educational experience. *(DS)*
• Student-athletes must also be encouraged to value education, not simply eligibility. *(DS)*

COURSES OF STUDY AND SPECIAL ACADEMIC PROGRAMS

• Athletic scholarship recipients who are considered at risk academically should be required to attend a six-week orientation program at the school prior to their freshman year. The school should provide an orientation, including academic and counseling evaluation of the educational needs of all incoming scholarship athletes. Intensive workshops dealing with study skills, reading and writing skills, use of the library, and basic computer skills could be presented during this orientation. *(DM)*
• All student-athletes should have the benefit of an annual seminar dealing with issues they will face, including academics, career counseling, injuries, drugs (recreational and performance-enhancing), race relations, and other relevant topics. *(CSSS)*
• Academic programs for student-athletes should have a good spread of major studies throughout the entire academic range. *(RS)*
• Scholarship athletes should also be required to attend a sport-and-society course to show them sport as it relates to many aspects of American life. It would offer a rich matrix for learning, particularly for those engaging in high-level athletic competition. *(DM, JH, CSSS)*

ATHLETIC SCHEDULING POLICIES DESIGNED TO BENEFIT
ACADEMIC ACHIEVEMENT

• Incoming student-athletes should not count on playing when they are freshmen. Either freshman eligibility should be eliminated or student-athletes should be informally apprised of the coach's policy. The result is a happier player who absorbs team and school spirit while adjusting to college academic and social life. *(RB, JB, CSSS)*
• The institution should restrict the number of games in a season (for example: football—10; basketball—25 plus post-season games; baseball—40 plus post-season games; and so forth. *(JF)*
• The institution should place a limit on the number of hours an athlete can practice. *(CG)*
• Athletic activities should not be scheduled on campuses in prime class time, between the hours of 7:30 A.M. and 1:30 P.M. Students should not be excused from class to attend or participate in these activities. *(JF)*
• There should be a maximum number of days that can be missed due to travel. *(CG)*
• Travel should not include more than two class days away from campus. *(JF)*
• A quiet study room should be available for student-athletes. *(CG)*
• The institution should not schedule any away games (preferably no games at all) during final exam week. *(JF)*
• Exit interviews should be conducted with student-athletes to determine if they felt there was adequate time to achieve their academic goals. *(CG)*

ACADEMIC SUPPORT SERVICES

• Academic support services must be available, including academic advisement, tutors, and counseling; it is critical that the student-athlete be able to get away from an athletic environment. *(JB, DS, RS, JS, RB, CSSS)*
• Academic guardians, appointed from the regular faculty, should stay in touch with players to provide encouragement and guidance. *(CSSS)*

• The goal of academic support services should be the integration of academics and athletics at both the individual and institutional levels. *(DS)*

• Academic support services should work toward integrating student-athletes into the academic life of the university rather than furthering their isolation as a subculture outside the mainstream of the university community. *(DS)*

• At the heart of this model of academic assistance programming for student-athletes lies the goal of creating an integrated system of services that encompasses both the resources available to all students and a set of services based on the athletic department that is designed to supplement those resources. *(DS)*

• Academic assistance is defined as the mutual responsibility of the faculty, the undergraduate dean's office, and the designated academic advisers within the athletic department. *(DS)*

ACADEMIC MONITORING POLICIES

• Make sure the player is going to class; if there is a problem, the best way to solve it is for the coach to suspend game participation. *(JB)*

• Coaches should stay in regular touch with families regarding all athletic and academic progress. *(CSSS)*

• A scholarship athlete's academic progress should be closely monitored by the school's academic advisers. Credits must be evaluated regularly: they must be real and not simply for eligibility; evaluation should be made of what courses athletes are taking and what their career interests are; and advisers should function as the athletes' ombudsmen. *(DM, JB, DS, JS)*

• Credit for athletic participation should match only the credits that can be earned from participation in physical education courses (usually four.) *(JF)*

• Reasonable progress should be maintained—exceeding NCAA requirements so that student-athletes will be as close as possible to graduation after eligibility has expired. *(CSSS)*

• Summer school should be available for those who need it to stay on the graduation track. *(CSSS)*

*CREATING A CONDUCIVE SOCIAL ENVIRONMENT TO REDUCE
THE IMPACT AND EFFECT OF THE ATHLETIC SUBCULTURE*

• The institution should eliminate athletic dormitories and/
or separate eating facilities. *(JF)*
• The institution should encourage involvement in university-
wide social and academic student activities. *(JF)*
• The institution should advise athletes to take responsibility
for their own affairs, both academic and social. They should
conduct their own business. *(CSSS)*
• The institution should offer professional career counseling
sessions to all athletes each year. *(CSSS)*
• The institution should encourage student-athletes to participate in summer internship programs to gain real-world
experience. *(CSSS)*
• The institution should ask student-athletes to give something back to young people by participating in educational
and drug-outreach programs in area schools. This will help
prepare future generations of student-athletes and reinforce
educational values in the athletes who carry out the programs. *(CSSS)*

POST-ELIGIBILITY DEGREE COMPLETION SUPPORT

• Scholarship athletes should be allowed to retain their athletic scholarships, including housing, meals, and books, for
a period of time after they complete their athletic eligibility. *(JB, DM, BW, AS, CSSS)*
   2. *Former athletes:*
• Former athletes who attended school on a scholarship in a
revenue sport in the previous ten-year period and have not
gotten their degrees but have used their eligibility may need
help. They should be able to return to complete their education at the expense of the university in exchange for community service. This policy should apply to former athletes
who have exhausted their eligibility and were unable to complete their degrees. It should not be a disincentive for current
student-athletes to complete their educations as soon as possible. *(CSSS)*
• Colleges should also try to help other former college athletes—professionals, Olympians, and others who never reached

either level—to complete their degrees or further their educations by creating special programs. These could include bridge programs such as those operated by the National Consortium coordinated by Northeastern University's Center for the Study of Sport in Society.

• In all cases in which athletes are receiving a continuing chance to complete their educations, controls should be built in that require the athlete to take a specified number of course hours and maintain a certain grade point average to retain the scholarship. *(DM, CSSS)*

High School and Middle School Levels

1. SCHOOL PROGRAMS

• Institutions should hold educational forums and assemblies for student-athletes, other students, coaches, teachers, and parents to sensitize them to issues faced by all those who might overemphasize any aspect of their lives. These forums and assemblies should be addressed by high-profile athletes who are role models for youngsters and can capture their attention with the message. Programs should take place throughout the year so that the message is constantly reinforced. The effectiveness of such programs should be measured to make workable adjustments. *(CSSS)*

• Institutionalized educational support services should combine coaches' mandatory study halls, home visits with parents by coaches to assess student-athletes' personal needs and to involve parents in academic as well as athletic preparation, faculty involvement as academic counselors and guardians, and tutoring by other students and teachers. *(CSSS)*

• Ongoing drug and alcohol abuse programs should extend beyond simple "say no" messages. Performance-enhancing drugs must be brought up in conjunction with these. *(CSSS)*

2. ACADEMIC POLICIES:

The introduction of increased academic standards is rapidly spreading around the country, and schools now expect as much academically from athletes as they do on the playing field. As such pass-and-play standards are introduced, caution must be taken that athletic programs are not severely dislocated and that student-athletes are not overly discouraged. Recommended pass-and-play policies would include:

(1) A simple C average in all subjects combined.
(2) A student would be allowed one F per year as long as the average remained at the C level.

(The first two provisions were suggested to avoid a situation in which a student could have 2 Bs, an A, and an F and be ineligible. This happened in several districts in Texas. As long as a C average was maintained, the student could get one F per year.)

(3) A student must take courses on a graduation track and make normal progress toward graduation.

(This would eliminate the apprehension that athletes who had to achieve a higher standard would take easier courses.)

(4) There would be one probationary period. Thus, if a student dropped below a C or 2.0, he or she would be put on probation and not become ineligible (for the first time only.)

(Provision 4 speaks to the problem of adequate warning. With Proposition 48 at the college level, students had warning and most were able to bring up their grades. Since this has generally not been the case at the high school level, the probationary period would alleviate the question of unfairness.)

(5) If the average continues below a C, that student is removed from that activity until the grades improve to meet the minimum standard.
(6) Once ineligible, athletes should receive academic help.

(Opponents of standards believed that ineligible athletes would drop out of school once they were out of the coaches' care.

In many districts, coaches themselves have acted as grade monitors and have set up mandatory study halls and tutorial programs where they were necessary. Such programs would not add cost to the school budgets if the coaches did this voluntarily, as they have done in many districts to date.)

(7) Exceptions should be made on an individualized basis for students with extenuating circumstances.

(Most agree that provisions should be made for students with learning disabilities, English as a second language, personal tragedy, or other circumstances that might merit such consideration.)

(8) Administration of the rules should be left up to each principal.

(The principals know the students better than some centralized agency. This question was the most controversial for the group surveyed.)

(9) Junior high or middle school students should receive nonmandatory warnings if they fall below a C average, noting that if they had been in high school they would be ineligible for extracurricular activities.

(The highest numbers of ineligible students where standards were in place were for freshmen and junior varsity athletes. Such warnings at earlier levels would have better prepared the freshman athletes for the new standards.)

3. MEDIA:

• The media should reconcile the conflict between being the conscience of intercollegiate athletics and at the same time acting as "one of its main publicity engines." *(SP)*
• The media need investigative reporters or staffs in their sports departments. *(SP)*
• The media need to be sensitive on issues and to give more balanced coverage to women and minorities. *(SP)*

• The media should stop promoting gambling interests. *(SP)*
• In their relationship with the media, coaches should be totally honest in all they say. They should also be accessible, with an openness that shows they have nothing to hide. The only qualification to this: coaches should refuse to cooperate with the media in discussing potential recruits during recruiting season. Speculative talk simply fuels the fires that already may be raging as alumni try to influence the coach or athlete. *(SP)*

4. AGENTS:

• The institution should establish a players' advisory committee. Every college or university should offer a committee that includes the athletic director, the president of a bank, a leading businessman, an attorney, an accountant, a coach, and a psychologist to educate the athlete and his family about the people, situations, and temptations they may encounter. This would also help the athlete to screen agents. *(BW)*
• The schools should provide an insurance program to counter enticements made by some agents. *(BW)*
• The school should encourage stricter rules regarding agents by players' associations.
• The school should require agents to be licensed. *(BW)*
• The school should supervise and monitor the actions of agents. *(BW)*
• The school should bar all agents from the campus for the purpose of recruiting a client until after the season has been completed. *(BW)*

5. DRUGS:

• Testing of athletes can be an effective deterrent *(JB)*, but constitutional issues still need to be resolved. *(JH)*
• The integrity of the administration of drug test procedures at both the national and international levels must be ensured. *(JH)*
• The media must be more honest in coverage and thus save lives. *(SP)*
• In college the emphasis should be on alcohol abuse as much as drugs. *(JB)*

• Increasing emphasis must be placed on performance-enhancing drugs. *(JH)*
• Educational programs must be offered at much earlier ages, including respected athletes counseling high school and middle school students about the dangers of drug abuse. *(CSSS)*

6. BETTER REPRESENTATION FOR THE ATHLETE

• An advisory committee should be formed at the level of the NCAA to help with issues concerning the welfare of the student-athlete. Committee opinions must be included in developing association policy. *(RS)*
• Student-athletes should be appointed to NCAA governing committees. Athletes should represent each institution at the NCAA meetings, and they should be allowed to caucus at these meetings in order to present a position on matters before the convention. *(JF)*
• Student-athletes should be represented on faculty athletic committees. *(JF)*
• An athletic council should be created on each campus to advise the president and the athletic director on programs and also to evaluate the programs. The council should include the president, the athletic director, athletes (to present the student-athlete point of view), nonathletes (to present the student point of view, which frequently is very different, and to create dialogue), selected coaches, a business leader, and a parent.

CONTRIBUTORS

Jack Bicknell. Jack Bicknell, Boston College's 29th head coach of football, has guided the Eagles to the highest levels of gridiron achievement in the school's long and glorious athletic history.

Under Mr. Bicknell's guidance, the football Eagles have gone to four bowls in the last six years. Bicknell is regarded as one of the keenest offensive strategists in the college game today. He has been a head coach for five years at the University of Maine and seven years at Boston College.

After receiving a football scholarship to Rutgers University, a neck injury cut short his grid career with the Scarlet Knights and he decided to finish his undergraduate degree at Montclair State University, where he received his BA in 1960.

Roscoe C. Brown, Jr. Roscoe C. Brown, Jr., is President of Bronx Community College of the City University of New York, and was formerly Director of the Institute of Afro-American Affairs at New York University. He holds a doctorate from NYU and has served as a Full Professor at NYU's School of Education. Dr. Brown's publications include *The Negro Almanac; Classical Studies in Physical Activity; New Perspectives of Man in Action.* He has written extensively on the problems of the black athlete and the role of sports in higher education.

213

Dr. Brown has recently completed his term on the Board of the American Council on Education (ACE) and chairs the ACE Interassociational President's Committee on Collegiate Athletics. A former varsity athlete at Springfield College, he has chaired the New York City Board of Education Chancellor's Committee on School Sports. He also serves on the Strategic Planning Committee of the National Junior College Athletic Association (NJCAA).

Charles S. Farrell. A graduate of Lincoln University with an MA in journalism from Northwestern University, Charles S. Farrell became a well known journalist in the area of college sports after he joined the staff of the *Chronicle of Higher Education*. While at the *Chronicle* he worked as an editor and minority affairs reporter before accepting the assignment to cover college athletics, which he did for more than three years. His investigative reporting helped the *Chronicle* win the Northeastern University Award for Excellence in Sports Journalism for 1986–87.

Charles Farrell currently works for the sports department of *The Washington Post* while serving as contributing editor for *Black Issues in Higher Education*, and has published articles in many other periodicals. He is President of Sports Perspectives International.

John M. Hoberman. John M. Hoberman received his Ph.D. in Scandinavian Languages and Literature from the University of California, Berkeley, in 1975. He has taught Scandinavian and European studies at the University of Wisconsin, Madison, Harvard University, and the University of Texas at Austin, where he is Associate Professor of Germanic Languages. He has taught courses on sport, politics, and the Olympic Games at Harvard and the University of Texas.

Dr. Hoberman is the author of *Sport and Political Ideology* (University of Texas Press, 1984) and *The Olympic Crisis: Sport, Politics, and the Moral Order* (Aristide D. Caratzass, 1986), which received the 1987 Olympic Book of the Year Award from the United States Olympic Committee Education Council. He has written and lectured widely within the area of sports studies and is an active sports journalist. He is currently at work on a book about the development of scientific sport.

Donna Lopiano. As Athletics Director at the University of Texas at Austin, Donna Lopiano has built what many believe is the premiere women's athletics program in the country. The department has claimed a total of 14 national championships since 1982. Lopiano's striving for excellence includes hiring a highly respected coaching staff made up of individuals who are esteemed as the very best in their fields and who embrace an impeccable standard of integrity regarding their positions as role models for student-athletes.

Dr. Lopiano received her BA from Southern Connecticut State University. A four-sport athlete, she was a star softball player. She earned All-America honors, played professionally, and was inducted into the Amateur Softball Association National Hall of Fame in 1984. Her commitment to expanding opportunities for women in sport led to her being named a trustee of the Women's Sports Foundation.

Lopiano holds master's and doctoral degrees from the University of Southern California.

David Meggyesy. David Meggyesy is the Western Director of the National Football League Players Association, AFL-CIO. He has taught courses at Stanford University and Columbia College. He is a graduate of Syracuse University where he was an all-American football player.

Considered to be one of the first professional athletes who dared to be critical of the athletic establishment, this former all pro NFL veteran shocked the sports world with his highly-acclaimed book, *Out of Their League.* He has written numerous articles on issues regarding college and professional sports and has long been considered a leading advocate of the rights of athletes.

Sandy Padwe. One of the nation's most respected sports journalists, Sandy Padwe is now Senior Editor for *Sports Illustrated.*

Mr. Padwe graduated with a BA in Journalism in 1961 from Penn State. He is a former winner of the Headliner

Club Sportswriter of the Year, which he won prior to becoming a sports editor. He wrote for both *Newsday* and the *Philadelphia Inquirer*.

Mr. Padwe's career as an editor began at *Newsday* in 1973 when he was named Deputy Sports Editor. Four years later he moved to *Sports Illustrated* as a senior editor where he became the investigations editor. He joined the *New York Times* in August of 1980 as Editor of Sports Monday and became Deputy Sports Editor in April 1981. Padwe returned to *Sports Illustrated* in January 1985 where he is now in charge of pro-basketball and investigations.

Allen L. Sack. Allen L. Sack is a Professor of Sociology and Director of the Honors Program at the University of New Haven. His articles on college sport have appeared in periodicals ranging from the *New York Times* and *Sporting News* to the *Sociology of Education* and the *Journal of Higher Education*. He is currently on the editorial boards of the *Sociology of Sport Journal* and the *Journal of Sport and Social Issues*.

Dr. Sack was a defensive end on Notre Dame's 1966 National Championship football team and was drafted by the Los Angeles Rams. From 1981 to 1983 he was director of the federally funded Center for Athletes Rights and Education, which worked on issues affecting athletes' rights. His areas of specialization in sociology are social stratification, social problems, and the sociology of sport.

Richard D. Schultz. Richard D. Schultz became the Executive Director of the NCAA in September of 1987. His appointment was hailed as an important signal for those seeking to reemphasize the proper place of athletics in education.

Dick Schultz was Athletic Director at Cornell (1976–81) and the University of Virginia (1981–87). Prior to these positions Schultz worked at the University of Iowa for 16 years as a coach including head Basketball Coach, and as Assistant to the President. He became very active in the NCAA and chaired both the Division I Men's Basketball Committee and the Special Television Negotiations Committee.

He did his undergraduate work at Central College (Iowa) and graduate studies at the University of Iowa.

Doug Single. Doug Single was named as Southern Methodist University's Director of Athletics in October 1987 in the wake of SMU's receiving the so-called death penalty from the NCAA. He was chosen largely because he had earned national acclaim during his seven-year tenure at Northwestern for heading an intercollegiate athletic program that brought athletic success to the university without sacrificing academic superiority.

Central to Mr. Single's administrative philosophy is the belief that student-athletes deserve a well-rounded program to enhance the athletic experience. A complete reevaluation and restructuring of the Athletic Department has taken place at SMU since his arrival.

Mr. Single, who graduated from Stanford, served as associate athletic director for two years and assistant football coach for six years at Stanford. He played in the 1972 Rose Bowl. He obtained his master's degree in political science from Stanford in 1977.

Bob Woolf. Bob Woolf has been hailed as the pioneer of sports law in this country. The *American Bar Association Journal* noted that ". . . the name in sports law is Bob Woolf. For a simple reason. Before Woolf, there was no such thing as sports law. Ever since former Red Sox pitcher, Earl Wilson chose Mr. Woolf to represent him in 1964, more than 500 other athletes have followed suit, thus establishing Mr. Woolf as the top sports attorney in the country." Mr. Woolf's clients have included such stars as: Carl Yastrzemski, John Havlicek, Jim Plunkett, Joe Thiesmann, Julius Erving, Thurman Munson, Derek Sanderson, and 1980 Olympic hero Jim Craig. Mr. Woolf also represents Larry Bird, one of the highest paid team professional athletes, 1984 Heisman Trophy winner Doug Flutie, 1986 Heisman Trophy winner Vinny Testaverde, Joe Montana, Dexter Manley, Anthony Carter, Dominique Wilkins, Byron Scott, Bernard King, Robert Parish and numerous other top professional athletes.

Mr. Woolf is the author of *Behind Closed Doors* and is now undertaking a major book on his experiences and negotiation skills.

Connee Zotos. Connee Zotos, who holds a Ph.D in Educational Administration, is presently an Assistant Professor in the Department of Kinesiology and Health Education at the University of Texas at Austin. She teaches graduate courses in sports administration and coordinates the undergraduate degree program in sports management.

Dr. Zotos is also employed by Austin Cablevision and Home Sports Entertainment. She uses her 6 years of college coaching experience to work as a television color commentator for women's Southwest Conference basketball games.

As coordinator of Women's Athletics at Philadelphia College of Textile and Science, Dr. Zotos was responsible for the organization and implementation of a five-sport intercollegiate program.

SOURCES AND NOTES

Chapter 1: Historical Overview

SOURCES

Denlinger, Kenneth, and Shapiro, Leonard. *Athletes for Sale.* New York: Thomas Y. Cromwell Co., 1975.

Edwards, Harry. *The Revolt of the Black Athlete.* New York: The Free Press, 1969.

Lapchick, Richard. *Broken Promises: Racism in American Sports.* New York: St. Martin's/Marek, 1984.

Lawrence, Paul R. *Unsportsmanlike Conduct: The National Collegiate Athletic Association and the Business of College Football.* New York: Praeger Publishers, 1987.

Novak, Michael. *The Joy of Sports: End Zones, Bases, Baskets, Balls, and the Consecration of the American Spirit.* New York: Basic Books, Inc., 1976.

Noverr, Douglas A., and Ziewacz, Lawrence. *The Games They Played: Sports in American History, 1865–1980.* Chicago: Nelson-Hall Publishers, 1983.

Rader, Benjamin G. *American Sports: From the Age of Folk Games to the Age of Spectators.* Englewood Cliffs, N.J.: Prentice-Hall, Inc., 1983.

Rooney, John F., Jr. *The Recruiting Game: Toward a New System of Intercollegiate Sports.* Lincoln: University of Nebraska Press, 1987.

Savage, Howard. *American College Athletics.* Boston: Merrymount Press, 1929.

Chapter 3: Equity and Policy Problems in Women's Intercollegiate Athletics

SOURCES

Acosta, R. V., and Carpenter, L. J. *Women in intercollegiate sport: A longitudinal study—Eleven year update, 1977-1988.* Unpublished manuscript, Brooklyn College, New York, 1988.

Aiken v. Lievallen, 39 Or. App. 779, 593 P.2d 1243 (1979).

Atwell, R. H., Grimes, B., and Lopiano, D. *The money game: Financing collegiate athletics.* Washington, D.C.: American Council on Education, 1980.

Berry, R. C., and Wong, G. M. *Law and business of the sports industries: Vol. 2, Common issues in amateur and professional sports.* Dover, Mass.: Auburn House, 1986.

Demo, D. H. Closing or widening the gender gap? Boys' and girls' interscholastic sports in Mississippi. *Studies in the Social Sciences,* 24, 1985.

Education Amendments of 1972, P.L. 92-318, Title IX–Prohibitions of Sex Discrimination, July 1, 1972 (now codified as 20 U.S.C. § 1681(a)).

Federal Register. (1979, December 11). 44(239), 71413-23.

Gelb, J. , and Palley, M. L. *Women and public policies.* Princeton, N.J.: Princeton University Press, 1982.

Gerry, M. *OCR interpretation of the Title IX Regulations as it concerns sex separate departments of physical education and athletics.* Letter from the Office of Civil Rights, Sept. 30, 1976.

Isaac, T. A. Sports—the final frontier: Sex discrimination in sports leadership. *Women Lawyers Journal,* 73 (4), 1987.

Lawmakers predict override of Reagan's civil-rights veto. *NCAA News,* 25(12), March 23, 1988.

Like she owns the earth. (PEER Report no. 4). Washington, D.C. 1985.

Lopiano, D. A. Statement of Donna A. Lopiano before the Subcommittee on Higher Education, Committee on Labor and Public Welfare, S. 2106, Sept. 18, 1975.

Lopiano, D. A. A fact-finding model for conducting a Title IX self-evaluation study in athletic programs. *Journal of Physical Education, Recreation and Dance,* 47(5), 1976.

Lopiano, D. A. Modern athletics: Directions and problems. *Thresholds in Education,* 8(4), 1980.

Lopiano, D. A. *Top ten survey.* Unpublished manuscript, University of Texas at Austin, 1983.

Lopiano, D. A. A political analysis of the possibility of impact alternatives for the accomplishment of feminist objectives within American intercollegiate sport. In R. E. Lapchick (ed.), *Fractured focus: Sport as a reflection of society.* Lexington, Mass.: Lexington Books, 1986.

Lopiano, D. A. A speech made at the NCAA President's Commission National Forum. *The Physical Educator,* 45(1), 1988.

More than education at stake in new Title IX battle. *WEAL Washington Report,* 16(3), 1987.

Mottinger, S. G., and Gench, B. E. Comparison of salaries of female and male intercollegiate basketball coaches: An equal opportunity study. *Journal of the National Association of Women Deans, Administrators and Counselors,* 47(2), 1984.

Mushier, C. Testimony before the U.S. Commission on Civil Rights, July 9, 1978.

Oglesby, C. A. *Women and sport: From myth to reality.* Philadelphia: Lea & Febiger, 1978.

Orleans, J. H. Aggressive pursuit of a legislative exemption under Title IX for revenue-producing men's sports is not in the best interests of athletes or colleges. *Educational Record,* 1982.

Otto, L. B., and Alwin, D. F. Athletics, aspirations and attainments. *Sociology of Education,* 42, 1977.

Parkhouse, B. L., and Lapin, J. *Women who win: Exercising your rights in sport.* Englewood Cliffs, N.J.: Prentice Hall, 1980.

Pogrebin, L. C. *Growing up free: Raising your child in the 80's.* Toronto: Bantam Books, 1980.

Sanders, M. T. *Comparison of various operation procedures in Division I women's athletics.* Unpublished manuscript, University of Tennessee, 1985.

Schafer, S. P. Women in coaching: Problems, possibilities. *American Coach,* Sept./Oct., 1987.

Title IX: More races to run. *Christian Science Monitor,* May, 1981.

Uhlir, G. A. Athletics and the university: The post-woman's era. *Academe,* 73(4), 1987.

Wong, G. M., and Ensor, R. J. Sex discrimination in athletics: A review of two decades of accomplishments and defeats. *Gonzaga Law Review,* 21(2), 1985–86.

Yudof, M. G., Kirp, D. L., van Geel, T., and Levin, B. *Educational policy and the law.* Berkeley, Calif.: McCutchan, 1982.

Chapter 4: Race on the College Campus

NOTE

1. Excludes the 18 predominantly black schools in Division I. Figures compiled from National Collegiate Athletic Association; *Chronicle of Higher Education; NCAA News; Broken Promises: Racism in American Sport.*

Chapter 5: Recruiting

NOTES

1. Richard N. Current et. al., *American History: A Survey, Vol. 2* (New York: Alfred A. Knopf, 1983), p. 724.
2. H. J. Vetter and J. Wright, *Introduction to Criminology* (Springfield, IL: Charles C. Thomas, 1974), pp. 13–14.
3. See Peter Monaghan, "Scandals and Allegations of Rules Violations Beset Members of the Southwest Conference," *The Chronicle of Higher Education* (October 16, 1985), p. 37; Gordon S. White, "Tennessee Wins despite Ban," *New York Times* (September 8, 1986); Douglas Lederman, "Football Troubles at Southern Methodist Boil Down to: Who Runs the University?" *The Chronicle of Higher Education* (January 7, 1987), p. 35; and John Bannon, "Ex Agent: No Clean Programs," *USA Today* (December 17, 1987), p. 1C.
4. Of the 22 institutions under NCAA sanctions as of July, 1986, the grounds for action in 17 cases were improper benefits to players. The discovery of an elaborate payment scheme to football players at Southern Methodist University has forced a dramatic reorganization of the school's board of governors. The governor of the state has admitted to being involved in funneling improper benefits to athletes. See Lederman, note 3.
5. Richard Pear, "Poverty Shows Slight Drop for 85, Census Bureau Says," *New York Times* (August 27, 1986), p. A17.
6. In 1968, there were 11 blacks on scholarship in the Southeastern Conference. In 1972, there were 100 blacks in football alone in the SEC. By 1983, 44 of the conference's 50 starters in basketball were black. Television and radio revenues have also increased dramatically during this period. See D. Stanley Eitzen and George Sage, *Sociology of North American Sport* (Dubuque: Wm. C. Brown, 1986), p. 265.
7. This study is based on data drawn from a national survey of college basketball players undertaken by the federally funded Center for Athletes' Rights and Education between 1983 and 1985.
8. Social class was measured by the use of the Hollingshead Two Factor Index of Social Position, which combines educational attainment with occupational status to create a measure of socioeconomic status.

9. PERCENTAGE OF COLLEGE ATHLETES WHO SEE NOTHING WRONG WITH ACCEPTING MONEY UNDER THE TABLE, BY CLASS, RACE, GENDER, DIVISION, AND SCHOLARSHIP STATUS[a,b]

Independent Variable	Is It Wrong?		Total	Chi-Square	df
	No	Yes			
	%	%	N		
Race					
Black	61.2	38.8	157	31.86**	1

9. PERCENTAGE OF COLLEGE ATHLETES WHO SEE NOTHING WRONG WITH ACCEPTING MONEY UNDER THE TABLE, BY CLASS, RACE, GENDER, DIVISION, AND SCHOLARSHIP STATUS[a,b]

Independent Variable	Is It Wrong?		Total	Chi-Square	df
	No	Yes			
	%	%	N		
White	34.4	65.6	360		
Gender					
Male	54.5	45.5	312	40.15**	1
Female	26.6	73.6	214		
Class					
Upper	32.5	67.5	200	16.26**	2
Middle	45.0	54.0	151		
Lower	55.0	45.0	120		
Division					
I	49.9	52.1	365	5.12	2
II	39.6	60.4	159		
III	36.7	63.3	109		
Scholarship					
Yes	50.9	49.1	265	13.48**	1
No	34.7	65.3	262		

** Significant at the .0002 level.

a. The "under-the-table" question was a contingency question answered only by athletes receiving some form of financial aid.

b. Table 1 is composed of five separate bivariate tables.

10. PERCENTAGE OF COLLEGE ATHLETES WHO SEE NOTHING WRONG WITH ACCEPTING MONEY UNDER THE TABLE, BY SEX, CLASS, AND RACE

Class[a]	White				Black				Total	
	Male		Female		Male		Female			
	%	N	%	N	%	N	%	N	%	N
Upper	42	(83)	18	(84)	50	(24)	33	(6)	32	(197)
Middle	49	(45)	28	(61)	62	(37)	75	(8)	45	(151)
Lower	60	(30)	33	(33)	67	(48)	40	(5)	54	(116)
TOTAL	47	(158)	24	(178)	61	(109)	53	(19)	42	(464)

a. A fairly large number of athletes did not report their father's occupation, thereby increasing the number of missing values in this table.

11. A separate analysis carried out to examine attitudes toward "under-the-table" payments by race and scholarship status revealed that when race was held constant, the effect of scholarship status was considerably diminished. However, regardless of scholarship status, blacks are more likely to support under-the-table payments than whites.

12. PERCENTAGE OF COLLEGE ATHLETES WHO AGREE THAT THEY DESERVE THE TV REVENUE THEY GENERATE, BY RACE, CLASS, AND GENDER[a]

	Male				Female					
Class	Black		White		Black		White		Total	
	%	N	%	N	%	N	%	N	%	N
Upper	68	(25)	28	(109)	50	(6)	31	(87)	34	(227)
Middle	61	(36)	29	(51)	100	(9)	44	(62)	46	(158)
Lower	80	(49)	46	(37)	67	(6)	39	(36)	58	(128)
TOTAL	71	(110)	32	(197)	76	(21)	37	(185)	43	(513)

a. The TV revenue question was a Likert scale item. The categories strongly agree and were combined in this table.

13. PERCENTAGE OF COLLEGE ATHLETES WHO AGREE THAT THEY HAVE A RIGHT TO SAME BENEFITS AS OTHER WORKERS, BY RACE, CLASS, AND GENDER[a]

	Males				Females					
Class	Black		White		Black		White		Total	
	%	N	%	N	%	N	%	N	%	N
Upper	48	(27)	33	(100)	83	(6)	28	(81)	35	(214)
Middle	56	(32)	34	(50)	25	(8)	39	(62)	40	(152)
Lower	64	(42)	50	(38)	100	(3)	25	(36)	49	(119)
TOTAL	57	(101)	37	(188)	59	(17)	31	(179)	40	(485)

a. The worker benefits question was a Likert scale item. The categories strongly agree and were combined in this table.

14. PERCENTAGE DISTRIBUTION OF RESPONSES TO THE QUESTION "WHAT IS YOUR PRIMARY REASON FOR PLAYING COLLEGE SPORT?" BY DIVISION AND RACE

	Fun	Pays Education	Other[a]	Total
	%	%	%	N
Division I	40	45	15	(276)
Black	23	56	21	(102)
White	50	39	11	(174)
Division II	62	28	10	(182)
Black	41	47	12	(37)
White	67	23	10	(145)
Division III	81	4	15	(158)
Black	72	7	21	(32)
White	84	4	12	(126)

a. The category Other includes: (1) I love the recognition; (2) it offers the promise of money I can make in the future; (3) it allows me to meet people.

15. William G. Sumner, *Folkways.* New York: Dover Publications, 1959.
16. Carole Gilligan, *In a Different Voice.* Cambridge, MA: Harvard University Press, 1982.
17. The NCAA has recently set up a $9 million scholarship fund for athletes who did not graduate but decided to return to school. This is a step in the right direction, but what is really needed is a guaranteed fifth year of scholarship aid for any athlete who completes four years of athletic eligibility.

Chapter 6: Drug Abuse

NOTES

1. "Drug Testing Wins Approval," *New York Times*, January 15, 1986.
2. "South Carolina Sports Chief Fired over Drug Tests," *Chronicle of Higher Education*, March 9, 1988. For a horrifying account of the physical and psychological effects of steroid abuse at the University of South Carolina, and the amorality of some college coaches and team physicians, see Tommy Chaikin with Rick Telander, "The Nightmare of Steroids," *Sports Illustrated*, October 24, 1988.
3. "NAIA Suspends 4 for Failing to Meet Drug-Plan Deadline," *Chronicle of Higher Education*, February 10, 1988; "4 Colleges File Drug Plans; NAIA Lifts Its Ban," *Chronicle of Higher Education*, February 17, 1988.
4. "24 Football Players Failed NCAA Drug Tests Last Fall," *Chronicle of Higher Education*, March 16, 1988.
5. "NCAA Considering Stricter Drug Testing," *USA Today*, October 7, 1987; "NCAA Approves Voluntary Drug Tests," *Austin American-Statesman*, January 14, 1988.
6. See Terry Todd and John M. Hoberman, "NCAA Finally Makes a Substantial Move against Drugs," *Austin American-Statesman*, January 3, 1988.
7. "Miami Appeal on Mira Reported," *New York Times*, December 29, 1987.
8. Tom Donohoe and Neil Johnson, *Foul Play: Drug Abuse in Sports* (Oxford and New York: Basil Blackwell, 1986), p. 31.
9. Jack A. Bell and Theodore C. Doege, "Athletes' Use and Abuse of Drugs," *The Physician and Sportsmedicine*, Vol. 15, No. 3 (March 1987), p. 103.
10. Ibid., p. 99.
11. See, for example, "As Ever More People Try Anabolic Steroids, Traffickers Take Over," *Wall Street Journal*, October 24, 1988; Charles E. Yesalis, Why Children Use Steroids," *New York Times*, December 4, 1988; "Study Suggests 500,000 Teens May Be Using Steroids," *Houston Chronicle*, December 16, 1988.
12. "Spreading Use of Steroids by Young Athletes Alarms Sports Medicine Specialists," *New York Times*, February 18, 1988; "Athletes Use and Abuse of Drugs, p. 105.

13. "Top Pick for Jets Took Steroids," *New York Times*, April 27, 1988.

14. "Meese Wants Broader Drug Testing," *New York Times*, April 28, 1988.

15. "Congress Urged to Ban Most Random Drug Testing,"*Dallas Morning News*, April 22, 1988.

16. "Justices to Rule on Drug-Testing Plan," *New York Times*, March 1, 1988.

17. Ibid.

18. "N.C.A.A. Plans to Test for Drugs despite Ruling," *New York Times*, November 21, 1987.

19. "Stanford Athletes' Drug-Test Victory Puts NCAA on Defensive," *Christian Science Monitor*, November 27, 1987.

20. Virginia S. Cowart, "Drug Testing Programs Face Snags and Legal Challenges," *The Physician and Sportsmedicine* (February 1988), pp. 167, 169.

21. "N.C.A.A. Plans to Test for Drugs despite Ruling."

22. "NCAA Proceeds with Plans for Drug Testing, despite Limits Imposed by California Court," *Chronicle of Higher Education*, December 2, 1987.

23. "NCAA's Drug Tests of Athletes at Stanford U. Barred by Cal. Judge," *Chronicle of Higher Education*,. September 1, 1988, p. A30.

24. "Federal Court Rules NCAA's Drug-Testing Program Does Not Violate College Athletes' Privacy Right," *Chronicle of Higher Education*, March 9, 1988.

25. "U. of Montana Revises Its Drug-Testing Program," *Chronicle of Higher Education*, April 20, 1988.

26. "Stanford Athletes' Drug-Test Victory Puts NCAA on Defensive."

27. "Drug Testing Programs Face Snags and Legal Challenges."

28. On the efficacy of anabolic steroids see, for example, William N. Taylor, M.D., "Synthetic Anabolic-Androgenic Steroids: A Plea for Controlled Substance Status," *The Physician and Sportsmedicine* (May 1977), pp. 140–47.

29. "Federal Court Rules NCAA's Drug-Testing Program Does Not Violate College Athletes' Privacy Right." In September 1988, the U.S. Court of Appeals for the Ninth Circuit overturned Judge McGovern's ruling on the grounds that the case belonged in state rather than federal court. See "Drug Case Sent to State Court," *Chronicle of Higher Education*, September 21, 1988, p. A43.

30. "N.C.A.A. Plans to Test for Drugs despite Ruling."

31. Robert O. Voy, M. C., "Education As a Means against Doping," *The Olympian* (December 1987), p. 45.

32. Adapted from John M. Hoberman, "Sport and the Technological Image of Man," in William J. Morgan and Klaus V. Meier, eds., *Philosophic Inquiry in Sport* (Champaign, Ill.: Human Kinetics Publishers, Inc., 1987), pp. 319–20.

33. See, for example, John M. Hoberman, "The Future of Scientific Sport." The R. Tait McKenzie Lecture, Cosponsored by the American Academy

of Physical Education and the American Alliance for Health, Physical Education, Recreation and Dance at the 102nd Anniversary National Convention, Caesars Palace Hotel, Las Vegas, April 13, 1987.

34. "Shorter Calls for Blood," *Track & Field News* (April 1988), p. 59.
35. "Doping ist wie ein Buschfeuer," *Süddeutsche Zeitung* (Munich), February 1, 1984.
36. "Unheilbarer Drang," *Der Spiegel*, April 8, 1985, p. 179.
37. "Gefahren durch Flickschusterei," *Der Spiegel*, November 4, 1985, p. 242.
38. "Education As a Means against Doping."
39. "Thompson Still Feisty," *Track & Field News* (May 1988), p. 51.
40. See, for example, William Oscar Johnson and Kenny Moore, "The Loser," *Sports Illustrated*, October 3, 1988.
41. "Generell lauwarm," *Der Spiegel*, December 12, 1988, p. 182.
42. W. Hollmann, "Risikofaktoren in der Entwicklung des Hochleistungssports," in H. Rieckert, ed., *Sportmedizin-Kursbestimmung* [Deutscher Sportärztekongress, Kiel, Oktober 16–19, 1986] [Berlin: Springer-Verlag, 1987], p. 15.

Chapter 14: Where Was the President

SOURCES

Durso, Joseph. *The Sports Factory: An Investigation into College Sports,* New York: Quadrangle/The New York Times Book Co., 1975.

Lucas, John A.; and Smith, Ronald A. *Saga of American Sport.* Philadelphia: Lea and Febiger, 1978.

NCAA Proceedings, Vol. 1, 1906.

Rudolph, Frederick. *The American College and University.* New York: Vintage Books, 1962.

INDEX